The Positioning of the Roman Imperial Legions

Jerome H. Farnum

BAR International Series 1458
2005

Published in 2016 by
BAR Publishing, Oxford

BAR International Series 1458

The Positioning of the Roman Imperial Legions

ISBN 978 1 84171 896 5

© J H Farnum and the Publisher 2005

The author's moral rights under the 1988 UK Copyright,
Designs and Patents Act are hereby expressly asserted.

All rights reserved. No part of this work may be copied, reproduced, stored,
sold, distributed, scanned, saved in any form of digital format or transmitted
in any form digitally, without the written permission of the Publisher.

BAR Publishing is the trading name of British Archaeological Reports (Oxford) Ltd.
British Archaeological Reports was first incorporated in 1974 to publish the BAR
Series, International and British. In 1992 Hadrian Books Ltd became part of the BAR
group. This volume was originally published by Archaeopress in conjunction with
British Archaeological Reports (Oxford) Ltd / Hadrian Books Ltd, the Series principal
publisher, in 2005. This present volume is published by BAR Publishing, 2016.

Printed in England

PUBLISHING

BAR titles are available from:

        BAR Publishing
        122 Banbury Rd, Oxford, OX2 7BP, UK
EMAIL   info@barpublishing.com
PHONE +44 (0)1865 310431
FAX   +44 (0)1865 316916
        www.barpublishing.com

TABLE OF CONTENTS

Foreword 2

I. The Positioning of the Legions 3

II. The Tables 14

    A. List of legions with a history of their names and locations..15

    B. Alphabetical list of legion bases and their garrisons 26

    C. Index of English/Roman and Roman/English legion base names 32

    D. Global legion movements 34

    E. Regional legion histories with maps..42
        1) Spain..42
        2) Gaul/Germany/Raetia/Noricum 43
        3) Britain..52
        4) Illyricum, Dalmatia, Pannonia, Dacia, Macedonia, Moesia 60
        5) The East...81
        6) Egypt and Africa...90

    F. Additions to and deletions from the legion list 30 B.C.- 250 A.D..................................94

    G. Distribution of the legions by region at various dates...95

    H. Chronology of campaigns and battles 30 B.C. - 300 A.D...98

III. Appendices...110

    A. The origin of the Augustan legions..110

    B. The importance of the legion's name 111

    C. The legionary eagles 112

    D. The tactics of territorial expansion...113

    E. When and why were legions disbanded?...116

IV. Bibliography 120

FOREWORD

The positioning of the legions of the Imperial Roman army provides a window into both the thinking and the course of events during the period from 30 B.C. to 300 A.D. When one can identify the locations and date the redeployments of the legions, it is possible to recreate the planning that caused the army to be so placed. One can think of the Empire as a giant chessboard. There were a finite number of pieces and they needed to be distributed in a rational and effective way. The analogy fails at a point because the permanent headquarters of a legion was an elaborate installation. A legion could not replace another legion until the first had moved away. At the same time, legionary bases were not placed in temporary mothballs. They were usually occupied continuously until they were abandoned. Even when the resident legion was off on campaign, a detachment would continue to maintain the base and deal with the legion's logistical problems until the campaigning elements returned. It would equally be a mistake to assume that legions could easily be permanently relocated. Such a movement required a substantial investment in new logistics, infrastructure and, in the case of the legionaries, good will. Consequently, a redeployment, of necessity, shows a major shift of events or a significant refocussing of the strategic thinking of the then ruling emperor at that particular moment. Datable historical events are therefore most useful in pinpointing the dates when legions moved. The basic work on the location of the legions, from which all historians have gone forward, is the 1925 article in the Realencyclopaedie des Klassischen Altertumswissenschaft written by Emil Ritterling. Since then, uncounted excavations and learned papers have added more and more fragments to the record.

From time to time, it is useful to draw a new picture. This book starts from the assumption that a legion's headquarters remained at a base until that legion was permanently posted to another base. A legion might temporarily serve in another province, even for more than a year, perhaps with its eagle present, but know that it would return to its permanent base. At any moment in time, a legion might have detachments serving in a variety of locations. Some of these detachments, or vexillations, might be separated from the parent legion for long periods of time at great distances from its permanent headquarters. This was particularly true during the Late Empire. The legion's commander and its eagle might accompany the detachment on a distant campaign, or a unit commander might be appointed with a vexillum, or unit standard, to show the identity of the legion to which the unit belonged. It appears that, at the end of the Empire, a detached unit might even acquire its own cognomen, or nickname, and be composed of legionaries who had never served with the parent legion. This book presupposes that a campaign was not a relocation and that a legion was based where its eagle was expected to return.

A great number of scholars have addressed the subject of legion locations, usually one legion or one province at a time. It is a truism, however, that one cannot study the movements of a single legion without reference to the locations of the other legions. It was usually the case that a legion was relocated in tandem with the movement of other legions to maintain a balance of military forces in the various provinces as far as possible. This book attempts to formulate a seamless web of legion locations, deducing from the evidence where the legions must have been during the period. It is a synthesis of what has been written before, and is written with the expectation that in the future new archeological evidence will further refine the information it contains. In consequence, the bibliography is limited to those works which broadly address parts of the puzzle and omits the usual endless citations and excavation reports justifying and supporting each molecule of the presentation.

THE POSITIONING OF THE LEGIONS

The Roman army was the primary instrument through which the sole ruler of the Empire controlled his Empire and its surroundings. There were other branches of government carrying out the wishes of the emperor, but their power to change events was inconsequential. The Senate in Rome was an example of those bodies who made formal decisions while knowing that there was but one ultimate power in the State. As long as the army stood behind the emperor of the moment, there could be no challenge to his authority. The emperor thus positioned his army where he needed it to protect against the internal and external dangers to his interests as he saw them. Knowing where the Imperial Roman legions were stationed and when and why they were moved gives a great insight into what was happening at any particular moment throughout the Empire. It enables the observer to see when and where the emperor believed that his Empire might be burning.

With the suicide of Antonius after the battle of Actium in 31 B.C., Octavian had all of the Roman armies in his hands. His former rivals were dead and the patrician class, who might have produced new rivals, was generally sick of civil war. It has been estimated that this collection of armies comprised about 60 legions containing some 250,000 men. All of the legions were understrength from casualties and general wear and tear. Perhaps 100,000 citizen and non-citizen auxiliaries from all over the Empire rounded out the armed forces of Rome. Octavian dealt with the question of how his new Roman army would now be organized in a series of related and logical decisions. There would be a permanent standing army controlled directly by the emperor. The legions were to be composed only of Roman citizens serving for a fixed period of time. Smaller units of citizen and non-citizen auxiliaries would be brigaded with each legion to serve as shock troops in battle or for specialized functions. The army would be repositioned outside Italy as soon as possible at strategic locations in certain sensitive provinces. Provinces in which legions were located were to be placed under the direct authority of Augustus himself. The army had made Octavian an emperor and having a permanent army meant that an emperor could be unmade by his army if a significant part of it turned against him. The mission of the new army was to control, expand and, when necessary, to defend the Empire for the benefit of the emperor.

One of Augustus' more important military reforms was the establishment and perfection of a logistics system that would feed and supply all parts of the army wherever they were serving. For an army whose field command structure consisted of amateur legates and tribunes, this was a remarkable achievement. Taxes in kind and requisitions paid for with the legions' cash would provide food and materials from the nearest provincial producers. Waterways and legion-built roads would bring them to wherever they would be consumed. Arms and equipment would flow from state factories farther away over the same transport system. The legions could now be based where they were needed and the supplies would come to them. In earlier times, the legions had been spread out during the non-campaigning season in camps where enough food could be found locally to feed them. This had proven to be both dangerous and inefficient as newly conquered territory could not support the legions needed to pacify and integrate that land into the Roman world.

There is good evidence that the following legions had served in Octavian's army at the time of Actium:

IV Macedonica, V Macedonica, VI Victrix, VII Macedonica, VIII (Augusta), IX Hispana, X Fretensis, XI, XIII Gemina, XIV Gemina, XV Apollinaris and XVI Gallica

The legions of Antonius that survived Octavian's reorganization were:

III Gallica, III Cyrenaica, IV Scythica, V Alaudae, VI Ferrata, X Gemina, XII Fulminata, XVII Classica, XVIII Libyca and XIX Paterna.

It is unclear where the legions I (Augusta), II (Augusta), III (Augusta), XX Valeria and XXI Rapax had stood although legions with their numbers certainly existed in 30 B.C.[1]

The oddity in the emperor's decision-making process was the setting of the size of the army at 27 legions. After discharging non-citizens and over-age veterans, the total of the legionaries from all of the units Octavian had inherited would have equalled about 27 legions at full strength. As foot soldiers have few political loyalties, it would be relatively easy to bring them together under new management into reorganized legions. Many, if not most, of the soldiers had found military life to be better than the available alternatives.

Octavian would appoint new officers for his legions from men that he knew personally in Rome. As he was paying for the army from the spoils he had acquired in the Civil War, this was the size of army that he wanted. Later, it was determined that the Empire could support the cost of 27 legions plus an approximately equal number of auxiliaries. Succeeding emperors for the next 200 years would limit the Empire's military forces to approximately

---

[1] II (Augusta) and XX Valeria appear to have been garrisoning Spain at the time of Actium and so missed participating in the battle. The Spanish garrison would have been on the side of Octavian.

this size. The reorganized legions were spread around the Empire about 30 B.C. as follows:

Legions formerly of	Octavian	Antonius	Uncertain
Nearer Spain	2	0	1^2
Farther Spain	3	2	0^2
Gaul	0	3	1^3
Italy	2	0	0^4
Illyricum	3	0	0^5
Macedonia	3	1	0^6
Syria	0	2	0^7
Egypt	0	2	0^8
Africa	1	0	1^9

This distribution shows a pattern:

1. Certain of the former legions of Antonius were retained intact in the post-Actium army, if under new management.
2. The ex-Antonian legions were, to a notable extent, employed in the provinces in which they had served before Actium and to which they had by now become acclimated.
3. Octavian felt more comfortable with his own legions closest to Rome, and stationed the surviving legions of Antonius at the edges of the Empire.
4. In most provinces, the garrison consisted of legions that had followed either one or the other of the final contenders for power. The implication is that the rivalry between their supporters had not completely disappeared.
5. Legions I, II, and III Augusta do not appear to have been at Actium and so did not receive their cognomen for valiant service there. Legions with these numbers certainly existed before Actium. It can be hypothesized that I, II and III Augusta were legions reconstituted with legionaries that had served under Octavian in legions he had disbanded and that the name Augusta was a notice to the rest of the army of their prior service with him.

The table also shows that 27 legions were about eight more than Octavian needed to merely control or to defend the Empire of 30 B.C. The only possible explanation for the 'extra' manpower is that Octavian had planned from the time of his accession to expand the western Empire through military conquest. These additional legions were not combined into a central striking force, however, which might have turned into a dangerous army serv-ing its own or a rival's ends.

Six legions were sent to Spain to join the two that had been permanently stationed there.[10] The legions in the Iberian Peninsula were separated into two military regions to prevent any unwanted joint political activity.[11] The Iberian army's mission was to conquer the area of the precious metal mines in the northwest quarter of the peninsula. The Iberian tribes were not capable of joining together to defend their tribal territories. The Roman forces could therefore advance in parallel capturing one local stronghold after another. The Roman problem was that the tribes rose up again as soon as the legions withdrew to their winter camps in the lowlands. The successive campaigns against the tribes occupied the eight legions during the decade from 29-19 B.C. In 26 B.C., Augustus traveled from Italy to join this army to ensure that they remembered for whom it was fighting. As the last Spanish resistance was thought to have been eliminated, manpower became available for a further expansion of the empire on another frontier.

At the same time as the Spanish campaign was beginning, Octavian's consular colleague of 30 B.C., Marcus Licinius Crassus, was sent as governor with four legions to Macedonia.[12] Two legions would have been the normal garrison of the province. The 'extra' two legions gave Crassus a chance to make military history. When the tribes to the north of the province became troublesome or, more probably, in a pre-planned campaign, Crassus attacked northwards and conquered the territory up to the Danube. This campaign was concluded in 27 B.C. Two of Crassus' four legions were then transferred to other provinces.[13] Two legions were considered to be a sufficient garrison for the new pacified province of Macedonia and the region to the north which would eventually be combined with it to become the province of Moesia.[14]

The histories record an uprising at Thebes in Upper Egypt in 29 B.C. VIII Augusta, which had been with Octavian at Actium and afterwards was being reorganized in Italy, was sent to Thebes to deal with it. It is worthy of note that Octavian decided to send a legion across the Mediterranean and not to call upon the ex-Antonian legions stationed in Lower Egypt.[15] The use of a 'loyal'

---

[2] Nearer Spain – Octavian: IV Macedonica, IX Macedonica; Uncertain: I (Augusta) Farther Spain – Octavian: II (Augusta), VI Hispaniensis, XX Valeria - Antonius - V Alaudae, X Gemina

[3] Antonius - XVII Classica, XVIII Libyca, XIX Paterna; Uncertain - XXI Rapax

[4] Octavian - VIII (Augusta), XVI Gallica; Surmised, as no locations have been identified

[5] Octavian - XIII Gemina, XIV Gemina, XV Apollinaris

[6] Octavian - V Macedonica, X Fretensis, XI Antonius - IV Scythica

[7] Antonius - III Gallica, VI Ferrata

[8] Antonius - III Cyrenaica, XII Fulminata

[9] Octavian – VII Macedonica; Uncertain - III (Augusta); Presumed as no bases have been identified

[10] I (Augusta), IV Macedonica, V Alaudae, VI Hispaniensis (Victrix), IX Macedonica (Hispana), X Gemina joined II (Augusta) and XX Valeria

[11] Nearer Spain – I (Augusta), II (Augusta), IX Macedonica (Hispana) Farther Spain – IV Macedonica, V Alaudae, VI Hispaniensis (Victrix), X Gemina, XX Valeria

[12] IV Scythica, V Urbana (Macedonica), X Fretensis, XI

[13] X Fretensis to Syria; XI to Illyricum

[14] IV Scythica, V Macedonica

[15] III Cyrenaica at Cairo, XII Fulminata at Alexandria; That VIII Augusta was transferred to Thebes is not proven, but is the product of a process of elimination. A legion garrisoned Thebes after the uprising. All other legions are accounted for. There is no base where VIII Augusta might have been "parked" for 30 years.

legion implies that the uprising was more than a local disturbance and could have spread down the river to threaten Imperial control of all of Egypt. Augustus' trust in the ex-Antonian legions appears to have had its limits. VIII Augusta remained at Thebes for more than three decades until it was transferred to the Danube.

In 25 B.C., a client king, Amyntas of Galatia in what is now Turkey, died. His kingdom was immediately annexed as a new Roman province. Two legions were sent to the capital city of Galatia, Antakya in modern Turkey, to ensure that the annexation would be peaceful.[16] The presence of the two legions in Galatia would provide its new Roman governor with overwhelming force and thus obviate the need for it. The Galatian royal army had been trained in the Roman manner under Amyntas' predecessor, Deiotarus. Some of the Galatian troops were now reorganized into a new Imperial legion incorporated into the Roman army.[17] The remainder were absorbed into other legions in the East away from their homeland. The new legion was sent to be a part of the Roman garrison in Egypt where it could not interfere with the absorbtion of Galatia into the Empire. Egypt, however, required a garrison of only two legions. The arrival of the Galatian legion released a legion for a transfer from Egypt to Syria where it became the fourth legion in that critical province.[18]

Augustus' next targets were the Alpine passes to the north of Italy and the areas along the upper Rhine and Danube. A peace treaty was negotiated with the Parthians in order that nothing in the East would interfere with the expansion northwards. In 25 B.C., the territory below the St. Bernard passes had been conquered. The last legion in Italy, which had participated in this campaign, was then sent further on to Gaul to assist in ensuring that that province was pacified once and for all.[19] In 16 B.C., Augustus moved to Gaul to supervise the Alpine conquest. Two legions arrived on the Rhine from Spain[20] to join the five which had been bringing order to Gaul.[21] This total of seven legions made up a northern army commanded by the future emperor Tiberius. Armies of this size were only assembled when a trusted member of the Imperial family was present. Augustus' stepson, Drusus, leading a southern army from Illyricum, also had seven legions including the four stationed in that province[22] plus one from Macedonia[23] and two transferred from Spain.[24] In 15 B.C., the two armies rolled over the tribes in the mountains and along the upper rivers and brought parts of what are now Bavaria, Switzerland and Austria into the Empire as the provinces of Raetia and Noricum.

The so-called Drusus War of 15 B.C. established a new frontier along the Rhine and the upper Danube. After the campaign was at an end, Tiberius' seven legions were spread along the Rhine from Vechten in the Netherlands to Dangstetten in southern Germany.[25] From Drusus' army, four legions remained in Illyricum as its permanent garrison.[26] One legion was advanced into the new province of Raetia to control the critical Brenner Pass.[27] The remaining two legions moved to neighboring Macedonia where they became that province's garrison on the lower Danube.[28] The rest of Noricum and Raetia was left to the auxiliaries to control. In 12 B.C., Tiberius used the four legions from Illyricum to conquer the region of Pannonia. These legions, however, returned at their previous bases in the hinterlands when the campaign was over and were not repositioned along the new frontier on the Danube.

In the years following the 15 B.C. campaign, Drusus led the Rhine legions eastwards each year along the tributaries of the Rhine. An advanced legionary base was established in 11 B.C. on the River Lippe at Oberaden with a two-legion garrison from which the next year's campaign could begin.[29] This series of efforts to conquer more of Germany ended with Drusus' accidental death in 9 B.C., and the defeat and resettlement of the German Sugambri by Tiberius on the west bank of the Rhine. The two legions based at Oberaden were then withdrawn in 8 B.C. to a new stronghold at Augsburg-Oberhausen in Raetia close to the upper Danube. Oberaden was replaced by a base for a single legion further into Germany at Haltern on the Lippe.[30] Campaigns against the German tribes continued, but at a lower intensity.

In 6 A.D., Tiberius prepared an army for a new campaign northwards toward Bohemia and Moravia. As the army moved out of Illyricum, the local tribes rose in revolt in its rear. The advance to the north was aborted. Subduing the Illyrians required three years of fighting with more than a few military setbacks. Tiberius used the four legions from Illyricum, the one from Raetia, and the two from Macedonia to repacify the region.[31]

The belief that disciplined well-trained legions could defeat any number of barbarians anywhere came to an

---

[16] V Macedonica from newly conquered Macedonia and VII Paterna (Macedonica) no longer needed to pacify Mauritania.
[17] as Legio XXII Deiotariana; The choice of the number XXII for the new legion shows that Legions XVI-XXI existed in 25 B.C. The name Deiotariana would not have been used had this legion been organized some years after the annexation of the province.
[18] XII Fulminata
[19] XVI Gallica
[20] I (now nameless after a disgrace in Spain) and V Alaudae
[21] XVI Gallica, XVII Classica, XVIII Libyca, XIX Paterna, XXI Rapax
[22] XI, XIII Gemina, XIV Gemina, XV Apollinaris
[23] IV Scythica
[24] IX Hispana, XX Valeria

[25] XVII Classica at Vechten, XVI Gallica and XVIII Libyca at Xanten, V Alaudae and XXI Rapax at Neuss, Germanica at Mainz, XIX Paterna at Dangstetten
[26] IX Hispana, XIII Gemina, XIV Gemina, XX Valeria
[27] XV Apollinaris
[28] IV Scythica, XI
[29] XVI Gallica, XXI Rapax
[30] XIX Paterna
[31] IX Hispana, XIII Gemina, XIV Gemina and XX Valeria from Illyricum; XV Apollinaris from Raetia; IV Scythica and XI from Macedonia

abrupt end in 9 A.D. with the annihilation of Varus and his three legions from lower Germany.[32] This shock brought a close to the expansionist policy of Augustus. The enormous blow to Roman self-confidence is best illustrated by the subsequent repositioning of the Rhine legions in two-legion fortresses in Germany and Raetia,[33] and Augustus' public admonition to Tiberius to forego further expansion of the Empire. The army no longer believed that a single legion, even behind walls, could successfully defend itself against all comers. Three fully trained legions had to be found immediately to reestablish the Rhine frontier and replace those that Varus had lost. At the same time, the Danube frontier had also to be strengthened to ensure that the pacification of Illyricum was complete. Newly formed legions would not be effective enough to carry out these missions even if enough volunteers had been available. The solution was a shuffle from east to west across the frontier. Four legions were transferred to Germany.[34] The Raetian and Illyrian legions that went to Germany were replaced by moving other legions westward along the frontier.[35] In the end, Germany gained one legion. Spain and Egypt each lost one[36] and Galatia lost both of its legions.[37]

During the succeeding three decades, the focus of the emperor and the army remained on the Rhine as confidence in Roman military prowess was progressively restored. The eight-legion Rhine garrison was divided into two separate military commands so that no single general would have more than four legions at his disposal.[38] The double legion bases at Augsburg-Oberhausen in Raetia and Cologne in lower Germany were eventually closed and the Rhine garrison began again to be spread along the river.[39] The turf and wood bases of the early Empire were slowly rebuilt in stone. The new bases had all the amenities of small cities. They were constructed by the legionaries themselves over a period of years and consumed time that the legions would normally have used for training and campaigning. They signified that the legions could expect to return to their established bases after each campaigning season in the German forests. And they provided the incentive for civilian centers – with personal connections to their legions – to grow up around the bases. This was the first step in a static mentality that crept into and eventually destroyed the usefulness of the Imperial legions.

In Egypt, Augustus decided that the only threat to that province would come from overseas. The two legions in its garrison now shared a combined base near Alexandria.[40] In Syria, a legion was moved eastwards in 18 A.D., to build a new legionary base at Belkis on the Euphrates River in a portion of the client kingdom of Commagene newly annexed to the province of Syria.[41] Belkis controlled the point at which the bulk of the commercial trade between the un-Romanized East and the Empire crossed the Euphrates.

Tiberius' successor, Caligula, formed two new legions in 39 A.D. and sent them to the Rhine for seasoning before he undertook a major German campaign.[42] Caligula's German campaign came to nothing, but the army on the Rhine had now been expanded to ten legions.[43]

The assassination of Caligula brought the unknown and, at the time, unrespected Claudius to the throne. It was Claudius who decided to make a military reputation for himself by invading Britain in 43 A.D. To ensure the success of the venture, Claudius detailed three seasoned Rhine and one Illyrian legion to the invasion army.[44] The Rhine legions heard the news of the new campaign and almost mutinied. The attraction of loot and action was not enough to overcome the ties to their permanent bases. After a tense confrontation, the legions finally marched to the English Channel. The three Rhine legions destined for Britain were replaced by the two new legions which had been formed by Caligula, now considered to be effective, and a legion transferred from Spain.[45] The Spanish garrison was thus reduced to two legions.[46] A Rhine legion was transferred to Pannonia to replace the one sent to Britain.[47] The Rhine garrison now comprised seven legions still divided into two military districts.[48] As a safety precaution for the emperor, the province of Illyricum was divided into Dalmatia and Pannonia, each with two legions.[49] The client kingdom of Moesia was annexed as a province. It gained a legion from Pannonia[50] and was for a time a three-legion province.[51] The Danube frontier had now been reorganized into three

---

[32] XVII Classica, XVIII Libyca, XIX Paterna
[33] V Alaudae and XXI Rapax at Xanten; I Germanica and XX Valeria at Cologne; II Augusta and XIV Gemina at Mainz; XIII Gemina and XVI Gallica at Augsburg-Oberhausen
[34] II Augusta from Spain, XXI Rapax from Raetia, XIV Gemina and XX Valeria from Illyria
[35] XIII Gemina from Illyricum to Raetia; VII Macedonica from Galatia to Illyricum; VIII Augusta from Egypt to Illyricum; XI from Moesia to Illyricum; XV Apollinaris from Raetia to Illyricum; V Macedonica from Galatia to Macedonia
[36] Spain - II Augusta; Egypt - VIII Augusta
[37] V Macedonica, VII Macedonica
[38] Upper Germany and Raetia - Mainz, Augsburg-Oberhausen; Lower Germany - Cologne and Xanten - See note 33
[39] II Augusta from Mainz opened Strasbourg 15 A.D.; XIII Gemina from Augsburg-Oberhausen opened Windisch 16 A.D.; I Germanica from Augsburg-Oberhausen opened Bonn, and XX Valeria reopened Neuss 35 A.D. Cologne was closed.
[40] III Cyrenaica and XXII Deiotariana
[41] X Fretensis
[42] XV Primigenia and XXII Primigenia. Their numbers seem to have been selected to fit into the row of legions already on the Rhine (XIII, XIV, XVI, XX, and XXI). The numbers XVII, XVIII and XIX were the Varian legions never to be mentioned again.
[43] I Germanica, II Augusta, V Alaudae, XIII Gemina, XIV Gemina, XV Primigenia, XVI Gallica, XX Valeria, XXI Rapax, and XXII Primigenia
[44] II Augusta, XIV Gemina, XX Valeria from Germany, and IX Hispana from Pannonia
[45] XV Primigenia and XXII Primigenia plus IV Macedonica from Spain
[46] VI Victrix, X Gemina
[47] XIII Gemina
[48] Upper Germany - IV Macedonica, XV Primigenia, XXII Primigenia; Lower Germany - I Germanica, V Alaudae, XVI Gallica, XXI Rapax
[49] Dalmatia – VII Claudia and XI Claudia; Pannonia – XIII Gemina and XV Apollinaris
[50] VIII Augusta
[51] IV Scythica, V Macedonica, VIII Augusta

new interlocking provinces, Dalmatia, Pannonia, and Moesia, none of which had a large enough garrison to be a threat to the emperor.

After an initial victory against the southeastern tribes in Britain, the four Claudian legions separated and proceeded to conquer the fertile portion of the island in separate campaigns. Wales and northern England were left alone for the time being until such time as the newly acquired territory had been sufficiently romanized to be left without a garrison. A first attempt to expand the province into Wales was abandoned abruptly when the supposedly pacified British tribes rose up behind the legions in 60-61 A.D. and slaughtered the Romanized civilian population in the province. Britain was repacified with a vengeance by the four legions already stationed there.

The next major wave of repositionings came in 62 A.D. during Nero's reign after the Parthians had invaded Armenia and badly defeated two legions under the command of the governor of Cappadocia.[52] With these two legions crippled for the moment and sent back to Syria to regroup, two legions from the Danube together with the three remaining Syrian legions were moved to Cappadocia to oppose the Parthians.[53] To fill the resulting gaps along the Danube frontier, Dalmatia lost one of its two legions and Spain its next to last.[54]

The Parthian threat to Armenia was resolved through negotiation. The build up of a serious army in Cappadocia and Armenia, however, led Nero to consider a new military adventure, perhaps to the south toward Ethiopia. The legions brought together to confront the Parthians left Cappadocia in 66 A.D. Three legions moved to Alexandria in Egypt to prepare for the new campaign.[55] One legion moved to Moesia for retraining in a Danube environment.[56] The remaining legion went back to its original base in Syria where it joined the two defeated legions.[57] Syria now had a three-legion garrison.[58]

Whatever plans Nero may have had for the army at Alexandria were aborted by the Jewish uprising of 66 A.D. The three legions from Alexandria moved to Palestine to help the Syrian legions crush the uprising. One of the three Syrian legions had already been ambushed by Jewish guerillas and had lost its eagle, its artillery and baggage train, and the remaining two legions plus auxiliaries were clearly inadequate.

To reinforce the embattled East, or perhaps to restart his Eastern expansion plan, Nero brought back one of the four British legions to Italy.[59] He also formed two new legions in Italy which would only be ready for active service in a year or so.[60] The conquering of the remainder of Britain was put in abeyance by the reduction of its garrison from four to three legions.[61] Britain was a triumph for Claudius, and not interesting to Nero. The revolt of Julius Vindex, the governor of Gallia Lugdunensis in 68 A.D., supported by the Gallic population but none of the legions, ended any plans for Nero's Eastern campaign. The Vindex revolt was quickly crushed at Besançon by the legions from upper Germany. One of Nero's new legions was sent from Italy to the scene of the revolt near Lyon to ensure that the province would remain quiet.[62] Nero's suicide shortly afterwards threw the Empire into the first of the succession convulsions.

When the dust had cleared at the end of 69 A.D., and the general from the East, Vespasian, was securely on the throne, he could survey an army that was as disorganized as that after Actium exactly 100 years earlier. Vespasian's new army organization was as carefully calculated and as subtle as Octavian's had been. His first priority was the Rhine where the Batavians and others of the local tribes were in full revolt. The Rhine legions that had actually opposed Vespasian's legions on the battlefield at Bedriacum in Italy were pardoned, re-officered, and sent farther away from Italy.[63] A new 7-legion German garrison was formed with the last two legions from Spain, and one each from Britain, Dalmatia and Pannonia together with the two Vitellian survivors now moved from upper to lower Germany.[64] A legion from Moesia was repositioned in the French Burgundy region to ensure that the Vindex problem would not arise again.[65] Four legions, officially at least, had disappeared.[66] Vespasian, however, formed a new IV Flavia, almost certainly with the legionaries of the former IV Macedonica, and a new XVI Flavia bearing the number of the disbanded XVI Gallica. Fresh officers were undoubtedly appointed to teach their legionaries new lessons of loyalty.

Another new legion formed by Galba in Spain in 68 A.D. had been battered in fightIng for Otho at the first battle of

---

[52] IV Scythica and XII Fulminata; IV Scythica was sent to Cappadocia in 55 A.D.
[53] V Macedonica from Moesia and XV Apollinaris from Pannonia;III Gallica, VI Ferrata and X Fretensis from Syria
[54] VII Claudia from Dalmatia to Moesia to replace V Macedonica; X Gemina from Spain to Pannonia to replace XV Apollinaris
[55] V Macedonica, X Fretensis and XV Apollinaris
[56] III Gallica
[57] VI Ferrata
[58] IV Scythica, VI Ferrata, XII Fulminata

[59] XIV Gemina
[60] I Adiutrix and I Italica; I Adiutrix was formed from marines from the fleet at Misenum. I Italica reportedly from Italians at least six feet tall. The centuriate of both legions would have been transferred from other legions, the taller to I Italica.
[61] II Augusta, IX Hispana, XX Valeria
[62] I Italica
[63] I Italica and V Alaudae to Moesia; XXI Rapax and XXII Primigenia to lower Germany
[64] I Adiutrix (Spain), VI Victrix (Spain), XIV Gemina (Britain via Italy), XI Claudia (Dalmatia), X Gemina (Pannonia), plus XXI Rapax and XXII Primigenia from the former German garrison
[65] VIII Augusta at Mirebeau-sur-Béze near Dijon
[66] XV Primigenia had been destroyed at Xanten, and I Germanica, IV Macedonica and XVI Gallica had sworn loyalty to the New Gallic Empire and were offically disbanded.

Bedriacum and exiled to Pannonia by Vitellius.[67] It was renamed Gemina, a certain sign that it had been combined with other units which could only have been I Germanica and XVI Gallica from the Rhine that had foresworn their oaths to Rome and had been disbanded by Vespasian. I Germanica is never heard of again. XVI Flavia was formed in the East and probably did not contain survivors of XVI Gallica. In 74 A.D., the reorganized VII Gemina returned to Spain. There it could digest its newly transferred legionaries and become an effective legion again. It would be the only legion in Spain until the end of the Empire. A further new legion, II Adiutrix was given the honorific Pia Fidelis and sent to Britain as the fourth legion for that province after the Batavian insurrection was crushed. The four new legions, II Adiutrix, IV Flavia, VII Gemina, and XVI Flavia replaced, numerically at least, the four legions that had disappeared. With Nero's two new legions, the army's size had now increased to 29 legions with a maximum of four under the control of any one provincial governor.[68]

Having restored the Rhine garrison and with the Batavian unrest settled, Vespasian turned his attention to the East. The client kingdoms of Commagene, Cappadocia and Lesser Armenia were annexed in 72 A.D. Cappadocia received a permanent two-legion garrison. The two transferred legions built new bases along the upper Euphrates from which they could oversee the annexations, control the client kingdom of Armenia, and defend Cappadocia against Alan raiders from the north.[69] Syria received back the legion sent to Moesia for retraining and saw it stationed in a new base on the upper Euphrates.[70] The Danube legions that had been sent from Alexandria to Palestine to help put down the Jewish uprising returned to their original provinces.[71] The Jewish uprising had been crushed except for a few isolated pockets of last gasp resistance. Vespasian separated Judaea from the province of Syria and made it into a new province, Syria Palaestina. He transferred one of the Syrian legions to Jerusalem as the province's first permanent garrison.[72] The population of Syria Palaestina was still prone to violence. Syria was now a three-legion province.[73] Moesia's garrison was increased to four legions although these included two former Vitellian legions that were still in the process of being reorganized.[74]

Vespasian's second son, Domitian started a campaign against the Chatti in Germany in 83-84 A.D. to put his name into the history books. A new legion was raised in Italy and sent to the Rhine.[75] Before the German campaign could be concluded, attacks of the Sarmatians and Dacians into Moesia caused Domitian to break off his expedition in order to reinforce the Danube frontier. The presence of the new legion on the Rhine permitted the transfer of a more experienced one from Germany to Pannonia.[76] Seven legions were still required to protect the Rhine frontier.[77] Any idea of conquering all of Britain was canceled when its fourth legion was withdrawn and also sent to reinforce Pannonia.[78] Britain was again a three-legion province[79] and would remain so until the end of the Empire. After a series of Roman defeats, including the destruction of one legion,[80] Pannonia was cleared of raiders in 88 A.D. by an army of eight legions from Pannonia and Moesia.[81] Britain and Dalmatia had each lost a legion to strengthen the Danube frontier.[82] Moesia was divided into Upper and Lower provinces each with two legions to avoid four legions delivering too much power into the hands of a governor.[83] Pannonia had its garrison increased from two to four legions.[84]

In 89 A.D., before Domitian could take final retribution against the Dacians, the governor of Upper Germany, Lucius Antonius Saturninus, led the two legions stationed in Mainz in a rebellion.[85] The rebellion did not spread to the remainder of the Rhine army as the governor had hoped, and it was quickly crushed. The remnant of one of the defeated legions was then exiled to Pannonia to become the fifth legion in that province.[86] Upper Germany received the legion previously in Gaul as a replacement.[87]

Domitian now decreed that there would be no more double legion bases. The risk of a rebellion by two legions in a single base had become too great. The only exception in the Empire would be Alexandria in Egypt where the governor was never a Senator and, so it was felt, could not aspire to the purple.

Trajan began his reign with a concentration of every available legion to conquer Dacia. He overcame the

---

[67] VII Galbiana had been formed by the future emperor Galba in Spain from provincial citizens. Its centuriate probably came primarily from VI Victrix, the last of the Spanish garrison legions.
[68] See Table G
[69] XII Fulminata at Malataya, still suffering from defeats by the Parthians and XVI Flavia at Kelkit
[70] III Gallica at Samsat
[71] V Macedonica returned to Gigen, Moesia to replace III Gallica which was going back to Syria XV Apollinaris returned to Petronell, Pannonia where it had been stationed before the Parthian campaign
[72] X Fretensis that had been temporarily at Alexandria before transferring to fight the Jewish uprising
[73] III Gallica, IV Scythica, VI Ferrata
[74] I Italica and V Alaudae, Vitellian legions from Germany, plus V Macedonica, VII Claudia

[75] I (Flavia) Minervia
[76] I Adiutrix
[77] Upper Germany – XI Claudia, XIV Gemina, XXI Rapax; Lower Germany – I (Flavia) Minervia, VI Victrix, X Gemina, XXII Primigenia
[78] II Adiutrix
[79] II Augusta, IX Hispana, XX Valeria
[80] V Alaudae
[81] Pannonia – I Adiutrix, II Adiutrix, XIII Gemina, XV Apollinaris; Moesia – I Italica, IV Flavia, V Macedonica, VII Claudia
[82] Britain – II Adiutrix; Dalmatia – IV Flavia
[83] Upper Moesia – IV Flavia, VII Claudia; Lower Moesia – I Italica, V Macedonica
[84] I Adiutrix, II Adiutrix, XIII Gemina, XV Apollinaris
[85] XIV Gemina, XXI Rapax
[86] XXI Rapax
[87] VIII Augusta from Mirebeau-sur-Beze reopened Strasbourg on the Rhine joining XI Claudia and XIV Gemina

growing legion immobility problem with stories of the great gold wealth of the Dacians and the prospect of each legionary becoming rich. Trajan had nine legions already in Pannonia and Moesia.[88] He supplemented these with a newly formed legion[89] and three legions from the Rhine.[90] The First Dacian War ended in 102 A.D. in a stalemate sealed by a temporary peace treaty. One of the legions from the Rhine, no longer combat ready, was sent back to Lower Germany to reorganize itself.[91] Trajan raised a second new legion to replace it.[92] A Pannonian legion was destroyed or disbanded either at the end of the First Dacian War or the beginning of the Second.[93] It was replaced in Trajan's army by a further legion from Upper Germany.[94] The Rhine garrison had now been reduced to the four legions it would have until the end of the Empire.[95] Trajan had served on the Rhine and was assuming that the German tribes were now controllable with the military power he still had available there. His focus and aims were elsewhere.

The Second Dacian War of 104-106 A.D. ended with the annexation of Dacia as a Roman province. The 13 legions that Trajan had used for the campaign remained on the Danube. Pannonia had been divided into Upper and Lower provinces, with three legions in the Upper province and one in the Lower.[96] Upper Moesia was now protected by the army in Dacia and required only a single legion.[97] Lower Moesia had an exposed frontier and was given a four-legions garrison.[98] Dacia's garrison was four legions.[99] The Danube frontier thus required nearly half of the entire Roman army.

By the end of the Dacian Wars, it is estimated that less than 2% of the legionary recruits were Italian, and a rapidly increasing percentage were non-citizens often enrolled under the gens Pollia, the Roman voting tribe to which newly made "citizens" were assigned. Whether this decline was because bread and circuses at home were more attractive than 25 years on the frontiers of the Empire is a matter of some debate. Some of the non-citizen legionaries would receive their citizenship diplomas only when they had completed their 25 years' service. In other cases, instant citizenship seems to have been used as an incentive for them to enlist.

As the proportion of Italian recruits fell, each legion became more responsible for finding its own replacement manpower. The logical place for their recruiting was the area where the legion was stationed. Sons of retired legionaries and young men from the neighborhood who were drawn to a military life joined "their" legion. At the end of the 1st Century and thereafter, it was common for a legion to find the majority of its recruits from the province in which it was then serving. Additionally, the legion became responsible for training its recruits from the day they swore their first oath. It would have been pointless to recruit a volunteer in Britain or Syria and then to send him to Italy for four months' basic training. Recruits would henceforth give their allegiance to the particular legion where they would probably begin and end their military careers. At the point in time when the majority of the legionaries came from the province in which their legion was stationed, there would be a problem with relocating that legion to another province. A resentful legion, particularly if its centuriate shared the feeling, would not be fully effective. Moreover, if a legion was transferred to a new frontier, it would have to be retrained to fight another sort of barbarian who would use different tactics and weapons. Until this training was complete, the legion would be less useful than one with local experience.

In the East, the Nabataean client king Rabbell II died unexpectedly in 106 A.D. His kingdom was immediately annexed as the Roman province of Arabia by the governor of Syria. A Syrian legion was transferred to Arabia with a strong force of auxiliaries to ensure that the absorbtion of the new province into the empire was peaceful.[100] The king's army became auxiliaries in the Roman army and were sent to other provinces. The garrison of Syria was thus reduced to two legions.[101]

Trajan then opened a campaign against the Parthians in 113 A.D. with all the eastern legions plus one legion transferred from Moesia and vexillations from the other Danube legions.[102] The campaign involved all or parts of 12 legions and left the eastern provinces with skeleton garrisons. Perhaps as a result, a Jewish uprising broke out in 116 A.D. and spread around the eastern Mediterranean. More uprisings blossomed in newly conquered Armenia and Mesopotamia. These uprisings, Trajan's failing health, and the lack of a conclusive success against the Parthians ended the campaign. The vexillations returned to their home bases and the eastern legions dedicated themselves to crushing the various uprisings. Trajan died at Antioch in 117 A.D. and Hadrian, a successful general from the Danube frontier

---

[88] The legions in Notes 84, 85 and 87
[89] XXX Ulpia
[90] VI Victris and X Gemina from Lower Germany and XI Claudia from Upper Germany
[91] VI Victrix
[92] II Traiana
[93] XXI Rapax
[94] XIV Gemina
[95] 106-122 A.D. – I Minervia and VI Victrix in Lower Germany; VIII Augusta and XXII Primigenia in Upper Germany. In 122 A.D., VI Victrix was transferred to Britain and was replaced by XXX Ulpia from Pannonia
[96] Upper Pannonia: XIV Gemina, XV Apollinaris and XXX Ulpia; Lower Pannonia: X Gemina
[97] VII Claudia
[98] I Italica, II Traiana, V Macedonica, XI Claudia
[99] I Adiutrix, II Adiutrix, IV Flavia, XIII Gemina

[100] VI Ferrata from Rafniyeh in Syria to Bosra in Arabia. III Cyrenaica from Egypt may have assisted in the takeover.
[101] III Gallica, IV Scythica
[102] East – III Gallica, IV Scythica, VI Ferrata, X Fretensis, XII Fulminata, XVI Flavia; Egypt – III Cyrenaica; Danube – II Traiana (transferred) from Moesia plus vexillations from I Adiutrix, II Adiutrix, XIII Gemina and XV Apollinaris

and Trajan's presumed successor, proceeded to reorder the army and the borders.

Hadrian's reorganization was the last Empire-wide repositioning of the old Roman Army. His purpose appears to have been an attempt to fix the frontiers of the Empire where they could be defended with the army he had available. Armenia, Mesopotamia and Assyria, which had been conquered by Trajan but not fully integrated into the Empire as provinces, were abandoned. Nine legions were shuffled along the frontiers without any apparent disciplinary problems.[103] It may be that the usual accession donative smoothed the relocations. Syria Palaestina and Upper Moesia each gained a legion,[104] and Dacia, now considered to be pacified, lost two of its four.[105] Otherwise, the number of legions in each provincial garrison remained the same. Shortly after the Hadrianic reorganization, one British legion disappeared but was replaced by shuffling three legions along the frontier from Dacia to Britain.[106] Dacia then lost its next to last legion. The other provinces had the same number of legions as before. Hadrian then issued a decree that, henceforth, no legion was to be permanently transferred away from the province where it was stationed. This was probably designed to aid recruiting. The legions now relied primarily on volunteers from their own provinces to fill their ranks, and recruits for the legions were more likely to come forward to serve in the areas where they were at home.

Legion transfers during the next three quarters of a century were minimal. A further Jewish revolt in 132-135 A.D. destroyed one of the two legions stationed in Egypt.[107] It was not replaced. Egypt was now a one-legion province and would remain so until the time of Diocletian.[108]

The accession of Marcus Aurelius, an emperor without any military experience, opened a decade and a half of continuous frontier warfare. In 161 A.D. the Parthians invaded Armenia and chased Rome's client king into exile. The governor of Cappadocia rode to the rescue of Armenia with one legion and was totally defeated.[109] A legion from Upper Germany and two from the Danube were immediately sent to Cappadocia to confront the Parthians.[110] This reinforcement, together with the Cappadocian and Syrian legions, enabled the Roman general, Avidius Cassius, to launch a counterstroke deep into Parthian territory. The campaign ended in 166 A.D. with the defeat of the Parthian army. The legions from the West returned home and left the eastern garrison as it had been before. The weakening of the Rhine garrison had encouraged the always aggressive Chatti to attack the Rhine limes in Upper Germany. They were repulsed with difficulty by the remaining garrison together with reinforcements from Britain.

In the meantime, Marcus Aurelius had formed two new legions for a campaign north of the Danube to conquer that always restive region.[111] The legions returning to the Danube from the Parthian campaign brought plague with them. It spread with particular ferocity through the tightly packed legionary bases. At the same time, the tribes across the Danube were being pushed southwards by other tribes from further to the north. The combination of sudden weakness in the Roman army, and a sense of desperation among the tribes, caused the major eruption of the Marcomanni War of 167-172 A.D. Raetia, Noricum, Pannonia, Dalmatia and parts of Italy were laid waste. A legion was advanced from Moesia to Dacia to reinforce the garrison there.[112] Other legions from as far away as Spain sent vexillations to contain the barbarians. By 173 A.D., the frontier had been stabilized again and peace treaties had been signed with the tribes. After the fighting ended, the two new legions were posted to Raetia and Noricum, where there had been no previous legionary garrisons.[113]

In 192 A.D., Marcus Aurelius' son and successor, Commodus, was strangled in his palace in Rome. This unleashed a new succession convulsion. The ultimate victor was Septimius Severus, the governor of Upper Pannonia. He secured the loyalty of the twelve Danube legions and proceeded to defeat the Eastern garrison led by Gaius Pescennius Niger in 194 A.D.[114] Severus then used Rhine and Danube legions to defeat the legions of Decimus Clodius Albinus, the governor of Britain, in 197 A.D.[115]

---

[103] IV Flavia from Dacia back to Upper Moesia; II Adiutrix from Dacia back to Lower Pannonia; X Gemina from Lower to Upper Pannonia; XIV Gemina within Upper Pannonia; XV Apollinaris from Upper Pannonia to Cappadocia; XVI Flavia from Cappadocia to Syria; II Traiana from Syria to Egypt; III Cyrenaica from Egypt to Arabia; VI Ferrata from Arabia to Syria Palaestina
[104] Syria Palaestina gained VI Ferrata; Upper Moesia gained IV Flavia
[105] Dacia lost II Adiutrix and IV Flavia. I Adiutrix and XIII Gemina remained.
[106] IX Hispana was transferred from York, Britain to Nijmegen on the lower Rhine after some form of disgrace, and then passes into oblivion. VI Victrix moved from the Rhine to Britain and XXX Ulpia from Pannonia to the Rhine. I Adiutrix returned from Dacia to Szony in Pannonia where it had been before the Dacian Wars to replace XXX Ulpia. This shuffle of legions confirms the theory that IX Hispana was no longer usable and had been disbanded.
[107] XXII Deiotariana
[108] II Traiana at Alexandria
[109] XV Apollinaris
[110] I Minervia from Upper Germany; II Adiutrix from Lower Pannonia and V Macedonica from Lower Moesia
[111] II Italica Pia and III Italica Concors
[112] V Macedonica from Iglitza-Turcoaia, Moesia to Turda, Dacia
[113] II Italica Pia to Noricum; III Italica Concors to Raetia
[114] Septimius Severus apparantly took parts or all of the following legions to the battlefield of Issus: III Italica from Raetia; II Italica from Noricum; I Adiutrix, II Adiutrix, and XIV Gemina from Pannonia; I Italica, IV Flavia, VII Claudia, and XI Claudia from Moesia. X Gemina was left to protect Pannonia and V Macedonica and XIII Gemina remained in Dacia. C. Pecennius Niger had XII Fulminata and XV Apollinaris from Cappadocia; III Gallica, IV Scythica and XVI Flavia from Syria; and X Fretensis from Syria Palaestina. III Cyrenaica in Arabia and VI Fretensis from Syria Palaestina were rewarded by Severus for having remained neutral.
[115] Severus– I Minervia, VIII Augusta, XXII Primigenia, XXX Ulpia, III Italica; Albinus– II Augusta, VI Victrix and XX Valeria

During these four years of internal warfare, the Parthians had taken the opportunity to regain the territory they had lost earlier to Roman expansion. Severus began a counterstroke against the Parthians within months after his defeat of Clodius Albinus. The times of moving entire legions from one part of the Empire to another were past. Severus founded three new legions in the East to reinforce the army there.[116] The centuriate for these legions came from existing legions. He reformed the Praetorian Guard with volunteers from the frontier legions and took it along as part of his army. These two actions removed the best and the bravest from the western frontier legions. Together with the legions and auxiliaries already stationed in the East,[117] Severus had an army approaching 120,000 men. The Parthian army was heavily defeated although certain of its major cities managed to beat off the invading Roman army.

Severus then divided the provinces that had opposed him.[118] The provinces of Mesopotamia and Osrhoene were formed and garrisoned, each with one of Severus' newly formed legions.[119] No governor of the newly made provinces would in the future be able to call upon more than two legions. The two legions from Syria Coele were moved south from the Euphrates to the edge of the Arabian Desert, but were still in the province of Syria Coele.[120] The East now comprised seven provinces with a total of ten legions.[121] The last of the new Severan legions returned to Italy.[122] Periodically, it would be called upon for a campaign in the East or the West. It was the first of the truly mobile legions in the Roman army. In the past, the Praetorian Guard had been the only available force for this purpose.

The Severan redeployment in the East was almost the last movement of the old Imperial legions. In 214 A.D., Caracalla redrew the borders of Upper and Lower Pannonia so that each province would have only a two-legion garrison. The legions in Pannonia, however, did not move their bases.[123] Until then, emperors had relied upon the army to keep them in power. The next half century was marked by a series of pretenders, most of whom were senators serving as generals on the frontier. Their candidature was put forward by one or another part of the army, and often at the initiative of the army rather than the general himself. It became the norm to pander to the will of the legions. One inconvenienced legions at one's peril, and relocation was a major inconvenience. Short lived emperors and would be emperors came and went. Factions of the army bled themselves white supporting or defending one or another candidate against the others. At the same time as the quality and training of the legions was being diluted by casualties and the need for ever more replacements, pressure was increasing on the frontiers from outside the Empire. And yet, for the most part, the frontier legions continued to exist and to attempt to carry out their mission of defending the borders of Roman civilization even as they refused relocation. Between 122 A.D. during the reign of Hadrian and 284 A.D., when Diocletian came to power, only three legions were transferred to different provinces.[124] Two of these eventually returned to their original provinces. Nineteen legions remained in the same bases for 180 years, two were destroyed,[125] and six moved within the same province.[126] By the end of the 3rd Century, the legions knew only their immediate surroundings and could hardly be employed for any other purpose. It is illuminating that the greatest pressure on the frontiers during the 3rd Century came from across the Rhine. No legions, however, were withdrawn from provinces that were less threatened. This reinforces the argument that the parameters of frontier defense were now being dictated more by the soldiers and less by the Emperor in Rome. Vexillations were the maximum that could be offered.

The only major repositioning in the first three quarters of the 3rd Century was the withdrawel by Aurelian in 270 A.D. of the two legions stationed in Dacia and the abandonment of that province to the Carpi and Goths. One of the Dacian legions, it would appear, had been seriously worn down in defending the province.[127] It was first posted far back from the border near an old base in Pannonia.[128] After a few years, during which its ranks were refilled and it was retrained, it was moved forward again to the Danube to become an active part of the frontier defenses.[129] The other Dacian legion was moved directly to a Moesian base as an additional frontier reinforcement.[130]

There is also evidence that III Cyrenaica was so badly defeated by the Palmyrene troops under Zenobia in 269 A.D. that it was no longer capable of further service. A new legion, IV Martia, was stationed in III Cyrenaica's former base at Bosra. IV Martia remained in Bosra until 288 A.D. when it was transferred to a new base at nearby

---

[116] I Parthica, II Parthica, III Parthica
[117] See table G
[118] Upper Britain – II Augusta, XX Valeria; Lower Britain – VI Victrix; Syria Phoenice – III Gallica; Syria Coele IV Scythica, XVI Flavia
[119] Mesopotamia – I Parthica; Osrhoene – III Parthica
[120] IV Scythica to Tayibeh; XVI Flavia to Sura
[121] See Table G
[122] II Parthica
[123] X Gemina and XIV Gemina in Upper Pannonia; I Adiutrix and II Adiutrix in Lower Pannonia
[124] V Macedonica from Lower Moesia to Lower Dacia 166 A.D. during the Marcommi War returning to Lower Moesia in 271 A.D. when Dacia was abandoned; III Gallica from Syria to Numidia in 238 A.D. to replace the disbanded III Augusta returning to Syria in 253 A.D. when III Augusta was reconstituted; XIII Gemina from Upper Dacia to Dacia Ripensis 268-270 A.D when Dacia was being abandoned
[125] XXII Deiotariana in Syria Palaestina between 132 and 135 A.D. in the Jewish uprising; VI Ferrata with Valerian in 260 A.D. by the Parthians
[126] III Augusta within Africa 128 A.D.; II Italica within Noricum 172 A.D. and 205 A.D.; IV Scythica and XVI Flavia within Syria Coele 198 A.D.; III Gallica within Syria Phoenice 219 A.D.; III Parthica within Osrhoene 219 A.D.
[127] XIII Gemina
[128] Ptuj which had last been garrisoned 150 years before. A new base for the legion would have been necessary as the old base had been turned into a veteran's colony at the end of the Dacian Wars.
[129] To Artscav, a base once garrisoned by IV Flavia 150 years before
[130] V Macedonica to Gigen

Al Lejum. III Cyrenaica seems to have been reconstituted and stationed again at Bosra.

Once the legion immobility problem had been recognized as serious and probably incurable, various emperors tried to modify the army organization to meet their military needs. Gallienus, about 260 A.D., determined that some sort of mobile reserve was required to reinforce threatened sectors of the frontiers. If he could not concentrate full legions to meet a barbarian or internal threat, the forces would have to be assembled from other sources. Vexillations, or legionary detachments, had been used since far earlier times to strengthen a part of the army at a moment of need. A vexillation at this earlier time would have consisted of one or more full cohorts sent as independent units under a flag but without the legionary eagle. They would serve under the commander of a combined force until the immediate crisis had been resolved. The vexillation would then return to its legion and disapear as a separate entity.

Gallienus initiated a system of taking vexillations from each of the legions in the provinces he controlled and retaining them indefinitely in a field army. The vexillations from the two legions stationed in a province served in a single paired formation of about 2000 men. It may have been this reorganization that caused the 3rd Century garrisons at the permanent legionary bases to shrink from the 5000 men at the end of the first quarter of the century to the 1500 at the beginning of the fourth quarter. These vexillations were probably made up of volunteer forces of younger and more ambitious men from throughout the legion rather than specifically detailed cohorts. There must have continued to be communication between these vexillations and their mother legions. One would expect that trained replacements would have flowed continuously from the home legion to its vexillation, and that the vexillation would not recruit and provide basic training in competition with other units in the area where the field army was operating. A fresh recruit sent directly into battle is a danger to his unit and his comrades. His basic training cannot be done in the field. It must be carried out in a settled encampment, most probably the fortress of the parent legion. When, at the end of the 3rd Century, the mobile army began to receive drafts of raw or barbarian recruits directly, the level of training and discipline inevitably fell. There were neither resources nor sufficient time to bring these recruits up to the standards of the early Empire. On the other hand, the better or more ambitious centurions would have been eager to join a vexillation in the hopes of gaining promotion. The time-servers would have remained behind. Over decades, the standard of training and the morale of the legion at its home base would have declined. No permanent base of Gallienus' mobile army has ever been located. This would reinforce the argument that the vexillations in his army were supported, for a time at least, by their parent legions.

At about this time, there was also a significant change in Roman military architecture. Previously, military fortresses had been built with towers whose front walls were flush with the outside fortress walls. Fighting was expected to be outside the walls and not on them. In the middle of the 3rd Century, fortress towers began to be built or reconstructed so that they projected outside the walls. Ostensibly, this was to enable artillery pieces to be mounted on the towers to fire along the walls. The immense effort that went into these tower improvements tends to support the theory that fortress garrisons had been sharply reduced throughout the Empire and that the remaining troops were only just sufficient to defend their bases. Although the size of the garrisons had shrunk, it would appear that the legions' artillery had remained at the permanent bases. The old tradition that the Roman army fought in the field and only wintered in its bases had passed.

The accession of Diocletian in 284 A.D., yet another of the Illyrian generals, would have seemed to the citizens of the Empire to be only an interlude in the descent into chaos. By a combination of luck and political skills, Diocletian survived long enough to actually bring the whole of the army and thus the entire empire under his control. Diocletian created a substantial number of new small legions which he scattered along the border of the empire from Germany to Egypt.[131] The border with the Parthian Empire was reset further to the east along the Tigris and old and new legions were posted along it.[132] The size of the bases that these legions built for themselves indicates that they were only half or less as big as the legions of Septimius Severus. It does not seem reasonable to assume that these bases were smaller because parts of the legion were stationed elsewhere. Periodically, the entire legion would come together, whether to celebrate its Natalis Aquilae, or for a military exercise. During that time, accommodations would be needed for the whole legion. If the new legions created by Diocletian were all smaller, then it is logical to assume that the old legions in their centuries old bases had also shrunk. Some of the shrinkage is undoubtedly attributable to the practice of sending vexillations of the frontier legions to a central field army. The core of the old legions, however, remained in their traditional bases, whether for the purpose of recruiting and training, or as a second class border defense.

Diocletian also separated the civil authority in a province from the military. The provincial governor would no longer have the authority to call out the troops or to block a transfer of troops from his province. The governor

---

[131] We know of I Pontica, I Jovia Scythica, I Armeniaca, I Martia, I Noricorum, II Herculea, II Flavia Constantia, III Diocletiana, III Herculea, IV Parthica, IV Jovia, V Parthica, V Jovia, VI Parthica and VI Herculea

[132] II Parthica at Cefae, Mesopotamia; III Parthica at Tel Araban, Osrhoene, IV Parthica at Beseira, Osrhoene; V Parthica at Diarbekir, Mesopotamia, and I Armeniaca at Klaudias, Cappadocia on the upper Euphrates

would now have to deal with a Dux, or chief miliary officer for the province. This may have lessened the risk of further civilian pretenders to the throne. It certainly reduced the authority of the governor to organize the protection of his province against attack, and the ability of the frontier legions to support themselves with public tax money raised in the civilian sector.

Diocletian inherited the field army begun by Gallienus and built it out further in the direction of a group of mobile armies. When the ursurper Carausius acquired the field army in Gaul about 286 A.D., it included vexillations from nine legions whose home bases stretched from Britain to Upper Moesia.[133] It is probable that the army led by Constantius against the Carausian stronghold of Boulogne in 293 A.D. contained further vexillations from these same legions. That soldiers from the same legions could be counted on to fight each other to the death indicates how far the vexillations had separated from their parents. The remainder of the field army was barbarian, hired or blackmailed into serving the emperor. Their methods of fighting were those of their homelands, and the field army came less and less to resemble that of the early Empire. The old legions in their border fortresses were now known as 'Ripenses'. The complete border army was referred to as 'Limitanei'. Both were becoming irrelevant to the military history of the period. The barbarian attacks were no longer raids, but had become full-fledged invasions. The frontier fortresses, with their shrunken garrisons, were now expected only to defend themselves and, when possible, to threaten the invader's rear. The field army would be responsible for turning back a barbarian invasion.

The final straw was the inability of the center to pay or to supply the frontier garrisons. The financial difficulties of the 4th Century left the emperors of the West without the means to finance both the field armies and the Limitanei on the frontiers. The provinces were also unable to raise additional taxes to pay the Limitanei. Without contact or support, the old Imperial legions faded into the mist. History tells us that all of the frontier legions were ordered to Italy in 405 A.D. to defend Rome against the Goths. Perhaps the legionary eagles were carried to Italy, but if any substantial forces from the old legions responded, they left no trace there. It is about at this time that a civilian occupation of the old legionary fortresses can be seen. Whether relatives of the soldiers who had been left behind, or merely wanderers, they saw the fortresses as defendable places to settle. Military buildings were cannibalized to construct new housing. And, although the fortress acqueduct systems soon failed for lack of skilled maintenance, life went on.

---

[133] II Augusta and XX Valeria from Upper Britain; I Minervia and XXX Ulpia from Lower Germany; VIII Augusta and XXII Primigenia from Upper Germany; II Parthica from Italy; IV Flavia and VII Claudia from Lower Moesia

II. THE TABLES

INTRODUCTION TO THE TABLES

1. Tables A and B indicate that the relocation of the legions had virtually stopped by the end of Hadrian's reign. Statistics show that the disappearance of Italian recruits by this time, and the sharp increase of recruits born in the neighborhood of the legions' bases seem to be related to this phenomenon. The Empire's wars continued, first on one front, and then on another. The legions' headquarters, however, remained where they had always been. The use of vexillations, and the later mobile army were emergency measures which eased the Empire's immediate military needs. They did not, however, bring the army back to its condition in the early Augustan years.

2. Table C is interesting because it shows how many of the names of Roman bases have been preserved down to modern times. This would indicate that these sites were never totally abandoned. There were always enough inhabitants left, after the fires had died down, to pass on the name of the place. The invaders or conquerers were seldom so overwhelming that they would impose their own names. Clearly, the Roman engineers had selected the most defensible or strategically desireable locations in the neighborhood. It is the continuity, however, that continues to impress. Only along the middle and lower Danube were the names universally lost and this may have been the result of the general Hunnish destruction at the end of the Empire.

3. The maps attached to Table E clearly show the methodical way in which the Roman army absorbed territory. The resemblance to a chess board is unmistakable. Legions were posted where they could support each other if an expansion became over-extended. Bases were sited, wherever possible, on navigable rivers so that supplies and movements to and from the bases were simplified. The rivers were less borders than they were transportation routes. The maps further show that most legions were not sited on the Imperial frontiers. They were located where they could easily move forward or laterally to undertake whatever limited objective was ordered.

4. Table G demonstrates that the number of legions in each province remained remarkably constant during the entire Imperial period. In the early decades, a maximum of four legions in a province was considered safe, unless the Emperor himself was present to campaign with a larger army. With four legions, it was felt that the provincial governor could defend his territory but could not become a serious threat to the Empire. At a later date, Emperors became less confident that governors would share their own good sense. The size of the army needed to defend the Empire had not changed, but experience showed that the ambitions of governors had. The practical solution selected was to leave the legions where they were - perhaps for other reasons - but to divide the provinces, and thus to appoint two governors for the four legions. It was assumed, or perhaps hoped, that the two governors, who were forbidden to meet with each other, would be unable to cooperate to combine their legions.

5. Table H indicates how the Roman army was almost continually in action during the entire 300 years. Various factors came together to intensify military activity: a) Emperors wanted to shine militarily for political reasons in Rome, b) Generals and governors sought riches and glory across the next frontier, c) Legions that were not kept active could become bored and restive with negative consequences for both the Empire and the Emperor, and d) in the 3rd Century, barbarians came to see the Empire as the land of milk and honey where they could either settle or steal in eternal happiness.

TABLE A
LIST OF LEGIONS WITH THE HISTORY OF THEIR NAMES AND LOCATIONS

I Germanica   Formed 41 B.C. by Octavian. No name known prior to 27 B.C. Named I Augusta ca. 27 B.C. Disgraced 19 B.C. in Spain (Mutiny or defeat) and lost the name Augusta. Renamed I Germanica after transfer to Germany 16 B.C. Symbol - Unknown

Naples, Italy 36 B.C., Nearer Spain 30-16 B.C. (Cantabrian conquest 29- 19 B.C.), Mainz (Moguntiacum) upper Germany 16 B.C.- 9 A.D. (Drusus War 15 B.C.), Cologne (Apud Arum Ubiorum) lower Germany 9-35 A.D., Bonn (Bonna) lower Germany 35-69 A.D., Swore allegiance to the New Gallic Empire 69 A.D., Disbanded 70 A.D.

I Italica   Formed 66 A.D. by Nero in Italy for a proposed Eastern campaign. Symbol - Boar + Bull

Italy 66-68 A.D., Lyon (Lugdunum) Gaul 68-69 A.D. (Defeated with the Vitellians at Bedriacum II 69 A.D.), Svistov (Novae) Moesia/Lower Moesia 70-316 A.D. (Defeated by Dacians 86 A.D.) (Tapae 88 A.D.) (Dacian Wars 101-106 A.D.) (Victorious with Septimius Severus at Issus 194 A.D.) (Parthian War 231-233 A.D.) (Defeated by Goths at Abrittus 251 A.D.) (Milan 260 A.D.) (Syria 300 A.D.), Destroyed ca. 317 A.D. in Syria by the Persians – A vexillation is recorded ca. 364 A.D., however, in Syria

I Adiutrix   Formed 68 A.D. by Nero from non-citizen marines at Misenum, Italy for a proposed Eastern campaign. "Adiutrix" = Supportive. I Adiutrix Pia Fidelis = Loyal and Faithful by Trajan ca. 102 A.D., perhaps in connection with the disbanding or disappearance of XXI Rapax. Symbol - Capricorn

Rome 68-69 A.D. (Defeated with Otho at Bedriacum I 69 A.D.), Near Merida Spain 69-70 A.D., Mainz (Moguntiacum) upper Germany 70-86 A.D. (Batavian campaign 70 A.D.) (Agri Decumates campaign 73-74 A.D.) (Chatti War 83-85 A.D.), Szony (Brigetio) Pannonia 86-101 A.D. (Dacian War 86-89 A.D.) (Tapae 88 A.D.) Dacian Wars 101-106 A.D., Alba Iulia (Apulum) Dacia 106-122 A.D. (Parthian War 114-116 A.D.), Szony (Brigetio) Upper Pannonia/Lower Pannonia 122-400 A.D. (Marcomanni War 167-172 A.D.) (Victorious with Septimius Severus at Issus 194 A.D.) (Parthian War 216-217 A.D.) (Dacian War 236-237 A.D.) (Defeated with Maximinus at Aquileia 238 A.D.) (Parthian War 256-260 A.D.)

I Macriana Liberatrix   Formed 68 A.D. by the legate of III Augusta, L. Clodius Macer, in Numidia to support the Vindex rebellion. Named for Macer.

Disbanded 69 A.D. by Galba, Reconstituted by Vitellius 69 A.D., Disbanded by Vespasian 69 A.D.

I Minervia   Formed 83 A.D. by Domitian for his proposed German campaign as I Flavia Minervia in honor of his family and the goddess. I Flavia Minervia Pia Fidelis Domitiana = Loyal and Faithful by Domitian after the Saturninus revolt of 88-89 A.D. After Domitian's assassination in 96 A.D., I Minervia Pia Fidelis. Symbol - Ram

Bonn (Bonna) Lower Germany 86-359 A.D. (Saturninus revolt 88-89 A.D.) (Dacian Wars 101-106 A.D.) (Parthian War 162-166 A.D.) (Lyon 197 A.D.) (Milan 260 A.D.) (Parthian War 359-360 A.D.), Destroyed at Balad Sinjar (Singara) Mesopotamia by the Parthians 360 A.D.

I Parthica Severiana   Formed 196 A.D. by Septimius Severus for his Parthian campaign. Also known as I Parthica Sagittarius as if it specialized in fighting as archers. Symbol - Centaur

Balad Sinjar (Singara) Mesopotamia 198-360 A.D. (Parthian Wars 216-217, 231-233, 242-244 A.D.) (Defeated by Parthians at Misikhe 244 A.D. and Barbalissus, Mesopotamia 252

	A.D.) (Parthian Wars 256-260, 359-360 A.D.) Destroyed at Balad Sinjar (Singara) Mesopotamia by the Parthians 360 A.D.
I Illyricorum	Formed 274 A.D. by Aurelian in Illyricum
	Palmyra, Syria Phoenice 274-350 A.D.
I Isaura	Formed 278 A.D. by Probus from Isaurians
	Seleucia, Isauria 353 A.D.
I Pontica	Formed ca. 288 A.D. by Diocletian and named for the province of Pontus where it served.
	Trabzon (Trapezus) Pontus 288-360 A.D.
I Jovia Scythica	Formed before 293 A.D. by Diocletian in Scythica
	Pannonia before 300 A.D., Isakca (Noviodunum) Scythica Minor 300-369 A.D.
I Maximiana Thebaeorum	Formed ca. 293 A.D. by Maximian for service at Thebes
	Pilae, Thebes, Egypt 293-388 A.D. (Thrace 354 A.D.)
I Armeniaca	Formed before 300 A.D. by Diocletian in Armenia
	Klaudias (Claudius-Claudiopolis) Cappadocia 300-363 A.D. (Parthian War 359-363 A.D.)
I Martia	Formed ca. 300 by Diocletian. 'Martia' = Warlike
	Kaiseraugst (Castrum Rauracense) Upper Germany 306-369 A.D. (Danube 350 A.D.) (Algeria 350 A.D.), Visegrad (Pone Navata) Upper Pannonia 371-372 A.D., Existed in Pannonia 395 A.D.
I Noricorum	Formed ca. 300 A.D. by Diocletian for service in Noricum
	Mautern (Favianis) Noricum 300-370 A.D.
II Augusta	Formed 48 B.C. by Julius Caesar. Originally II Gallica for service in Gaul. Reformed 43 B.C. by Pansa in Sabine country and then known as II Sabina. II Augusta about 27 B.C. Symbols - Pegasus + Capricorn
	Gaul 47 B.C., Apollonia, Macedonia 47-44 B.C., Italy 44 B.C. (With Antonius at Forum Gallorum 44 B.C. - lost eagle), Discharged 44 B.C., Reformed 43 B.C. (Mutina 43 B.C. - lost eagle), Nearer Spain 42 B.C.- 9 A.D. (Cantabrian conquest 29-19 B.C.), Mainz (Moguntiacum) upper Germany 10-15 A.D. (Mutiny 14 A.D.), Strasbourg (Argentorate) upper Germany 15-43 A.D. (Idistaviso 16 A.D.), Britain 43 A.D., Chichester (Noviomagus Regnorum) Britain 44-46 A.D., Silchester (Calleva Atrebatum) Britain 46-49 A.D., Lake Farm, Britain 49-55 A.D., Exeter (Isca Dumnoniorum) Britain 55-67 A.D., Gloucester (Glevum) Britain 67-74 A.D., Caerleon (Isca Silurum) Britain/Upper Britain 74-296 A.D. (Defeated with Clodius Albinus at Lyon 197 A.D.) (Defeated with Allectus 296 A.D.), Richborough (Rutupiae) Upper Britain 296-410 A.D.
II Adiutrix	Formed 70 A.D. by Gaius Licinius Mucianus from non-citizen marines at Ravenna, Italy. "Adiutrix" = Supportive. II Adiutrix Pia Fidelis = Loyal and Faithful by Vespasian in 70 A.D. Symbol - Pegasus
	Nijmegen (Noviomagus) lower Germany 70-71 A.D. (Batavian campaign 70 A.D.), Lincoln (Lindum) Britain 71-78 A.D., Chester (Deva) Britain 78-86 A.D., Budapest (Aquincum) Pannonia 86-101 A.D. (Tapae 88 A.D.) (1st Dacian War 101-102 A.D.), Ulpia Traiana, Dacia 102-104 A.D. (2nd Dacian War 105-106 A.D.), Varhély

(Sarmizegethusa) Dacia 106-120 A.D. (Parthian War 114-116 A.D.), Budapest (Aquincum) Lower Pannonia 120-405 A.D. (Jewish uprising 132-135 A.D.) (Parthian War 162-166 A.D.) (Victorious with Septimius Severus at Issus 194 A.D.) (Parthian War 198-199 A.D.) (German campaign 213-214 A.D.) (Parthian Wars 216-218 A.D., 256-260 A.D.)

II Traiana

Formed 102 A.D. by Trajan for his 2nd Dacian War. II Traiana Fortis = Courageous by Trajan in 106 A.D. for service in the 2nd Dacian War. Symbol - Hercules

Svistov (Novae) Lower Moesia 104-113 A.D. (2nd Dacian War 105-106 A.D.), Samsat (Samosata) Syria 113-120 A.D. (Parthian War 114-116 A.D.), Alexandria Kasr Kayasire (Nicopolis) Egypt 120-388 A.D. (Jewish uprising 132-135 A.D.) (Defeated by Avidius Cassius 174 A.D.) (German campaign 213-214 A.D.) (Mutiny 231 A.D.)

II Italica

Formed 165 A.D. by Marcus Aurelius in Italy as II Italica Pia for a Danube campaign. II Italica Pia Fidelis = Loyal and Faithful by Septimius Severus in 197 A.D. when the legion refused to join the revolt of Clodius Albinus. Symbol – She wolf

Lotschitz/Locica, Noricum 167-172 A.D. (Marcomanni War 168-172 A.D.), Albing, Noricum 172-205 A.D. (Victorious with Septimius Severus at Issus 194 A.D.), Enns-Lorch (Lauriacum) Noricum 205-400 A.D. (Dacian War 236-237 A.D.) (Milan 260 A.D.), Numidia ca. 423 A.D.?

II Parthica Severiana

Formed 196 A.D. by Septimius Severus on the Danube for his Parthian campaign. II Parthica Antoniana Pia Fidelis Aeterna by Caracalla ca. 215 A.D. Symbol – Centaur

Albanum (Alba) Italy 198-299 A.D. (Parthian War 198-199 A.D.) (German campaign 213-214 A.D.) (Parthian War 216-217 A.D.) (Victorious at Inmae, Syria 218 A.D.) (Parthian War 231-233 A.D.) (Rhine 234-236 A.D.) (Parthian War 242-244 A.D.) (Defeated at Misikhe 244 A.D.) (Milan 260 A.D.) (Mauritania 298-299 A.D.), Cefae (Kiphas) Mesopotamia 300 A.D., Defeated and probably destroyed by the Parthians at Bezabde, Mesopotamia 360 A.D.

II Isaura

Formed 278 A.D. by Probus from Isaurians

Seleucia, Isauria 353 A.D.

II Herculea

Formed 293 A.D. by Diocletian.

Iglitza-Turcoaia (Troesmi) Scythica Minor 300-360 A.D., Isakca (Noviodunum) Scythica Minor 367 A.D.

II Flavia Constantia

Formed 296 A.D. by Diocletian

Pilae, Thebes, Egypt 297-390 A.D. (Thrace 354 A.D.) (Cusas 360 A.D.) (Worms (Borbetomagus) France ca. 365 A.D.)

III Gallica

Formed 48 B.C. by Julius Caesar in Gaul. Named for its origin and service in Gaul by 42 B.C. Symbol - Bull

Spain 46-45 B.C. (Munda 45 B.C.), Gaul 45-42 B.C. (Mutina 43 B.C.) (With Antonius at Philippi 42 B.C.), With Antonius in the East 41-31 B.C. (Parthian War 38-34 B.C.) (With Antonius at Actium 31 B.C.), Antioch (Antiochea) Syria 30 B.C.- 62 A.D., Armenia 62-66 A.D., Gigen (Oescus) Moesia 67-69 A.D. (Victorious with Primus at Bedriacum II 69 A.D.), Capua, Italy 69 A.D. (Rhoxolani battle in Pannonia 69 A.D.), Samsat (Samosata) Syria 72-106 A.D., Rafniyeh (Raphanaea) Syria/Syria Phoenice 106-219 A.D. (Parthian War 114-116 A.D.) (Jewish uprising 132-135 A.D.) (Parthian War 162-165 A.D.) (Defeated with Gaius Pescennius Niger at Issus 194 A.D.), Damascus (Danaba) Syria Phoenice 219-238 A.D., Lambese (Lambaesis) Numidia 238-253 A.D., Damascus (Danaba) Syria Phoenice 253-350 A.D., Existed 400 A.D.

III Augusta	Formed ca. 43 B.C. by Pansa. III Augusta from ca. 27 B.C. III Augusta Pia Vindex = Loyal Avenger by Septimius Severus ca. 193 A.D. and "Pia Fidelis" = Loyal and Faithful at a later date. Symbol - Pegasus
	Haidra (Ammaedara) Africa 30 B.C.- 75 A.D. (Mauritania 25-24 B.C.) (Tacfarinas uprising 17-24 A.D.), Tebessa (Theveste) Africa 75-128 A.D., Lambese (Lambaesis) Africa/Numidia 128-238 A.D., Disbanded by Gordian III 238 A.D., Reformed by Valerian 253 A.D., Lambese (Lambaesis) Numidia 253-290 A.D., Existed 373 A.D. in combination with II Traiana in Legio Tertioaugustani in the field army in Numidia
III Cyrenaica	Formed ca. 40 B.C. by M Aemilius Lepidus in Africa. Named III Cyrenaica for service in that province. III Cyrenaica Severiana by Septimius Severus in 194 A.D. when it did not support Gaius Pescennius Niger. Symbol – Ram
	Cyrenaica 31 B.C., Cairo (Babylon) Egypt 30 B.C.- 14 A.D., Alexandria Kasr Kayasire (Nicopolis) Egypt 14-120 A.D. (Parthian War 114-116 A.D.), Bosra (Nova Trajana Bostra) Arabia 120-395 A.D. (Jewish uprising 132-135 A.D.) (Parthian War 256-260 A.D.) (defeated in Palmyrene War 269 A.D.)
III Italica Felix	Formed 166 A.D. as III Italica Concordia by Marcus Aurelius in Italy for a Danube campaign. "Concordia" = Concord. "Felix" = Fortunate. Symbol – Stork
	(Marcomanni War 167-172 A.D.), Regensburg (Castra Regina) Raetia 179-450 A.D. (Victorious with Septimius Severus at Lyon 197 A.D.) (German campaign 213 A.D.) (Parthian War 216-217 A.D.) (Milan 260 A.D.)
III Parthica Severiana	Formed 196 A.D. by Septimius Severus for his Parthian campaign. Symbol – Centaur
	Viransehir (Constantina), Osrhoene 198-219 A.D. (Parthian War 216-217 A.D.), Rhesenae (Apamca) Osrhoene 219-300 A.D. (Parthian Wars 231-234 A.D., 240-244 A.D.) (Defeated at Misikhe 244 A.D.), Tel Araban (Arbana) Osrhoene 300-355 A.D., Viransehir (Constantina), Osrhoene 362 A.D.
III Isaura	Formed 278 A.D. by Probus from Isaurians
	Seleucia, Isauria 353 A.D., Existed 360 A.D.
III Diocletiana Thebaeorum	Formed 296 A.D. by Diocletian in Egypt.
	Andaro (Schabur) Egypt 296-388 A.D.
III Herculea	Formed 293 A.D. by Diocletian
	Mauritania 298 A.D., Iglitza-Turcoaia (Troesmi) Lower Moesia
IV Macedonica	Formed 48 B.C. by Julius Caesar. Named for service in that province. Symbols – Bull + Capricorn
	Apollonia, Macedonia 47-44 B.C., Italy 44-39 B.C. (With Octavian at Forum Gallorum 44 B.C.) (With Octavian at Mutina 43 B.C.) (With Antonius at Philippi 42 B.C.) (Perugia 41 B.C.) (With Octavian at Actium 31 B.C.), Farther Spain 30-23 B.C., Herrera de Pisuerga (Pisoraca) Farther Spain/Nearer Spain 23 B.C.- 43 A.D. (Cantabrian conquest 29-19 B.C.), Mainz (Moguntiacum) upper Germany 43-69 A.D., Swore allegiance to the New Gallic Empire 69 A.D., Disbanded 70 A.D.
IV Scythica	Formed before 32 B.C. by Antonius and named for service in Scythia 29-27 B.C. Symbol - Capricorn
	(With Antonius at Actium 31 B.C.), Nis (Naissus) Macedonia 30 B.C.- 9 A.D. (Macedonian conquest 29-27 B.C.) (Drusus War 15 B.C.) (Thracian War 13-11 B.C.)

(Pannonian uprising 6-9 A.D.), Silistra (Durosturum) Moesia 9-55 A.D., Cappadocia 55-62 A.D. (Parthian War 55-58 A.D.) (Defeated by the Parthians at Rhandeia, Armenia 62 A.D.), Belkis (Zeugma) Syria/Syria Coele 62-198 A.D. (Parthian Wars 114-116 A.D., 161-165 A.D.) (Defeated with Gaius Pescennius Niger at Issus 194 A.D.), Tayibeh (Oresa) Syria Coele 198-400 A.D. (Defeated with Macrinus at Inmae, Syria 218 A.D.) (Parthian War 231-233 A.D.)

IV Flavia Felix — Formed 70 A.D. by Vespasian from remnants of IV Macedonica. Named after Vespasian. "Felix' = Fortunate. Symbol - Lion

Kistanje (Burnum) Dalmatia 71-86 A.D., Artschav/Arcar (Ratiara) Upper Moesia 86-106 A.D. (Tapae 88 A.D.) (Dacian Wars 101-106 A.D.), Resita (Berzobis) Dacia 106-120 A.D., Belgrade (Singidunum) Upper Moesia 120-337 A.D. (Victorious with Septimius Severus at Issus 194 A.D.) (Milan 260 A.D.)

IV Martia — Formed ca. 274 A.D. by Aurelian. "Martia" = Warlike

Bosra (Nova Trajana Bostra) Arabia 274-288 A.D., Al Lejum (Betthoro) Syria Palaestina 288-532 A.D., Disbanded ca. 532 A.D.

IV Parthica — Formed ca. 300 A.D. by Diocletian for a Parthian campaign.

Beseira (Circesium) Osrhoene 300-360 A.D., Aleppo (Beroea) Syria Coele 586 A.D.

IV Jovia — Formed ca. 300 A.D. by Diocletian.

Lower Pannonia

V Alaudae — Formed 52 B.C. by Julius Caesar from Gallic militia. Originally known as V Gallica 47 B.C. The "Alaudae", meaning Larks, was a nickname that had become official by 44 B.C. Symbol - Elephant

Gaul 52-49 B.C., Italy 48 B.C. (Pharsalus 48 B.C.), Spain 48-45 B.C. (Uzita 47 B.C.) (Thapsus 46 B.C.) (Munda 45 B.C.), Italy 44-43 B.C. (With Antonius at Forum Gallorum 44 B.C.) (Mutina 43 B.C.) (With Antonius at Philippi 42 B.C.), With Antonius in the East 41-31 B.C. (With Antonius at Actium 31 B.C.), Farther Spain 30-17 B.C. (Cantabrian conquest 29-19 B.C.), Neuss (Novaesium) lower Germany 17 B.C.- 9 A.D. (Lost eagle to Sugambri near Neuss 17 B.C.) (Drusus War 15 B.C.), Xanten (Vetera) lower Germany 9-69 A.D. (Mutiny 14 A.D.) (With the Vitellians at Bedriacum I and II 69 A.D.) (Xanten garrison destroyed by Civilis 69 A.D.), Silistra (Durosturum) Moesia 69-86 A.D., Destroyed in Dacia 86 A.D., Eagle recovered 102 A.D.

V Macedonica — Formed 43 B.C. by Pansa. First known as V Urbana referring to an origin in Rome. Renamed V Macedonica for service during the Macedonian conquest 29-27 B.C. V Macedonica Pia Fidelis = Loyal and Faithful by Commodus ca. 186 A.D. after the Maternus revolt. Symbols – Bull + Eagle

(Philippi 42 B.C.) (With Octavian at Actium 31 B.C.), Nis (Naissus) Moesia 30-25 B.C. (Macedonian conquest 29-27 B.C.), Antakya (Antiochia) Galatia 25 B.C.- 9 A.D. (Thracian War 13-11 B.C.), Kostolac (Viminacum) Moesia 9-62 A.D., Armenia 62-66 A.D. (Alexandria 66 A.D.), Imwas (Emmaus-Nicopolis) Syria 68-72 A.D. (Jewish uprising 66-70 A.D.), Gigen (Oescus) Moesia/Lower Moesia 72-106 A.D. (Defeated by Dacians 86 A.D.) (Tapae 88 A.D.) (Dacian Wars 101-106 A.D.), Iglitza-Turcoaia (Troesmi) Lower Moesia 106-166 A.D. (Jewish uprising 132-135 A.D.) (Parthian War 162-167 A.D.), Turda (Potaissa) Lower Dacia 167-271 A.D. (Marcomanni War 167-172 A.D.) (Victorious with Septimius Severus at Issus 194 A.D.), Gigen (Oescus) Lower Moesia 271-388 A.D. (Milan 260 A.D.), (Egyptian campaign 399 A.D.) Existed 6th Century.

V Jovia — Formed ca. 294 A.D. by Diocletian.

	Srijemska Mitronica (Sirmium) Lower Pannonia 294 A.D., Novi Banovci (Burgenae) Lower Pannonia ca. 360 A.D., Iglitza-Turcoaia (Troesmi) Lower Moesia 367 A.D.
V Parthica	Formed ca. 300 by Diocletian.
	Diarbekir (Amida) Mesopotamia 300-360 A.D., Destroyed there by the Parthians 360 A.D.
VI Ferrata	Formed 52 B.C. by Julius Caesar in Cisalpine Gaul. "Ferrata" = Ironclad by 42 B.C. VI Ferrata Fidelis Constans = Faithful and Steadfast by Septimius Severus in 194 A.D. when it did not support Gaius Pescennius Niger. Symbol – Wolf
	Gaul 52-49 B.C., Spain 49 B.C. (Pharsalus 48 B.C.), Alexandria Kasr Kayasire (Nicopolis) Egypt 48-47 B.C. (Zela 47 B.C.), Italy 47 B.C. (Munda 45 B.C.), Discharged 45 B.C., Reformed by Lepidus 44 B.C., (With Antonius at Philippi 42 B.C.), Latakia (Laodicea ad Mare) Syria 41 B.C.-69 A.D. (Parthian War 38-34 B.C.) (With Antonius at Actium 31 B.C.) (Jewish uprising 3 B.C.) (Cappadocia 62-66 A.D.), Gigen (Oescus) Moesia 69 A.D. (Defeated the Dacians 69 A.D.), Italy 69-72 A.D., Rafniyeh (Raphanaea) Syria 73-106 A.D., Bosra (Nova Trajana Bostra) Arabia 106-120 A.D. (Parthian War 114-116 A.D.), Legio-Kefar Otnay (Caparcotna) Syria Palaestina 120-260 A.D. (Jewish uprising 132-135 A.D.) (Mauritanian campaign 145-148 A.D.) Disappeared ca. 260 A.D. – Probably destroyed by the Parthians near Edessa, Osrhoene with Valerian.
VI Victrix	Formed 41 B.C. by Lepidus for Octavian. Named VI Hispaniensis for service in Spain. Renamed VI Victrix for victories in Spain. VI Victrix Pia Fidelis Domitiana = Loyal and Faithful by Domitian after the Saturninus revolt of 88-89 A.D. After Domitian's assassination in 96 A.D., VI Victrix Pia Fidelis. Symbol - Bull?
	(Perugia 41 B.C.), (With Octavian at Actium 31 B.C.), Farther Spain 30-23 B.C., Leon (Legio) Farther Spain/Nearer Spain 23 B.C.- 70 A.D. (Cantabrian conquest 29-19 B.C.), Neuss (Novaesium) lower Germany/ Lower Germany 70-102 A.D. (Batavian campaign 70 A.D.) (Saturninus revolt 88-89 A.D.) (1st Dacian War 101-102 A.D.), Xanten (Vetera) Lower Germany 102-122 A.D., York (Eburacum) Britain/Lower Britain 122-383 A.D. (Defeated with Clodius Albinus at Lyon 197 A.D.) (Dacian War 213 A.D.) Defeated with Maximus in Gaul 383 A.D. and disbanded or destroyed.
VI Herculea	Formed ca. 294 A.D. by Diocletian.
	Mitronica (Sirmium) Lower Pannonia 294 A.D., Isakca (Noviodunum) Scythica Minor 4th Century, Dalj (Teutoburgium) Lower Pannonia ca. 360 A.D.
VI Parthica	Formed ca. 300 A.D. by Diocletian.
	Cefae (Kiphas) Mesopotamia 359 A.D., Disbanded ca. 383 A.D.
VII Macedonica	Formed prior to 59 B.C. First known as VII Paterna for its service under Julius Caesar. Renamed VII Macedonica for service in Macedonia during the Thracian War 13-11 B.C. VII Claudia Pia Fidelis = Loyal and Faithful by Claudius in 42 A.D. for changing sides during the revolt of Camillus Scribonianus. Symbol - Bull
	Aquileia, Cisalpine Gaul 59 B.C., Gaul 59-49 B.C. (Bibracte 58 B.C.) (Brittany 57-56 B.C.) (Britain 55 and 54 B.C.), Spain 49-48 B.C. (Pharsalus 48 B.C.), Italy 48 B.C. (Thapsus 46 B.C.), Discharged 46 B.C., Reformed by Ventidius Bassus for Octavian in Campania 44 B.C. (Forum Gallorum 44 B.C.) (Mutina 43 B.C.) (With Antonius at Philippi 42 B.C.), Italy 42 B.C. (Perugia 41 B.C.) (Sicilian Channel 36 B.C.), Discharged ca. 35 B.C., Reformed and fought with Octavian at Actium 31 B.C., Italy 31 B.C., Mauritania 30-25 B.C., Antakya (Antiochia) Galatia 25 B.C.- 9 A.D. (Thracian War 13-11 B.C.) (Pannonian uprising 6-9 A.D.), Gardun (Tilurium) Illyricum/ Dalmatia 9-62 A.D. (Scribonianus revolt 42 A.D.), Kostolac (Viminiacum) Moesia/ Upper Moesia 62-400 A.D. (Victorious with Primus at Bedriacum II 69 A.D.) (Defeated by Dacians 86 A.D.) (Tapae

88 A.D.) (Dacian Wars 101-106 A.D.) (Victorious with Septimius Severus at Issus 194 A.D.) (Milan 260 A.D.)

VII Gemina Formed 68 A.D. by Galba in Spain as VII Galbiana. Renamed VII Hispana by Vespasian in 70 A.D. Renamed VII Gemina probably when it received remnants of I Germanica and XVI Gallica from Germany in 70 A.D. VII Gemina Felix = Fortunate by Vespasian in 73 A.D. after the Agri Decumates campaign. VII Gemina Pia Felix = Loyal and Fortunate by Septimius Severus in 197 A.D. when it refused to join Clodius Albinus.

Spain 68 A.D., Petronell (Carnuntum) Pannonia 69 A.D. (Victorious with Primus at Bedriacum II 69 A.D.), Petronell (Carnuntum) Pannonia 70-74 A.D. (Agri Decumates campaign 73-74 A.D.), Leon (Legio) Farther Spain 74-400 A.D.

VIII Augusta Formed prior to 59 B.C. First named VIII Gallica for service in Gaul. Reformed by Ventidius Bassus for Octavian from its discharged veterans in 44 B.C. as VIII Veterana. Renamed VIII Mutinensis for valor at Mutina 43 B.C. VIII Augusta ca. 27 B.C. VIII Augusta Pia Fidelis Constans Commoda = Loyal, Faithful and Steadfast by Commodus ca. 186 A.D., Symbol - Bull

Aquileia, Cisalpine Gaul 59 B.C., Gaul 58-49 B.C. (Bibracte 58 B.C.), Italy 48 B.C. (Pharsalus 48 B.C.) (Thapsus 46 B.C.), Discharged 45 B.C., Reformed 44 B.C. in Campania (Forum Gallorum 44 B.C.) (Mutina 43 B.C.) (With Antonius at Philippi 42 B.C.), Italy 41 B.C. (Perugia 41 B.C.), (With Octavian at Actium 31 B.C.), Italy 31-30 B.C., Thebes, Egypt 29 B.C.- 6 A.D. (Theban uprising 29 B.C.), Pannonian uprising 6-9 A.D., Ptuj (Poetovio) Illyricum/Pannonia 10-45 A.D. (Mutiny 14 A.D.), Svistov (Novae) Moesia 45-69 A.D. (Victorious with Primus at Bedriacum II 69 A.D.), Mirebeau-sur-Béze, Dijon, Gaul 70-90 A.D. (Batavian campaign 70 A.D.) (Agri Decumates campaign 73-74 A.D.), Strasbourg (Argentorate) Upper Germany 90-406 A.D. (Lyon 197 A.D.) (Milan 260 A.D.), Destroyed ca. 406 A.D. by the Vandals

IX Hispana Formed prior to 59 B.C. First named IX Triumphalis for victories under Julius Caesar. Renamed IX Macedonica probably for service in that province prior to 30 B.C. Renamed IX Hispana after 30 B.C. for service in Spain. Symbol – Neptune

Aquileia, Cisalpine Gaul 59 B.C., Gaul 58-49 B.C. (Bibracte 58 B.C.) (Britain 54 B.C.) (Ilerda 49 B.C.) (Pharsalus 48 B.C.), Italy 48 B.C. (Uzita 47 B.C.) (Thapsus 46 B.C.), Discharged 45 B.C., Reformed by Ventidius Bassus for Octavian in Italy 43 B.C., With Antonius in the East 39-32 B.C., (With Octavian at Actium 31 B.C.), Nearer Spain 30-16 B.C. (Cantabrian conquest 29-24 B.C.) (Mauritania 24-19 B.C.), Gardun (Tilurium) Illyricum 15 B.C.- 9 A.D. (Drusus War 15 B.C.) (Pannonian uprising 6-9 A.D.), Sisak (Siscia) Illyricum 9-43 A.D. (Mutiny 14 A.D.) (campaign against Tacfarinas in Mauritania 20-24 A.D.), Britain 43 A.D., Newton-on-Trent, Britain 45-66 A.D. (Defeated by Boudicca 60 A.D.), Lincoln (Lindum) Britain 66-71 A.D., York (Eburacum) Britain 71-121 A.D. (Stanwick 73 A.D.) (Apparently defeated by the Brigantes ca. 121 A.D.), Nijmegen (Noviomagus) Lower Germany 121 A.D., Disbanded there.

X Gemina Formed prior to 59 B.C. Known as X Equestris before 50 B.C. from service as mounted infantry under Julius Caesar. Reformed by Lepidus 44 B.C. from its discharged veterans as X Veneria. X Gemina Equestris after Actium in 31 B.C. when it apparently absorbed contingents from discharged legions and shortly thereafter X Gemina. X Gemina Pia Fidelis Domitiana = Loyal and Faithful by Domitian after the Saturninus revolt of 88-89 A.D.. After Domitian's assassination in 96 A.D., X Gemina Pia Fidelis. Symbol - Bull

Narbonne (Narbo) Transalpine Gaul 59 B.C., Gaul 58-49 B.C. (Bibracte 58 B.C.) (Britain 55 and 54 B.C.) (Gergovia 52 B.C.), Rosinos de Vidrialis (Paetavonium) Farther Spain 49-48 B.C. (Pharsalus 48 B.C.), Italy 48-47 B.C. (Uzita 47 B.C.) (Thapsus 46 B.C.) (Munda 45 B.C.), Discharged 45 B.C., Reformed 44 B.C., (With Antonius at Philippi 42 B.C.), With Antonius in the East 41-31 B.C. (With Antonius at Actium 31 B.C.), Farther Spain 30 B.C.- 26 B.C., Astorga (Asturica Augusta) Farther Spain 26-23 B.C., Rosinos de Vidrialis (Petavonium) Farther Spain/Nearer Spain 23 B.C.–63 A.D. (Cantabrian conquest

	29-19 B.C.) (Mauritania 24 B.C.), Petronell (Carnuntum) Pannonia 63-69 A.D., Spain 69 A.D., Kleve-Rindern (Arenacum) lower Germany 70-71 A.D. (Batavian campaign 70 A.D.), Nijmegen (Noviomagus) lower Germany/Lower Germany 71-101 A.D. (Saturninus revolt 88-89 A.D.), Budapest (Aquincum) Pannonia/Lower Pannonia 101-120 A.D. (Dacian Wars 101-106 A.D.), Vienna (Vindobona) Upper Pannonia 120-360 A.D. (Parthian War 256-260 A.D.), Vexillations appear in the East 360-388 A.D.
X Fretensis	Formed 40 B.C. by Octavian. Named X Fretensis after victories in the Fretum Siculum or Sicilian Channel against Sextus Pompeius in 36 B.C. Symbols - Bull, Dolphin, Galley, Boar
	Naulochus, Sicily 38-36 B.C. (Sicilian Channel 36 B.C.), Illyria 36 B.C., Sicily 36-31 B.C. (With Octavian at Actium 31 B.C.), Macedonia 30-27 B.C. (Macedonian conquest 29-27 B.C.), Kuros (Cyrrhus) Syria 27 B.C.- 18 A.D., Belkis (Zeugma) Syria 18-62 A.D. (Parthian War 55-58 A.D.), Armenia 62-66 A.D., Alexandria 66 A.D., Jewish uprising 66-73 A.D., Jerusalem (Aelia Capitolina) Syria Palaestina 73-290 A.D. (Parthian War 114-116 A.D.) (Jewish uprising 132-135 A.D.) (Defeated with Gaius Pescennius Niger at Issus 194 A.D.), Aqaba (Aela) Syria Palaestina 290-360 A.D., Existed 400 A.D.
XI	Formed 58 B.C. by Julius Caesar. Renamed XI Claudia Pia Fidelis = Loyal and Faithful by Claudius in 42 A.D. for changing sides during the revolt of Camillus Scribonianus. Symbol - Neptune
	Gaul 58-49 B.C. (Bibracte 58 B.C.), (Pharsalus 48 B.C.), Italy 48 B.C., Discharged 45 B.C., Reformed by Octavian 41 B.C., Italy 41-31 B.C. (Perugia 41 B.C.) (Sicilian Channel 36 B.C.) (With Octavian at Actium 31 B.C.), Nis (Naissus) Moesia 30-27 B.C. (Macedonian conquest 29-27 B.C.), Gardun (Tilurium) Illyricum 27-16 B.C., Kostolac (Viminiacum) Moesia 15 B.C.- 9 A.D. (Drusus War 15 B.C.) (Thracian War 13-11 B.C.) (Pannonian uprising 6-9 A.D.), Kistanje (Burnum) Illyricum/Dalmatia 9-69 A.D., Italy 69 A.D. (Batavian campaign 70 A.D.), Windisch (Vindonissa) upper Germany/Upper Germany 70-101 A.D. (Agri Decumates campaign 73-74 A.D.) (Chatti War 83-85 A.D.) (Saturninus revolt 88-89 A.D.), Szony (Brigetio) Pannonia/Upper Pannonia 101-106 A.D. (Dacian Wars 101-106 A.D.), Silistra (Durosturum) Lower Moesia 106-400 A.D. (Jewish uprising 132-135 A.D.) (Victorious with Septimius Severus at Issus 194 A.D.) (Milan 260 A.D.) (Aquilea 288 A.D.) (Mauritania 298-299 A.D.) (Mesopotamia 300 A.D.)
XII Fulminata	Formed 58 B.C. by Julius Caesar. Named XII Paterna ca. 46 B.C. to commemorate service under Julius Caesar. Renamed XII Victrix ca. 41 B.C. Renamed XII Antiqua ca. 33 B.C. to emphasize its age. XII Fulminata = "Thunderbolt" after 27 B.C. XII Fulminata Firma Constans = Sure and Steadfast by Marcus Aurelius ca. 175 A.D. when it did not join the revolt of Avidius Cassius. Symbol - Thunderbolt
	Gaul 58-49 B.C. (Bibracte 58 B.C.) (Defeated in the Valais, Switzerland 57 B.C.), Italy 49-45 B.C. (Pharsalus 48 B.C.), Discharged 45 B.C., Reformed by Lepidus 44 B.C. (with Antonius at Philippi 42 B.C.) (Perugia 41 B.C.), With Antonius in the East 41-31 B.C. (With Antonius at Actium 31 B.C.), Alexandria Kasr Kayasire (Nicopolis) Egypt 30-25 B.C., Rafniyeh (Raphanaea) Syria 25 B.C.- 72 A.D. (Defeated by the Parthians at Rhandeia, Armenia 62 A.D.) (Defeated in the Beth-Horon Pass, Palestine 66 A.D.), Malataya (Melitene) Cappadocia 72-337 A.D. to 5th Century (Parthian War 114-116 A.D.) (Jewish uprising 132-135 A.D.) (Marcomanni War 167-172 A.D.) (Defeated with Gaius Pescennius Niger at Issus 194 A.D.)
XIII Gemina	Formed 57 B.C. by Julius Caesar. XIII Gemina following Actium 31 B.C. Symbol - Lion
	Gaul 57-50 B.C. (Gergovia 52 B.C.), Aquileia 50-48 B.C. (Pharsalus 48 B.C.)(Uzita 47 B.C.) (Thapsus 46 B.C.), Discharged 45 B.C., Reformed by Octavian 41 B.C., Italy 36 B.C., Reformed 36 B.C. after campaign against Sextus Pompeius, (With Octavian at Actium 31 B.C.), Kistanje (Burnum) Illyricum 30-16 B.C. (Drusus War 15 B.C.), Ljubljana (Emona) Illyricum 15 B.C.-9 A.D. (Pannonian uprising 6-9 A.D.), Augsburg-Oberhausen (Augusta Vindelicum) Raetia 10-16 A.D., Windisch (Vindonissa) upper

Germany 16-45 A.D., Ptuj (Poetovio) Pannonia 45-89 A.D. (Defeated with Otho at Bedriacum I 69 A.D.) (Victorious with Primus at Bedriacum II 69 A.D.) (Batavian campaign 70 A.D.), Vienna (Vindobona) Pannonia/Upper Pannonia 89-106 A.D. (Dacian Wars 101-106 A.D.), Alba Iulia (Apulum) Dacia/ Upper Dacia 106-268 A.D. (Parthian War 114-116 A.D.) (Dalmatia 150 A.D.) (Milan 260 A.D.), Ptuj (Poetovio) Lower Pannonia 268-270 A.D., Artschav/ Arcar (Ratiaria) Dacia Ripensis 270-400 A.D.

XIV Gemina Formed 57 B.C. by Julius Caesar. XIV Gemina following Actium 31 B.C. XIV Gemina Martia Victrix = Warlike and Victorious by Nero in 62 A.D. following victory over Boudicca's army in Britain. Symbols - Capricorn + Eagle

Gaul 57-53 B.C., Destroyed 54 B.C. by the Eburones at Tongres, Gaul, Reformed by Julius Caesar 53 B.C., Defeated again by Germans at Tongres, Gaul 53 B.C. (Pharsalus 48 B.C.), Italy 48 B.C. (Uzita 47 B.C.) (Thapsus 46 B.C.), Macedonia 44 B.C., Italy 44 B.C., Wrecked at sea 41 B.C., Reformed by Octavian 41 B.C., (With Octavian at Actium 31 B.C.), Ptuj (Poetovio) Illyricum 30 B.C.- 9 A.D. (Drusus War 15 B.C.) (Pannonian uprising 6-9 A.D.), Mainz (Moguntiacum) upper Germany 10-43 A.D. (Idistaviso 16 A.D.), Britain 43 A.D., Towcester (Lactodurum) Britain 45-48 A.D., Mancetter (Manduessedum) Britain 48-56 A.D., Wroxeter (Viroconium Cornoviorum) Britain 56-65 A.D. (Defeated Boudicca 61 A.D.), Italy 66-69 A.D. (Defeated with Otho at Bedriacum I 69 A.D.), Britain 69 A.D., Mainz (Moguntiacum) upper Germany/Upper Germany 70-102 A.D. (Batavian campaign 70 A.D.) (Agri Decumates campaign 73-74 A.D.) (Defeated in Saturninus revolt 89 A.D.), Ptuj (Poetovio) Pannonia/Upper Pannonia 102-106 A.D. (2nd Dacian War 105-106 A.D.), Vienna (Vindobona) Upper Pannonia 106-120 A.D., Petronell (Carnuntum) Upper Pannonia 120-405 A.D. (Victorious with Septimius Severus at Issus 194 A.D.) (Milan 260 A.D.)

XV Apollinaris Formed 43 B.C. for Octavian. The name Apollinaris, from the god Apollo, appears to have been granted in the 40's B.C. XV Apollinaris Pia Fidelis = Loyal and Faithful by Marcus Aurelius ca. 176 A.D. when it did not join the revolt of Avidius Cassius. Symbol - Unknown

Illyrian Wars 35-33 B.C. (With Octavian at Actium 31 B.C.), Ljubljana (Emona) Illyricum 30-15 B.C. (Drusus War 15 B.C.), Brenner Pass, Raetia 15 B.C.- 6 A.D. (Pannonian uprising 6-9 A.D.), Ljubljana (Emona) Illyricum 9-14 A.D. (Mutiny 14 A.D.), Petronell (Carnuntum) Illyricum/Pannonia 14-62 A.D., Armenia 62-66 A.D., Alexandria 66 A.D., Jewish uprising 66-70 A.D., Petronell (Carnuntum) Pannonia/Upper Pannonia 74-120 A.D. (Dacian Wars 101-106 A.D.) (Parthian War 114-116 A.D.), Kelkit (Satala) Cappadocia 120-400 A.D. (Defeated by the Parthians at Elegeia 161 A.D.) (Defeated with Gaius Pescennius Niger at Issus 194 A.D.)

XV Primigenia Formed ca. 39 A.D. by Caligula. "Primigenia" = First Born and is derived from the goddess Fortuna Primigenia.

Mainz-Weisenau, upper Germany 39-46 A.D., Xanten (Vetera) lower Germany 46-69 A.D., Destroyed by Civilis at Xanten 69 A.D.

XVI Gallica Formed 43 B.C. for Octavian. Named for service in Gaul 25-17 B.C. Symbol - Lion

(With Octavian at Actium 31 B.C.), Italy 30-25 B.C. (Salassi campaign 25 B.C.?), Gaul 25-17 B.C., Xanten (Vetera) lower Germany 17-11 B.C. (Drusus War 15 B.C.), Oberaden (Aliso) lower Germany 11-8 B.C., Anreppen, lower Germany 8 B.C., Augsburg-Oberhausen (Augusta Vindelicum) Raetia 8 B.C.- 15 A.D. (Pannonian uprising 6-9 A.D.), Mainz (Moguntiacum) upper Germany 15-43 A.D., Neuss (Novaesium) lower Germany 43-69 A.D., Swore allegiance to the New Gallic Empire 69 A.D., Disbanded 70 A.D.

XVI Flavia Firma Formed 70 A.D. by Vespasian in the East. Named for the Flavian dynasty with the added honorific (or warning) "Firma" = Sure. XVI Flavia Firma Pia Fidelis = loyal and faithful when it failed to join Pecennius Niger in 194 A.D. Symbol - Lion

	Kelkit (Satala) Cappadocia 72-120 A.D. (Parthian War 114-116 A.D.), Samsat (Samosata) Syria 120-198 A.D. (Parthian War 162-165 A.D.) Souriya (Sura) Syria Coele 198-400 A.D.
XVII Classica	Formed by Octavian 41 B.C. The name comes from service aboard ships before 33 B.C. It can be assumed that the legions lost with Varus had names before 9 A.D. and no other name is forthcoming.
	With Antonius in the East 41-31 B.C. (With Antonius at Actium 31 B.C.) Aquitania 28-17 B.C., Vechten (Fectio) lower Germany 17 B.C.- 7 A.D. (Drusus War 15 B.C.), Nijmegen (Noviomagus) lower Germany 7-9 A.D., Destroyed in the Teutoberger Forest by the Cherusci 9 A.D.
XVIII Libyca	Formed by Octavian 41 B.C. The name comes from service in Libya. It can be assumed that the legions lost with Varus had names before 9 A.D. and no other name is forthcoming.
	With Antonius in the East 41-31 B.C. (With Antonius at Actium 31 B.C.), Gaul 30-17 B.C., Xanten (Vetera) lower Germany 17 B.C.- 9 A.D. (Drusus War 15 B.C.), Destroyed in the Teutoberger Forest by the Cherusci 9 A.D.
XIX Paterna	Formed by Octavian 41 B.C.. The name refers to Julius Caesar's honorific "Father of the country". It can be assumed that the legions lost with Varus had names before 9 A.D. and no other name is forthcoming.
	With Antonius in the East 41-31 B.C. (With Antonius at Actium 31 B.C.), Gaul 28-17 B.C., upper Germany 17-14 B.C., (Drusus War 15 B.C.), Dangstetten, upper Germany 14-8 B.C., Haltern, lower Germany 8 B.C.- 8 A.D., Cologne (Apud Arum Ubiorum) lower Germany 8-9 A.D., Destroyed in the Teutoberger Forest by the Cherusci 9 A.D. Eagle recovered 16 A.D.
XX Valeria Victrix	Formed 41 B.C. by Octavian. XX Valeria Victrix = Valiant and Victorious by Nero in 62 A.D. following victory over Boudicca's army in Britain. Symbol – Boar
	Farther Spain 32-17 B.C. (Cantabrian conquest 29-19 B.C.), Kistanje (Burnum) Illyricum 15 B.C.- 9 A.D. (Drusus War 15 B.C.) (Pannonian uprising 6-9 A.D.), Cologne (Apud Arum Ubiorum) lower Germany 9-35 A.D. (Mutiny 14 A.D.), Neuss (Novaesium) lower Germany 35-43 A.D., Britain 43 A.D., Shrewsbury, Britain 43 A.D., Colchester (Camulodunum) Britain 44-49 A.D., Kingsholm, Britain 49-56 A.D. (Defeated in Wales 53 A.D.), Usk (Burrium) Britain 56-66 A.D. (Defeated Boudicca 61 A.D.), Wroxeter (Viroconium Cornoviorum) Britain 66-85 A.D. (Stanwick 73 A.D.), Inchtuthill (Pinnata Castra) Britain 85-87 A.D., Chester (Deva) Britain/Upper Britain 87-383 A.D. (Defeated with Clodius Albinus at Lyon 197 A.D.) (Defeated with Allectus 296 A.D.), Defeated with Maximus in Gaul 383 A.D. and destroyed or disbanded
XXI Rapax	Formed 41 B.C. by Octavian. The name "Rapax" is Augustan = Grasping. Symbol - Capricorn
	Gaul 30-17 B.C., Neuss (Novaesium) Germany 17-11 B.C. (Drusus War 15 B.C.), Oberaden, (Aliso) lower Germany 11-8 B.C., Augsburg-Oberhausen (Augusta Vindelicum) Raetia 8 B.C.- 10 A.D. (Pannonian uprising 6-9 A.D.), Xanten (Vetera) lower Germany 10-46 A.D. (Mutiny 14 A.D.), Windisch (Vindonissa) upper Germany 46-69 A.D. (Victorious with the Vitellians at Bedriacum I, and defeated at Bedriacum II 69 A.D.), Bonn (Bonna) lower Germany 70-86 A.D. (Batavian campaign 70 A.D.) (Chatti War 83-85 A.D.), Mainz (Moguntiacum) Upper Germany 86-89 A.D. (Defeated in Saturninus revolt 88-89 A.D.), Ptuj (Poetovio) Pannonia 89-102 A.D., Destroyed or disbanded ca. 102 A.D during the Dacian Wars.
XXII Deiotariana	A legion formed with Galatian troops and taken into the Roman army ca. 25 B.C. Named after King Deiotarus of Galatia.

	Alexandria Kasr Kayasire (Nicopolis) Egypt 25 B.C.- 132 A.D., Destroyed in Palestine during the Jewish uprising of 132-135 A.D.
XXII Primigenia	Formed 39 A.D. by Caligula. "Primigenia" = First Born and is derived from the goddess Fortuna Primigenia. XXII Primigenia Pia Fidelis Domitiana = Loyal and Faithful by Domitian after the Saturninus revolt of 88-89 A.D. After Domitian's assassination in 96 A.D., XXII Primigenia Pia Fidelis. Symbols - Capricorn + Hercules
	Mainz-Weisenau, upper Germany 39-43 A.D., Mainz (Moguntiacum) upper Germany 43-69 A.D. (Defeated with the Vitellians at Bedriacum II 69 A.D.), Petronell (Carnuntum) Pannonia 70 A.D., Xanten (Vetera) lower Germany/Lower Germany 70-102 A.D., Mainz (Moguntiacum) Upper Germany 102-355 A.D., (Victorious with Septimius Severus at Lyon 197 A.D.) Destroyed 355 A.D. on the Rhine
XXX Ulpia	Formed 99 A.D. by Trajan for his 1st Dacian campaign and named in honor of his family. XXX Ulpia Victrix Traianus = Victorious by Trajan in 106 A.D. after the 2nd Dacian War. XXX Ulpia Victrix Severiana Pia Fidelis = Loyal and Faithful by Septimius Severus in 197 A.D.when the legion refused to join Clodius Albinus. Symbols - Neptune, Capricorn + Jupiter
	(Dacian Wars 101-106 A.D.), Szony (Brigetio) Upper Pannonia 106-122 A.D. (Parthian War 114-116 A.D.), Xanten (Vetera) Lower Germany 122-355 A.D. (Lyon 197 A.D.) (Milan 260 A.D.) (Diarbekir (Amida) Mesopotamia under Constantine II), Destroyed 355 A.D. on the Rhine, Reformed by Valentinian.

TABLE B
LIST OF LEGIONARY BASES AND THEIR GARRISONS

Alba Iulia (Apulum) Dacia/Upper Dacia from 120 A.D. - Command and control center for the pacification and rule of Dacia - I Adiutrix 106-122 A.D., XIII Gemina 106-268 A.D.

Albano (Albanum) Italy - Septimius Severus' mobile reserve close, but not too close, to Rome - II Parthica 198-299 A.D.

Albing, Noricum - Established by Marcus Aurelius on the Upper Danube at the mouth of the Enns to defend Noricum against the Marcomanni - II Italica 172-205 A.D.

Alexandria Kasr Kayasire (Nicopolis) Egypt - 3 miles to the east of the third largest city of the Empire, the entrance to and exit from Egypt - XII Fulminata 30-25 B.C., XXII Deiotariana 25 B.C.- 132 A.D., III Cyrenaica 14-120 A.D., II Traiana 120-388 A.D.

Al Lejum (Betthoro) Syria Palaestina - Diocletian's defense of Palestine against attacks from the east - IV Martia 288-532 A.D.

Andaro (Schabur) Egypt - III Diocletiana Thaebaeorum 296-388 A.D.

Anreppen, Lower Germany - An offensive base built near the headwaters of the Lippe, the main invasion route from Xanten into northern Germany - XVI Gallica 8 B.C.

Antakya (Antiochia) Galatia - Establishment of Roman rule in the newly acquired province - V Macedonica 25 B.C. - 9 A.D., VII Macedonica 25 B.C. - 9 A.D.

Antioch (Antiochea) Syria - The largest city in the East and the second largest in the Empire - III Gallica 30 B.C.- 62 A.D.

Aqaba (Aela) Syria Palaestina - At the head of the Red Sea. The southern anchor for Diocletian's Arabian defense line of Bosra-Al Lejum-Aqaba - X Fretensis 290-360 A.D.

Artschani/Arcar (Ratiaria) Upper Moesia/Dacia Ripensis from 270 A.D. - The final link in the chain of bases on the south bank of the Danube on the shortest route from the Adriatic to Dacia - IV Flavia 86-106 A.D., XIII Gemina 270-400 A.D.

Astorga (Asturica Augusta) Farther Spain – Cantabrian War base – X Gemina 26-23 B.C.

Augsburg-Oberhausen (Augusta Vindelicum) Raetia - The northern defense of Raetia after abandonment of the plan to conquer all of Germany - XVI Gallica 8 B.C.- 15 A.D., XXI Rapax 8 B.C.- 10 A.D., XIII Gemina 10-16 A.D.

Balad Sinjar (Singara) Mesopotamia - Septimius Severus' outpost against the Parthians in the corner of the Arabian desert and the Tigris - I Parthica 198-360 A.D., I Mineriva 360 A.D.

Belgrade (Singidunum) Upper Moesia - Hadrian's reinforcement of the Danube line where the Sava enters the Danube - IV Flavia 120-337 A.D.

Belkis (Zeugma) Syria - The first advance from Syria to the major crossing of the Euphrates - X Fretensis 18-62 A.D., IV Scythica 62-198 A.D.

Beseira (Circesium) Osrhoene - Part of Diocletian's defense line at the northern edge of the Arabian desert east of the Euphrates - IV Parthica 300-360 A.D.

Bonn (Bonna) lower Germany/Lower Germany from 85 A.D. - Successor to Cologne on the Rhine at the mouth of the Sieg River across from the Chatti - I Germanica 35-69 A.D., XXI Rapax 70-86 A.D., I Minervia 86-359 A.D.

Bosra (Nova Trajana Bostra) Arabia - Establishment of Roman rule in the new province of Arabia where the Spice Road from the Red Sea divides to go to Gaza or Syria - VI Ferrata 106-120 A.D., III Cyrenaica 120-395 A.D., IV Martia 274-288 A.D.

Area of the Brenner Pass, Raetia - Pacification of Raetia after the Drusus War - XV Apollinaris 15 B.C.- 6 A.D.

Budapest (Aquincum) Pannonia/Lower Pannonia from 103 A.D. - Domitian's Danube line across from the Sarmatians - II Adiutrix 86-101 A.D., X Gemina 101-120 A.D., II Adiutrix 120-405 A.D.

Caerleon (Isca Silurum) Britain/Upper Britain from 198 A.D. - The final control point for southern Wales - II Augusta 74-296 A.D.

Cairo (Babylon) Egypt - Early control of Middle Egypt - III Cyrenaica 30 B.C.- 14 A.D.

Cefae (Kiphas) Mesopotamia - Part of Diocletian's defense line along the Tigris - II Parthica 300 A.D.

Chester (Deva) Britain/Upper Britain from 198 A.D. - The key to northern Wales and the Northwest coast of Britain - II Adiutrix 78-86 A.D., XX Valeria 87-383 A.D.

Chichester (Noviomagus Regnorum) Britain - Phase 1 in the campaign to conquer the southern coast of Britain - II Augusta 44-46 A.D.

Colchester (Camulodunum) Britain - The tribal center intended to become the Roman capital city of Britain - XX Valeria 44-49 A.D.

Cologne (Apud Arum Ubiorum) lower Germany - Rhine base closed in favor of Bonn and Neuss - XIX Paterna 8-9 A.D., I Germanica 9-35 A.D., XX Valeria 9-35 A.D.

Damascus (Danaba) Syria Phoenice - A major population center between Syria and Palestine - III Gallica 219-238 A.D., III Gallica 253-350 A.D.

Dangstetten, upper Germany - Built to control southern Germany after the Drusus War – XIX Paterna 14-8 B.C.

Diarbekir (Amida) Mesopotamia - The northern end of Diocletian's Tigris defense line against the Parthians - V Parthica 300-360 A.D.

Enns-Lorch (Lauriacum) Noricum - Successor to Albing at the border of Raetia and Noricum to defend against the Marcomanni - II Italica 205-400 A.D.

Exeter (Isca Dumnoniorum) Britain - Pacification of southwestern Britain - II Augusta 55-67 A.D.

Gardun (Tilurium) Illyricum/Dalmatia from 41 A.D. - Built at the headwaters of rivers flowing toward both the Danube and the Adriatic to control southern Dalmatia - XI 27-16 B.C., IX Hispana 15 B.C.- 9 A.D., VII (Macedonica) Claudia 9-62 A.D.

Gigen (Oescus) Moesia/Lower Moesia from 85 A.D. - The center of the Danube defense line for Moesia except when Dacia was Roman - III Gallica 67-69 A.D., VI Ferrata 69 A.D., V Macedonica 72-106 A.D., V Macedonica 271-388 A.D.

Gloucester (Glevum) Britain - Base for control of the southern frontier with Wales - II Augusta 67-74 A.D.

Haidra (Ammaedara) Africa - The initial base for the control of North Africa - III Augusta 30 B.C.- 75 A.D.

Haltern (Aliso) lower Germany - East of Xanten on the Lippe replacing Oberaden - XIX Paterna 8 B.C.- 8 A.D.

Herrera de Pisuerga (Pisoraca) Farther Spain/Nearer Spain from 16 B.C. - Control of the Cantabri and Asturians in Northwest Spain - IV Macedonica 23 B.C.-43 A.D.

Iglitza-Turcoaia (Troesmi) Lower Moesia/Scythica Minor - Trajan's eastern base to protect Dacia - V Macedonica 106-167 A.D., II Herculea 300-360 A.D.

Imwas (Emmaus-Nicopolis) Syria - A base of operations during the 1st Jewish uprising - V Macedonica 68-72 A.D.

Inchtuthill (Pinnata Castra) Britain - Intended to control the Scottish Lowlands after Julius Agricola's campaigns. Never completed - XX Valeria 85-87 A.D.

Isakca (Noviodunum) Scythica Minor - Diocletian's defense line to the north of Moesia near to the Black Sea - I Jovia Scythica 300-369 A.D.

Jerusalem (Aelia Capitolina) Syria Palaestina - Vespasian's need to garrison the largest and most inflammable city in Palestine - X Fretensis 73-290 A.D.

Kelkit (Satala) Cappadocia – At one of the two major crossroads in Cappadocia - XVI Flavia 72-120 A.D., XV Apollinaris 120-400 A.D.

Kingsholm, Britain - First base at the south border of Wales - XX Valeria 49-56 A.D.

Kistanje/Suplja Crkva (Burnum) Illyricum/Dalmatia from 41 A.D. - Control point for central Dalmatia - XIII Gemina 30-16 B.C., XX Valeria 15 B.C.- 9 A.D., XI Claudia 9-69 A.D., IV Flavia 71-86 A.D.

Klaudias (Claudias-Claudiopolis) Cappadocia - Diocletian's reinforcement of the Euphrates line against the Parthians - I Armeniaca 300-363 A.D.

Kleve-Rindern (Arenacum) lower Germany - Temporary base during the Batavian campaign X Gemina 70-71 A.D.

Kostolac (Viminiacum) Moesia from 44 A.D./Upper Moesia from 85 A.D. – At the juncture of the Morava and the Danube, the key to the defense of Dalmatia, Macedonia, and Moesia against attacks across the Danube from Augustan times until the end of the Empire - XI 15 B.C.- 9 A.D., V Macedonica 9-62 A.D., VII Claudia 62-400 A.D.

Kuros (Cyrrhus) Syria - The northernmost of the early Syrian bases - X Fretensis 27 B.C.- 18 A.D.

Lake Farm, Britain - The third base in the conquest of southwestern Britain - II Augusta 49-55 A.D.

Lambese (Lambaesis) Africa/Numidia from 198 A.D.- The final legionary base in Africa established near the border between Africa and Mauritania to protect agricultural Africa from the Berbers - III Augusta 128-238 A.D., III Gallica 238-253 A.D., III Augusta 253-290 A.D.

Latakia (Laodicea ad Mare) Syria - An early coastal base in Syria - VI Ferrata 41 B.C.- 69 A.D.

Legio-Kefar Otnay (Caparcotna) Syria Palaestina - Hadrian's second garrison in Palestine - VI Ferrata 120-260 A.D.

Leon (Legio) Farther Spain/Nearer Spain from 16 B.C. - The permanent garrison of Spain guarding the northwestern mines - VI Victrix 23 B.C.- 70 A.D., VII Gemina 74-400 A.D.

Lincoln (Lindum) Britain - The northern garrison of eastern Britain from the end of the Boudiccan revolt until Wales was conquered - IX Hispana 66-71 A.D., II Adiutrix 71-78 A.D.

Ljubljana (Emona) Illyricum - At the crossing of the Amber Road over the Sava - XV Apollinaris 30-15 B.C., XIII Gemina 15 B.C.- 9 A.D., XV Apollinaris 9-14 A.D.

Lotschitz/Locica, Noricum - First base for the newly formed II Italica east of Ljubljana guarding the Carnatic Alps from the Marcomanni - II Italica 167-172 A.D.

Mainz (Moguntiacum) upper Germany/Upper Germany from 85 A.D. - The key to the Rhine frontier at the mouth of the Main leading into central Germany - I Germanica 16 B.C.- 9 A.D., XIV Gemina 10-43 A.D., II Augusta 10-15 A.D., XVI Gallica 15-43 A.D., IV Macedonica 43-69 A.D., XXII Primigenia 43-69 A.D., XIV Gemina 70-102 A.D., I Adiutrix 70-86 A.D., XXI Rapax 86-89 A.D., XXII Primigenia 102-355 A.D.

Mainz-Weisenau, upper Germany - Base for working up Caligula's new legions - XV Primigenia 39-46 A.D., XXII Primigenia 39-43 A.D.

Malataya (Melitene) Cappadocia – At one of the two main crossroads in Cappadocia – XII Fulminata 72-337 A.D.

Mancetter (Manduessedum) Britain - The base in central Britain for operations in Phase 2 of the conquest - XIV Gemina 48-56 A.D.

Mautern (Favianis) Noricum – Diocletianic defense of Noricum – I Noricorum 300-370 A.D.

Mirebeau-sur-Béze, Gaul - Base to control eastern Gaul after the Vindex revolt - VIII Augusta 70-90 A.D.

Neuss (Novaesium) lower Germany/Lower Germany from 85 A.D. - Rhine base garrisoned before and after Cologne - XXI Rapax 17-11 B.C., V Alaudae 17 B.C.- 9 A.D., XX Valeria 35-43 A.D., XVI Gallica 43-69 A.D., VI Victrix 70-102 A.D.

Newton-on-Trent, Britain – The northern headquarters in Phase 1 of the conquest of Britain with a forward base at Longthorpe – IX Hispana 45-66 A.D.

Nijmegen (Noviomagus) lower Germany/Lower Germany from 85 A.D. - Base occupied and reoccupied to control the Batavians - XVII Classica 7-9 A.D., II Adiutrix 70-71 A.D., X Gemina 71-101 A.D., IX Hispana 121 A.D.

Nis (Naissus) Moesia - Command and control base for the conquest of Macedonia - IV Scythica 30 B.C.- 9 A.D., V Macedonica 30-25 B.C., XI 30-27 B.C.

Oberaden, lower Germany - Double legion offensive base between Haltern and Anreppen on the Lippe aimed at the Sugambri and closed when the Sugambri were relocated west of the Rhine - XVI Gallica 11-8 B.C., XXI Rapax 11-8 B.C.

Palmyra, Syria Phoenice - Base established to control the Palmyrenes after an initial garrison was massacred - I Illyriacorum 274-350 A.D.

Petronell (Carnuntum) Illyricum/Pannonia from 44 A.D./Upper Pannonia from 103 A.D. – At the crossing of the Amber Road over the Danube - XV Apollinaris 14-62 A.D., X Gemina 63-69 A.D., VII Galbiana 69 A.D., XXII Primigenia 70 A.D., VII Gemina 70-74 A.D., XV Apollinaris 74-120 A.D., XIV Gemina 120-405 A.D.

Ptuj (Poetovio) Illyricum/Pannonia from 44 A.D./Lower Pannonia from 103 A.D. - A second line of defense for Italy from Augustan times until Trajan's Dacian Wars - XIV Gemina 30 B.C.- 9 A.D., VIII Augusta 10-45 A.D., XIII Gemina 45-89 A.D., XXI Rapax 89-102 A.D., XIV Gemina 102-106 A.D., XIII Gemina 268-270 A.D.

Rafniyeh (Raphanaea) Syria/Syria Phoenice from 198 A.D. - The southernmost of the original Syrian bases garrisoned until the opening of Damascus in the 3rd Century - XII Fulminata 25 B.C.- 72 A.D., VI Ferrata 73-106 A.D., III Gallica 106-219 A.D.

Regensburg (Castra Regina) Raetia - Marcus Aurelius' defense of eastern Raetia against the Marcomanni -III Italica 179-450 A.D.

Resita (Berzobis) Dacia – Built on the bank of the Birzava for the pacification of south-western Dacia - IV Flavia 106-120 A.D.

Rhesenae (Apamea) Osrhoene - Part of Diocletian's defense line on the Chaboras against the Parthians - III Parthica 219-300 A.D.

Richborough (Rutupiae) Britain – Coastal defense of Britain – II Augusta 296-410 A.D.

Rosinos de Vidrialis (Paetavonium) Farther Spain/Nearer Spain from 16 B.C. - Sited in the territory of the Vaccaei in northwest Spain to control the Astures and Cantabri X Gemina 23 B.C.- 63 A.D.

Samsat (Samosata) Syria - Vespasian's advance to the Euphrates - III Gallica 72-106 A.D., II Traiana 113-120 A.D., XVI Flavia 120-198 A.D.

Silchester (Calleva Atrebatum) Britain – Second base for the conquest of southern Britain - II Augusta 46-49 A.D.

Silistra (Durosturum) Macedonia/Moesia from 44 A.D./Lower Moesia from 85 A.D. – Defense of eastern Moesia against the Dacians and later against tribes to the east of Dacia at a major river crossing - IV Scythica 9-55 A.D., V Alaudae 69-86 A.D., XI Claudia 106-400 A.D.

Sisak (Siscia) Illyricum/Pannonia - Base near the border of Dalmatia and Pannonia - IX Hispana 9-43 A.D.

Souriya (Sura) Syria Coele - Severan reinforcement of the Euphrates line against the Parthians - XVI Flavia 198-400 A.D.

Strasbourg (Argentorate) upper Germany/Upper Germany from 85 A.D. - On the Rhine at the mouth of the Kinzing leading into southern Germany - II Augusta 15-43 A.D., VIII Augusta 90-406 A.D.

Svistov (Novae) Moesia/Lower Moesia from 85 A.D.- Primary base on the Danube for the protection of eastern Moesia - VIII Augusta 45-69 A.D., I Italica 70-316 A.D., II Traiana 104-113 A.D.

Szony (Brigetio) Pannonia/Upper Pannonia from 103 A.D./Lower Pannonia from 214 A.D. Domitian's base on the Danube between Petronell and Budapest opposite the Sarmatians - I Adiutrix 86-101 A.D., XI Claudia 101-106 A.D., XXX Ulpia 106-122 A.D., I Adiutrix 122-400 A.D.

Tayibeh (Oresa) Syria Coele - Part of Diocletian's southern defense line between the Euphrates and Syria - IV Scythica 198-400 A.D.

Tebessa (Theveste) Africa - The westward movement of III Augusta to be closer to the Atlas Mountains - III Augusta 75-128 A.D.

Tel Araban (Arbana) Osrhoene - Part of Diocletian's southern defense line at the edge of the Arabian desert between the Tigris and the Euphrates - III Parthica 300-355 A.D.

Thebes, Egypt - The southern garrison in Egypt at the beginning and end of the Empire - VIII Augusta 29 B.C.- 6 A.D., I Maximiana Thebaeorum 293-388 A.D., II Flavia Constantia 297-390 A.D.

Towcester (Lactodurum) Britain - Phase 1 of the conquest of central Britain - XIV Gemina 45-48 A.D.

Trabzon (Trapezus) Pontus - Diocletian's defense of the Black Sea coast against the Alans - I Pontica 288-360 A.D.

Turda (Potaissa) Lower Dacia - Reinforcement of the Dacian garrison until the abandonment of the province - V Macedonica 167-271 A.D.

Usk (Burrium) Britain - Base at the southern edge of Wales - XX Valeria 56-66 A.D.

Varhély (Sarmizegethusa) Dacia - The former capital of the Dacians - II Adiutrix 106-120 A.D.

Vechten (Fechtio) lower Germany - Early campaigns to conquer the Batavians - XVII Classica 17 B.C.- 7 A.D.

Vienna (Vindobona) Pannonia/Upper Pannonia from 103 A.D. - The western anchor of the Danube bases in Pannonia from the time of Domitian until the end of the Empire - XIII Gemina 89-106 A.D., XIV Gemina 106-120 A.D., X Gemina 120-360 A.D.

Viransehir (Constantina) Osrhoene – Part of Septimius Severus' garrisoning of Osrhoene – III Parthica 198-219 A.D., III Parthica 363 A.D.

Windisch (Vindonissa) upper Germany/Upper Germany from 85 A.D. - Defense of eastern Gaul and Raetia from the aftermath of the Varian Disaster until Trajan's Dacian Wars - XIII Gemina 16-45 A.D., XXI Rapax 46-69 A.D., XI Claudia 70-101 A.D.

Wroxeter (Viroconium Cornoviorum) Britain - The center of the line around Wales from the first campaign until the region was pacified - XIV Gemina 56-65 A.D., XX Valeria 66-85 A.D.

Xanten (Vetera) lower Germany/Lower Germany from 85 A.D. - The anchor of the Rhine frontier at the mouth of the Lippe from the Drusus War until the end of the Empire - XVI Gallica 17-11 B.C., XVIII Libyca 17 B.C.- 9 A.D., V

Alaudae 9-69 A.D., XXI Rapax 10-46 A.D., XV Primigenia 46-69 A.D., XXII Primigenia 70-102 A.D., VI Victrix 102-122 A.D., XXX Ulpia 122-355 A.D.

York (Eburacum) Britain/Lower Britain from 198 A.D.- The northern base on the east coast of Britain from Vespasian until the end of the Roman occupation - IX Hispana 71-121 A.D., VI Victrix 122-383 A.D.

Table C
Index of Latin/Modern and Modern/Latin base Names

A. Latin/Modern

Aela	Aqaba	Laodicea ad Mare	Latakia
Aelia Capitolina	Jerusalem	Lauriacum	Enns-Lorch
Albanum	Albano	Legio	Leon
Aliso	Haltern	Lindum	Lincoln
Amida	Diarbekir	Manduessedum	Mancetter
Ammaedara	Haidra	Melitene	Malataya
Antiochea	Antioch	Moguntiacum	Mainz
Antiochia	Antakya	Naissus	Nis
Apamca	Rhesenae	Nicopolis	Alexandria Kasr
Apud Arum Ubiorum	Cologne		Kayasire
Apulum	Alba Iulia	Novae	Svistov
Aquincum	Budapest	Novaesium	Neuss
Arbana	Tel Araban	Nova Trajana Bostra	Bosra
Arenacum	Kleve-Rindern	Noviodunum	Isakca
Argentorate	Strasbourg	Noviomagus	Nijmegen
Asturica Augusta	Astorga	Noviomagus Regnorum	Chichester
Augusta Vindelicum	Augsburg-Oberhausen	Oescus	Gigen
Babylon	Cairo	Oresa	Tayibeh
Berzobis	Resita	Paetavonium	Rosinos de
Betthoro	Al Lejum		Vidriales
Bonna	Bonn	Pinnata Castra	Inchtuthill
Brigetio	Szony	Pisoraca	Herrera de
Burnum	Kistanje		Pisuerga
Burrium	Usk	Poetovio	Ptuj
Calleva Atrebatum	Silchester	Potaissa	Turda
Camulodunum	Colchester	Raphanaea	Rafniyeh
Carnuntum	Petronell	Ratiaria	Artschani/Arcar
Capercotna	Legio-Kefar Otnay	Rutupiae	Richborough
Castra Regina	Regensburg	Samosata	Samsat
Circesium	Beseira	Sarmizegethusa	Varhely
Claudiopolis Claudius	Klaudias	Satala	Kelkit
Constantina	Viransehir	Schabur	Andaro
Cyrrhus	Kuros	Singara	Balad Sinjar
Danaba	Damascus	Singidunum	Belgrade
Deva	Chester	Siscia	Sisak
Durosturum	Silistra	Sura	Souriya
Eburacum	York	Theveste	Tebessa
Emmaus-Nicopolis	Imwas	Tilurium	Gardun
Emona	Ljubljana	Trapezus	Trabzon
Favianis	Mautern	Troesmi	Iglitza-Turcoaia
Fechtio	Vechten	Vetera	Xanten
Glevum	Gloucester	Viminiacum	Kostolac
Isca Dumnoniorum	Exeter	Vindobona	Vienna
Isca Silurum	Caerleon	Vindonissa	Windisch
Kiphas	Cephae	Viroconium Cornoviorum	Wroxeter
Lactodurum	Towcester	Zeugma	Belkis
Lambaesis	Lambese		

B. Modern/Latin

Alba Iulia	Apulum	Kuros	Cyrrhus
Albano	Albanum	Lambese	Lambaesis
Alexandria Kasr Kayasire	Nicopolis	Latakia	Laodicea ad Mare
		Legio-Kefar Otnay	Caparcotna
Al Lejum	Betthoro	Leon	Legio
Andaro	Schabur	Lincoln	Lindum
Antakya	Antiochia	Ljubljana	Emona
Antioch	Antiochea	Mainz	Moguntiacum
Aqaba	Aela	Malataya	Melitene
Artschav/Arcar	Ratiaria	Mancetter	Manduessedum
Astorga	Asturica Augusta	Mautern	Favianis
Augsburg-Oberhausen	Augusta Vindelicum	Neuss	Novaesium
Balad Sinjar	Singara	Nijmegen	Noviomagus
Belgrade	Singidunum	Nis	Naissus
Belkis	Zeugma	Petronell	Carnuntum
Beseira	Circesium	Ptuj	Poetovio
Bonn	Bonna	Rafniyeh	Raphanaea
Bosra	Nova Trajana Bostra	Regensburg	Castra Regina
Budapest	Aquincum	Resita	Berzobis
Caerleon	Isca Silurum	Rhesenae	Apamca
Cairo	Babylon	Richborough	Rutupiae
Cefae	Kiphas	Rosinos de Vidrialis	Paetavonium
Chester	Deva	Samsat	Samosata
Chichester	Noviomagus Regnorum	Silchester	Calleva Atrebatum
Colchester	Camulodunum	Silistra	Durosturum
Cologne	Apud Arum Ubiorum	Sisak	Siscia
Damascus	Danaba	Souriya	Sura
Diarbekir	Amida	Strasbourg	Argentorate
Enns-Lorch	Lauriacum	Svistov	Novae
Exeter	Isca Dumnoniorum	Szony	Brigetio
Gardun	Tilurium	Tayibeh	Oresa
Gigen	Oescus	Tebessa	Theveste
Gloucester	Glevum	Tel Araban	Arbana
Haidra	Ammaedara	Towcester	Lactodurum
Haltern	Aliso	Trabzon	Trapezus
Herrera de Pisuerga	Pisoraca	Turda	Potaissa
Iglitza-Turcoaia	Troesmi	Usk	Burrium
Imwas	Emmaus-Nicopolis	Varhely	Sarmizegethusa
Inchtuthill	Pinnata Castra	Vechten	Fechtio
Isakca	Noviodunum	Vienna	Vindobona
Jerusalem	Aelia Capitolina	Viransehir	Constantia
Kelkit	Satala	Windisch	Vindonissa
Kistanje	Burnum	Wroxeter	Viroconium Cornoviorum
Klaudias	Claudius-Claudiopolis		
Kleve-Rindern	Arenacum	Xanten	Vetera
Kostolac	Viminiacum	York	Eburacum

TABLE D
GLOBAL LEGIONARY MOVEMENTS

OCTAVIAN AUGUSTUS (31 B.C. - 14 A.D.)

30 B.C.	Octavian distributes the post-Actium army
29 B.C.	Uprising in Thebes, Egypt VIII from Italy opens Thebes; Egypt
27 B.C.	Macedonia is conquered and made a client kingdom; X Fretensis from Macedonia opens Kuros, Syria; XI from Nis, Moesia opens Gardun, Illyricum
25 B.C.	Galatea annexed as a province; V Macedonica from Nis, Macedonia opens Antakya, Galatia; VII Macedonica from Mauritania to Antakya, Galatia to join V Macedonica
	XII Fulminata from Alexandria Kasr Kayasire, Egypt opens Rafniyeh, Syria; XXII Deiotariana (new) from Galatia to Alexandria Kasr Kayasire to replace XII Fulminata
	Salassi conquered to open the Lesser St. Bernard Pass; XVI Gallica from Italy to Gaul
24 B.C.	Mountain tribes attack Mauritania IX Hispana from Nearer Spain to Mauritania
19 B.C.	Mauritania pacified. Uprising in Spain IX Hispana from Mauritania to Nearer Spain
17-16 B.C.	Spain pacified and reorganized; Build-up for the Alpine campaign I ex-Augusta (to be Germanica) from Nearer Spain opens Mainz, upper Germany XIX Paterna from Gaul to upper Germany XXI Rapax from Gaul opens Neuss, lower Germany V Alaudae from Farther Spain joins XXI Rapax at Neuss XVI Gallica and XVIII Libyca from Gaul open Xanten, lower Germany XVII Classica from Aquitania opens Vechten, lower Germany
	IX Hispana and XX Valeria from Spain to Illyricum
15-14 B.C.	Aftermath of the Drusus War XI from Gardun, Illyricum opens Kostolac, Macedonia IX Hispana to Gardun to replace XI
	XV Apollinaris from Ljubljana, Illyricum to the Brenner Pass, Raetia XIII Gemina from Kistanje, Illyricum to Ljubljana to replace XV Apollinaris XX Valeria to Kistanje to replace XIII Gemina
	XIX Paterna from upper Germany opens Dangstetten, upper Germany
11 B.C.	Change to an offensive posture in Germany XVI Gallica leaves XVIII Libyaca at Xanten, lower Germany, and opens Oberaden, lower Germany XXI Rapax leaves V Alaudae at Neuss, lower Germany to join XVI Gallica at Oberaden
9 B.C.	Drusus dies. The German offensive is abandoned; Sugambri resettled XVI Gallica and XXI Rapax close Oberaden, lower Germany to open Augsburg-Oberhausen, Raetia XIX Paterna closes Dangstetten, upper Germany to open Haltern, lower Germany
6-9 A.D.	Pannonian uprising VIII Augusta closes Thebes, Egypt to Illyricum V Macedonica and VII Macedonica close Antakya, Galatia to Illyricum and Macedonia

7 A.D.	XVII Classica closes Vechten, lower Germany to open Nijmegen, lower Germany
8 A.D.	XIX Paterna closes Haltern, lower Germany to open Cologne, lower Germany
9-10 A.D.	Tiberius crushes the uprising in Illyricum; Varian disaster in Germany XVII Classica from Nijmegen, XVIII Libyca from Xanten, and XIX Paterna from Cologne, all in lower Germany, are destroyed Nijmegen, lower Germany is closed I Germanica from Mainz, upper Germany to Cologne, lower Germany to replace XIX Paterna XX Valeria from Kistanje, Illyricum to Cologne to join I Germanica XI from Kostolac, Moesia to Kistanje to replace XX Valeria V Macedonica to Kostolac to replace XI II Augusta from Nearer Spain to Mainz, upper Germany to replace I Germanica XIV Gemina from Ptuj, Illyricum to Mainz to join II Augusta VIII Augusta to Ptuj to replace XIV Gemina V Alaudae closes Neuss, lower Germany to Xanten, lower Germany to replace XVIII Libyaca XXI Rapax from Augsburg-Oberhausen, Raetia to Xanten to join V Alaudae XIII Gemina from Ljubljana, Illyricum to Augsburg-Oberhausen, Raetia to replace XXI Rapax XV Apollinaris from Brenner Pass, Raetia to Ljubljana to replace XIII Gemina Double legion bases at Xanten and Cologne in lower Germany, Mainz in upper Germany, and Augsburg-Oberhausen, Raetia IX Hispana from Gardun, Illyricum opens Sisak, Illyricum VII Macedonica from Galatia to Gardun to replace IX Hispana. IV Scythica closes Nis, Macedonia to open Silistra, Macedonia on the Danube

TIBERIUS (14-37 A.D.)

14 A.D.	III Cyrenaica closes Cairo, Egypt to Alexandria Kasr Kayasire, Egypt to join XXII Deiotariana XV Apollinaris closes Ljubljana, Dalmatia to open Petronell, Illyricum on the Danube
15-16 A.D.	II Augusta from Mainz, upper Germany opens Strasbourg, upper Germany XVI Gallica from Augsburg-Oberhausen, Raetia to Mainz to replace II Augusta XIII Gemina from Augsburg-Oberhausen opens Windisch, upper Germany Augsburg-Oberhausen is closed
18 A.D.	Belkis is separated from Commagene and attached to Syria X Fretensis closes Kuros, Syria to open Belkis, Syria on the Euphrates
35 A.D.	Garrisons spread on the Middle Rhine I Germanica from Cologne, lower Germany opens Bonn, lower Germany XX Valeria from Cologne, lower Germany reopens Neuss, lower Germany Cologne is closed

CALIGULA (37-41 A.D.)

39 A.D.	The Rhine army expanded for a new German campaign XV Primigenia (new) and XXII Primigenia (new) open Mainz-Weisenau, upper Germany

CLAUDIUS (41-54 A.D.)

43 A.D.	Invasion of Britain with II Augusta from Strasbourg, upper Germany, IX Hispana from Sisak, Pannonia, XIV Gemina from Mainz, upper Germany, and XX Valeria from Neuss, lower Germany Strasbourg, upper Germany and Sisak, Pannonia are closed XVI Gallica from Mainz, upper Germany to Neuss to replace XX Valeria IV Macedonica from Herrera de Pisuerga, Nearer Spain to Mainz to replace XVI Gallica XXII Primigenia from Mainz-Weisenau to Mainz to replace XIV Gemina
44-45 A.D.	Phase 1 of the British campaign II Augusta opens Chichester, Britain IX Hispana opens Newton-on-Trent, Britain XIV Gemina opens Towcester, Britain XX Valeria opens Colchester, Britain
45-46 A.D.	Moesia becomes a province; The client kingdom of Thrace is annexed VIII Augusta from Ptuj, Pannonia opens Svistov, Moesia on the Danube XIII Gemina from Windisch, upper Germany to Ptuj to replace VIII Augusta XXI Rapax from Xanten, lower Germany to Windisch to replace XIII Gemina XV Primigenia from Mainz-Weisenau, upper Germany to Xanten to replace XXI Rapax Mainz-Weisenau is closed
46 A.D.	II Augusta closes Chichester, Britain to open Silchester, Britain
48-49 A.D.	Caratacus uprising in Britain II Augusta closes Silchester, Britain and opens Lake Farm, Britain XIV Gemina closes Towcester, Britain and opens Mancetter, Britain XX Valeria closes Colchester, Britain and opens Kingsholm, Britain

NERO (54-68 A.D.)

55 A.D.	The Parthians invade Armenia IV Scythica closes Silistra, Moesia to Cappadocia
55-56 A.D.	Campaign to conquer Wales in Britain II Augusta closes Lake Farm, Britain and opens Exeter, Britain XIV Gemina closes Mancetter, Britain and opens Wroxeter, Britain XX Valeria closes Kingsholm, Britain and opens Usk, Britain
62-63 A.D.	Parthian victory at Rhandeia, Armenia III Gallica closes Antioch, Syria to Armenia V Macedonica from Kostolac, Moesia to Armenia VII Claudia closes Gardun, Dalmatia to Kostolac to replace V Macedonica X Fretensis from Belkis, Syria to Armenia IV Scythica defeated at Rhandeia to Belkis to replace X Fretensis XV Apollinaris from Petronell, Pannonia to Armenia X Gemina from Rosinos de Vidriales, Nearer Spain to Petronell, Pannonia to replace XV Apollinaris
66 A.D.	Nero reduces the British garrison XIV Gemina from Wroxeter, Britain to Italy for an Eastern campaign XX Valeria closes Usk, Britain to Wroxeter to replace XIV Gemina IX Hispana closes Newton-on-Trent, Britain to open Lincoln, Britain Parthian Settlement. Jewish uprising in Palestine V Macedonica from Armenia via Alexandria to the Jewish uprising X Fretensis from Armenia via Alexandria to the Jewish uprising XV Apollinaris from Armenia via Alexandria to the Jewish uprising
67 A.D.	III Gallica from Armenia opens Gigen, Moesia

II Augusta closes Exeter, Britain to open Gloucester, Britain

68 A.D. Pacification of Judaea
V Macedonica involved in suppressing the Jewish uprising opens Imwas, Syria

Aftermath of the Vindex revolt in Gaul
I Italica (new) from Italy to Lyon, Gaul

69 A.D. Year of the 4 Emperors
Galba brings VII Galbiana (new) from Spain
X Gemina from Petronell to Spain

Vitellius disperses Otho's legions after Bedriacum I
I Adiutrix (new) to Spain
XIII Gemina from Ptuj, Pannonia held in Italy
XIV Gemina from Italy sent back to Britain

VESPASIAN (69-79 A.D.)

Vitellius' Rhine legions defeated at Bedriacum II in Italy; Civilis uprising in Gaul
VI Ferrata from Latakia, Syria stationed in Italy

70 A.D. XV Primigenia in Xanten destroyed by Civilis;
XVI Gallica in Neuss, I Germanica in Bonn, all in lower Germany, and
IV Macedonica from Mainz, upper Germany, are disbanded

The surviving Vittellian legions are dispersed
I Italica from Lyon, Gaul to Svistov, Moesia to replace VIII Augusta
V Alaudae from Xanten, lower Germany reopens Silistra, Moesia
XXI Rapax from Windisch, upper Germany to Bonn, lower Germany to replace I Germanica
XXII Primigenia from Mainz, upper Germany via Petronell, Pannonia to Xanten, lower Germany to replace V Alaudae

The Rhine garrison is replaced; The Civilis uprising is suppressed
II Adiutrix (new) reopens Nijmegen, lower Germany
VIII Augusta from Svistov, Moesia opens Mirebeau-sur-Beze, Gaul

X Gemina from Petronell, Pannonia via Spain opens Kleve-Rindern, lower Germany
VII Gemina (ex-VII Galbiana, new) to Petronell, Pannonia to replace X Gemina

XIV Gemina from Britain via Italy and Britain to Mainz, upper Germany to replace XXII Primigenia
I Adiutrix from Spain to Mainz, upper Germany to join XIV Gemina

VI Victrix closes Leon, Nearer Spain to Neuss, lower Germany to replace XVI Gallica

XI Claudia from Kistanje, Dalmatia to Windisch, upper Germany to replace XXI Rapax
IV Flavia (new) to Kistanje to replace XI Claudia

XIII Gemina from Italy returns to Ptuj, Pannonia

71 A.D. Expansion northwards in Britain
IX Hispana from Lincoln, Britain opens York, Britain
II Adiutrix from Nijmegen, lower Germany to Lincoln to replace IX Hispana
X Gemina from Kleve-Rindern, lower Germany to Nijmegen to replace II Adiutrix

72-73 A.D. Cappadocia and Commagene annexed as Roman provinces; End of the Jewish uprising; Syria Palaestina separated from Syria
XVI Flavia (new) opens Kelkit, Cappadocia
XII Fulminata from Rafniyeh, Syria opens Malataya, Cappadocia
VI Ferrata from Italy to Rafniyeh to replace XII Fulminata

	III Gallica from Gigen, Moesia via Italy returns to Syria to open Samsat on the upper Euphrates V Macedonica closes Imwas, Syria to Gigen, Moesia to replace III Gallica
73 A.D.	X Fretensis opens Jerusalem, Syria Palaestina
74 A.D.	Wales conquered II Augusta closes Gloucester, Britain to open Caerleon, Britain Spain receives its permanent garrison VII Gemina from Petronell, Pannonia reopens Leon, Spain XV Apollinaris from Syria Palaestina returns to Petronell to replace VII Gemina
75 A.D.	III Augusta closes Haidra, Africa to open Tebessa, Africa
78 A.D.	Agricola's campaign to conquer the rest of Britain II Adiutrix closes Lincoln, Britain to open Chester, Britain

DOMITIAN (81-96 A.D.)

85 A.D.	Lowland Scotland conquered XX Valeria closes Wroxeter, Britain to open Inchtuthill, Britain
86-88 A.D.	Dacians attack Moesia and are eventually defeated V Alaudae from Silistra, Lower Moesia is destroyed. Silistra is closed I Adiutrix from Mainz, Upper Germany opens Szony, Pannonia XXI Rapax from Bonn, Lower Germany to Mainz to replace I Adiutrix I Minervia (new) to Bonn to replace XXI Rapax IV Flavia closes Kistanje, Dalmatia to open Artschav, Upper Moesia British garrison reduced to reinforce the Danube II Adiutrix from Chester, Britain opens Budapest, Pannonia XX Valeria abandons Inchtuthill, Britain to Chester to replace II Adiutrix
89-90 A.D.	Saturninus revolt with XIV Gemina and XXI Rapax in Upper Germany XIII Gemina from Ptuj, Pannonia opens Vienna, Pannonia XXI Rapax from Mainz, Upper Germany to Ptuj to replace XIII Gemina VIII Augusta closes Mirebeau-sur-Béze, Gaul to open Strasbourg, Upper Germany

TRAJAN (98-117 A.D.)

101 A.D.	First Dacian War I Adiutrix from Szony, Pannonia and II Adiutrix from Budapest, Pannonia to Dacia XI Claudia closes Windisch, Upper Germany to Szony to replace I Adiutrix X Gemina closes Nijmegen, Lower Germany to Budapest to replace II Adiutrix operating in Dacia
102-104 A.D.	XXI Rapax from Ptuj, lower Pannonia is disbanded or destroyed XIV Gemina from Mainz, Upper Germany to Ptuj to replace XXI Rapax XXII Primigenia from Xanten, Lower Germany to Mainz to replace XIV Gemina VI Victrix back from the Dacian War closes Neuss, Lower Germany to Xanten to replace XXII Primigenia II Traiana (new) to Svistov, Lower Moesia to join I Italica
106 A.D.	Aftermath of the Dacian Wars XIII Gemina from Vienna, Upper Pannonia opens Alba Iulia, Dacia XIV Gemina closes Ptuj, Lower Pannonia to Vienna to replace XIII Gemina I Adiutrix joins XIII Gemina at Alba Iulia, Dacia II Adiutrix opens Varhély, Dacia IV Flavia closes Artschav, Upper Moesia to open Resita, Dacia V Macedonica closes Gigen, Lower Moesia to open Iglitza-Turcoaia, Lower Moesia

XI Claudia from Szony, Upper Pannonia reopens Silistra, Lower Moesia
XXX Ulpia (new) to Szony to replace XI Claudia

Annexation of the Nabataean Kingdom as the province of Arabia
VI Ferrata from Rafniyeh, Syria opens Bosra, Arabia
III Gallica closes Samsat, Syria to Rafniyeh to replace VI Ferrata

113 A.D.   Parthian War
II Traiana from Svistov, Lower Moesia reopens Samsat, Syria

HADRIAN (117-138 A.D.)

120 A.D.   Frontiers reorganized
VI Ferrata from Bosra, Arabia opens Legio-Kefar Otnay, Syria Palaestina
III Cyrenaica from Alexandria Kasr Kayasire, Egypt to Bosra to replace VI Ferrata
II Traiana from Samsat, Syria to Alexandria Kasr Kayasire to replace III Cyrenaica
XVI Flavia from Kelkit, Cappadocia to Samsat to replace II Traiana
XV Apollinaris from Petronell, Upper Pannonia to Kelkit to replace XVI Flavia
XIV Gemina from Vienna, Upper Pannonia to Petronell to replace XV Apollinaris
X Gemina from Budapest, Lower Pannonia to Vienna to replace XIV Gemina
II Adiutrix closes Varhély, Dacia and returns to Budapest to replace X Gemina
IV Flavia closes Resita, Dacia to open Belgrade, Upper Moesia

121-122 A.D.   Aftermath of a tribal uprising in Britain
IX Hispana from York, Britain seems to have been transferred and disbanded at   Nijmegen, Lower Germany
VI Victrix from Xanten, Lower Germany to York to replace IX Hispana
XXX Ulpia from Szony, Lower Pannonia to Xanten to replace VI Victrix
I Adiutrix from Alba Iulia, Dacia returns to Szony to replace XXX Ulpia

128 A.D.   III Augusta closes Tebessa, Africa to open Lambese, Africa

132-135 A.D.   2nd Jewish uprising
XXII Deiotariana from Alexandria Kasr Kayasire, Egypt destroyed in Syria Palaestina

MARCUS AURELIUS (161-180 A.D.)

167 A.D.   Marcomanni War
V Macedonica closes Iglitza-Turcoaia, Lower Moesia to open Turda, Lower Dacia
II Italica (new) opens Lotschitz/Locica, Noricum

172-179 A.D.   Aftermath of the Marcomanni War
II Italica closes Lotschitz/Locica, Noricum to open Albing, Noricum
III Italica (new) opens Regensburg, Raetia on the upper Danube

SEPTIMIUS SEVERUS (193-211 A.D.)

198 A.D.   Aftermath of Parthian campaign
I Parthica (new) opens Balad Sinjar, Mesopotamia
II Parthica (new) opens Albano, Italy
III Parthica (new) opens Constantina, Osrhoene
IV Scythica closes Belkis, Syria Coele to open Tayibeh, Syria Coele
XVI Flavia closes Samsat, Syria Coele to open Souriya, Syria Coele

205 A.D.   II Italica closes Albing, Noricum to open Enns-Lorch, Noricum

ELAGABALUS (218-222 A.D.)

218-219 A.D.   Gannys defeats Macrinus at Inmae, Syria
III Gallica closes Rafniyeh, Syria Phoenice to open Damascus, Syria Phoenice

III Parthica closes Constantina, Osrhoene to open Rhesenae, Osrhoene

GORDIAN III (238-244 A.D.)

238 A.D.	Gordian I's revolt in Africa is crushed by III Augusta
	III Augusta disbanded by Gordian III at Lambese, Numidia
	III Gallica closes Damascus, Syria Phoenice to Lambese to replace III Augusta

VALERIAN (253-260 A.D.)

253 A.D.	III Augusta is reformed at Lambese, Numidia
	III Gallica from Lambese reopens Damascus, Syria Phoenice
260 A.D.	Valerian defeated by the Parthians at Edessa, Osrhoene
	VI Ferrata probably destroyed . Legio-Kefar Otnay, Syria Palaestina is closed

CLAUDIUS GOTHICUS (268-270 A.D.)

268 A.D.	Decision made to abandon Dacia
	XIII Gemina closes Alba Iulia, Dacia to reopen Ptuj, Lower Pannonia
270 A.D.	XIII Gemina closes Ptuj, Lower Pannonia to reopen Artschav/Arcar, Dacia Ripensis

AURELIAN (270-275 A.D.)

271 A.D.	Dacia evacuated
	V Macedonica closes Turda, Dacia to reopen Gigen, Lower Moesia
274 A.D.	Zenobia of Palmyra defeats III Cyrenaica from Bosra, Arabia and is in turn defeated
	I Illyriacorum (new) opens Palmyra, Syria Phoenice
	IV Martia (new) occupies Bosra, Arabia

PROBUS (276-282 A.D.)

278 A.D.	Unrest in Issauria
	I Issaurus (new), II Issaurus (new), and III Issaurus (new) garrison Seleucia, Issauria

DIOCLETIAN (284-305 A.D.)

288 A.D.	Defense against the Alans from the Caucausus
	I Pontica (new) opens Trabzon, Pontus on the Black Sea
	IV Martia from Bosra, Arabia opens Al Lejum, Syria Palaestina
290 A.D.	X Fretensis closes Jerusalem, Syria Palaestina to open Aqaba, Syria Palaestina
293 A.D.	I Maximiana Thebaeorum (new) opens Pilae, Thebes, Egypt
294 A.D.	V Jovia (new) and VI Herculea (new) open Mitronica, Lower Pannonia
296 A.D.	III Diocletiana Thebaeorum (new) opens Andaro, Egypt
	II Augusta closes Caerleon, Britain to open Richborough, Britain on the Saxon Shore
297 A.D.	II Flavia Constantia (new) to Thebes to join I Maximiana Thebaeorum
298 A.D.	III Herculea (new) to Mauritania

300 A.D. New garrisons on the Tigris
I Armeniaca (new) opens Klaudias, Cappadocia
II Parthica from Albano, Italy opens Cefae, Mesopotamia on the Tigris
III Parthica closes Rhesenae, Osrhoene and opens Tel Araban, Osrhoene
IV Parthica (new) opens Beseira, Osrhoene on the Euphrates
V Parthica (new) opens Diarbekir, Mesopotamia on the Tigris

I Noricorum (new) opens Mautern, Noricum

II Herculea (new) reopens Iglitza-Turcoaia, Scythica Minor

TABLE E
REGIONAL LEGIONARY HISTORY

1) Spain

    OCTAVIAN AUGUSTUS (31 B.C. – 14 A.D.)

29 B.C.	Octavian decides to conquer the rest of Spain Legions available: Nearer Spain: I, II, IX Macedonica (Hispana) Farther Spain: IV Macedonica, V Alaudae, VI Hispana (Victrix), X Gemina, XX Valeria
24 B.C.	Uprising in Mauritania IX Hispana from Nearer Spain to Mauritania
23 B.C.	Permanent bases in Farther Spain are established IV Macedonica at Herrera de Pisuerga VI Hispana (Victrix) at Leon X Gemina at Rosinos de Vidrialis
19 B.C.	Uprising in Spain I Augusta loses its cognomen - Mutiny or defeat? IX Hispana returns from Mauritania to Nearer Spain
17-16 B.C.	Spain pacified and reorganized – Baetica and Lusitania become senatorial provinces, Farther Spain merged into Nearer Spain - Drusus War I (ex-Augusta) and V Alaudae to Germany IX Hispana and XX Valeria to Illyricum
9 A.D.	Varian Disaster II Augusta to Germany

    CLAUDIUS (41-54 A.D.)

43 A.D.	Invasion of Britain IV Macedonica from Herrera de Pisuerga to Germany

    NERO (54-68 A.D.)

63 A.D.	Parthian War X Gemina from Rosinos de Vidriales to Pannonia
68 A.D.	Galba, the governor of Spain, becomes Emperor VII Galbiana raised in Spain to Italy X Gemina from Pannonia to Spain I Adiutrix (new) from Italy to Spain for field training

    VESPASIAN (69-79 A.D.)

70 A.D.	Vitellian legions are replaced in Germany VI Victrix, the last of the original Spanish legions, from Leon to Germany X Gemina to Leon to replace VI Victrix
71 A.D.	Batavian campaign in lower Germany I Adiutrix to Germany X Gemina from Leon to lower Germany Spain is without legions
74 A.D.	VII Gemina (ex-Galbiana) from Pannonia replaces X Gemina at Leon

2) Gaul/Germany/Raetia/Noricum

OCTAVIAN AUGUSTUS (31B.C.-14 A.D.)

17-16 B.C.   Build-up for the invasion of the Alpine regions
XVII Classica from Aquitania opens Vechten, Germany
XVI Gallica and XVIII Libyca from Gaul open Xanten, Germany
V Alaudae from Spain and XXI Rapax from Gaul open Neuss, Germany
I (Germanica) from Spain opens Mainz, Germany
XIX Paterna from Gaul to Germany
Gaul is without legions

15-14 B.C.   Aftermath of the Drusus War – Germany divided into upper and lower military districts; Vechten, Xanten and Neuss are lower Germany, Mainz is upper Germany
XIX Paterna from upper Germany opens Dangstetten, upper Germany
XV Apollinaris from Illyricum to the Brenner Pass, Raetia

lower Germany 5, upper Germany 2, Raetia 1

11 B.C.   Change to an offensive posture in lower Germany
XVI Gallica from Xanten and XXI Rapax from Neuss, lower Germany open Oberaden, lower Germany

9 B.C.   Drusus dies. The expansion into Germany is abandoned; Sugambri resettled west of the Rhine
XVI Gallica and XXI Rapax close Oberaden, lower Germany to open Augsburg-Oberhausen, Raetia
XIX Paterna closes Dangstetten, upper Germany and opens Haltern, lower Germany

Lower Germany 3, upper Germany 1, Raetia 3

7 A.D.   XVII Classica closes Vechten, lower Germany to open Nijmegen, lower Germany

8 A.D.   XIX Paterna closes Haltern, lower Germany to open Cologne, lower Germany

9 A.D.   Varian Disaster
XVII Classica, XVIII Libyca, and XIX Paterna, all from lower Germany, are destroyed in the Teutoberger Forest

Surviving on the Rhine Frontier are V Alaudae at Neuss, lower Germany, I Germanica at Mainz upper Germany, and XVI Gallica and XXI Rapax at Augsburg-Oberhausen, Raetia
Nijmegen, Xanten, and Cologne are now empty

As a first reaction, V Alaudae moves from Neuss, lower Germany to Xanten, lower Germany and I Germanica from Mainz, upper Germany to Cologne, lower Germany

New legions are transferred to Germany:
II Augusta from Spain to Mainz to replace I Germanica
XIV Gemina from Illyricum to Mainz to join II Augusta
XX Valeria from Illyricum to Cologne to join I Germanica
XXI Rapax from Augsburg-Oberhausen to Xanten to join V Alaudae
XIII Gemina from Illyricum to Augsburg-Oberhausen to replace XXI Rapax

XV Apollinaris from the Brenner Pass, Raetia to Illyricum

The new strategy is double legion bases at Xanten and Cologne, lower Germany, Mainz, upper Germany, and Augsburg-Oberhausen, Raetia

lower Germany 4, upper Germany 2, Raetia 2

TIBERIUS (14-37 A.D.)

15 A.D.   II Augusta from Mainz, upper Germany opens Strasbourg, upper Germany

XVI Gallica from Augsburg-Oberhausen, Raetia to Mainz to replace II Augusta

Augsburg-Oberhausen, Raetia and Strasbourg, upper Germany are now
1 legion bases. Xanten, Cologne and Mainz remain 2 legion bases.

16 A.D.   Raetia is considered safe
XIII Gemina closes Augsburg-Oberhausen and opens Windisch, upper Germany

lower Germany 4, upper Germany 4, Raetia 0

35 A.D   I Germanica from Cologne, lower Germany opens Bonn, lower Germany
XX Valeria from Cologne reopens Neuss, lower Germany
Cologne, lower Germany is closed

Xanten and Mainz remain 2 legion bases.

CALIGULA (37-41 A.D.)

39 A.D.   Rhine army expanded for a new German campaign
XV Primigenia (new) and XXII Primigenia (new) open Mainz-Weisenau, upper Germany

CLAUDIUS (41-54 A.D)

43 A.D.   Invasion of Britain
II Augusta from Strasbourg, upper Germany, XIV Gemina from Mainz, upper Germany, and XX Valeria from Neuss, lower Germany, are part of the invasion force
XVI Gallica from Mainz to Neuss to replace XX Valeria
XXII Primigenia from Mainz-Weisenau to Mainz to replace XIV Gemina
IV Macedonica from Spain to Mainz to replace XVI Gallica
Strasbourg is closed

45-46 A.D.   Organization of the new Danube provinces
XIII Gemina from Windisch, upper Germany to Pannonia
XXI Rapax from Xanten to Windisch to replace XIII Gemina
XV Primigenia from Mainz-Weisenau, upper Germany to Xanten to replace XXI Rapax
Mainz-Weisenau is closed

NERO (54-68 A.D.)

68 A.D.   Vindex revolt in Gaul
I Italica (new) from Italy to Lyon, Gaul

lower Germany 4, upper Germany 3, Gaul 1

VESPASIAN (69-79 A.D.)

69-71 A.D.   Aftermath of the Year of the 4 Emperors
In 69 A.D., V Alaudae and XV Primigenia were based at Xanten; XVI Gallica was at Neuss; I Germanica was at Bonn; IV Macedonica and XXII Primigenia were at Mainz, XXI Rapax was at Windisch, I Italica was at Lyon. All these legions supported Vitellius. Vitellius was killed in Rome by supporters of Vespasian.
XV Primigenia was besieged and annihilated by Civilis at Xanten, lower Germany
I Germanica, IV Macedonica and XVI Gallica had sworn allegiance to the New Gallic Empire
These 4 legions officially disappeared
V Alaudae and I Italica were sent to Moesia
XXI Rapax and XXII Primigenia were relocated to lower Germany
IV Flavia (new), probably a reconstituted IV Macedonica, sent to Dalmatia

71-74 A.D.   The new Rhine garrison after the Batavian uprising was suppressed was:
Nijmegen, lower Germany reopened with X Gemina from Spain

Xanten, lower Germany received XXII Primigenia from Mainz
Neuss, lower Germany received VI Victrix from Spain
Bonn, upper Germany received XXI Rapax from Windisch
Mainz, upper Germany received XIV Gemina from Britain and I Adiutrix from Spain
Windisch, upper Germany received XI Claudia from Moesia

Mirebeau-sur-Béze, Gaul opened with VIII Augusta from Moesia

lower Germany 4, upper Germany 3, Gaul 1 as in 69 A.D.

DOMITIAN (81-96 A.D.)

86 A.D. Sarmatian War in Pannonia
Germany formally divided into Lower and Upper provinces
I Adiutrix from Mainz, Upper Germany to Pannonia
XXI Rapax from Bonn, Lower Germany to Mainz to replace I Adiutrix
I Minervia (new) to Bonn to replace XXI Rapax

89-90 A.D. Saturninus revolt with XIV Gemina and XXI Rapax from Mainz is crushed
XXI Rapax from Mainz, Upper Germany to Pannonia
VIII Augusta closes Mirebeau-sur-Béze, Gaul to open Strasbourg, Upper Germany

Lower Germany 4, Upper Germany 3, Gaul 0

TRAJAN (98-117 A.D.)

101 A.D. 1st Dacian War
X Gemina closes Nijmegen, Lower Germany to Pannonia
XI Claudia closes Windisch, Upper Germany to Moesia

102 A.D. XIV Gemina from Mainz, Upper Germany to Pannonia
XXII Primigenia from Xanten, Lower Germany to Mainz to replace XIV Gemina
VI Victrix returns from the Dacian War, closes Neuss, Lower Germany to Xanten to replace XXII Primigenia

Lower Germany 2, Upper Germany 2

HADRIAN (117-135 A.D.)

121-122 A.D. Tribal uprising in Britain
IX Hispana from Britain seems to have been transferred to Nijmegen, Lower Germany, briefly before disappearing
VI Victrix from Xanten, Lower Germany to Britain
XXX Ulpia from Pannonia to Xanten to replace VI Victrix

MARCUS AURELIUS (161-180 A.D.)

167 A.D. Marcomanni War
II Italica (new) opens Lotschitz/Locica, Noricum

172 A.D. II Italica closes Lotschitz/Locica, Noricum and opens Albing, Noricum

179 A.D. III Italica (new) opens Regensburg, Raetia

205 A.D. II Italica closes Albing, Noricum and opens Enns-Lorch, Noricum

DIOCLETIAN (284-305 A.D.)

300 A.D. I Noricorum (new) opens Mautern, Noricum

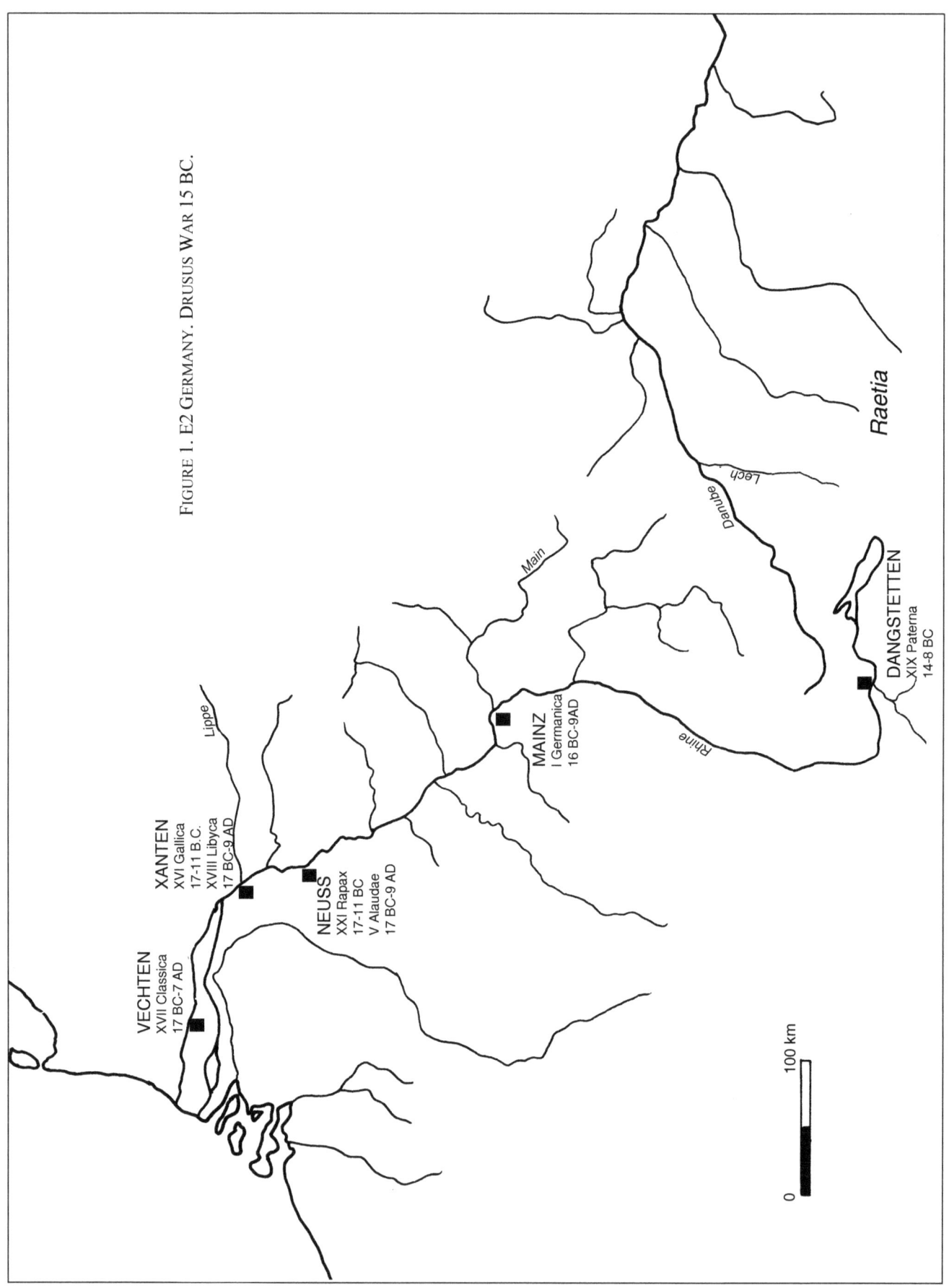

Figure 1. E2 Germany. Drusus War 15 BC.

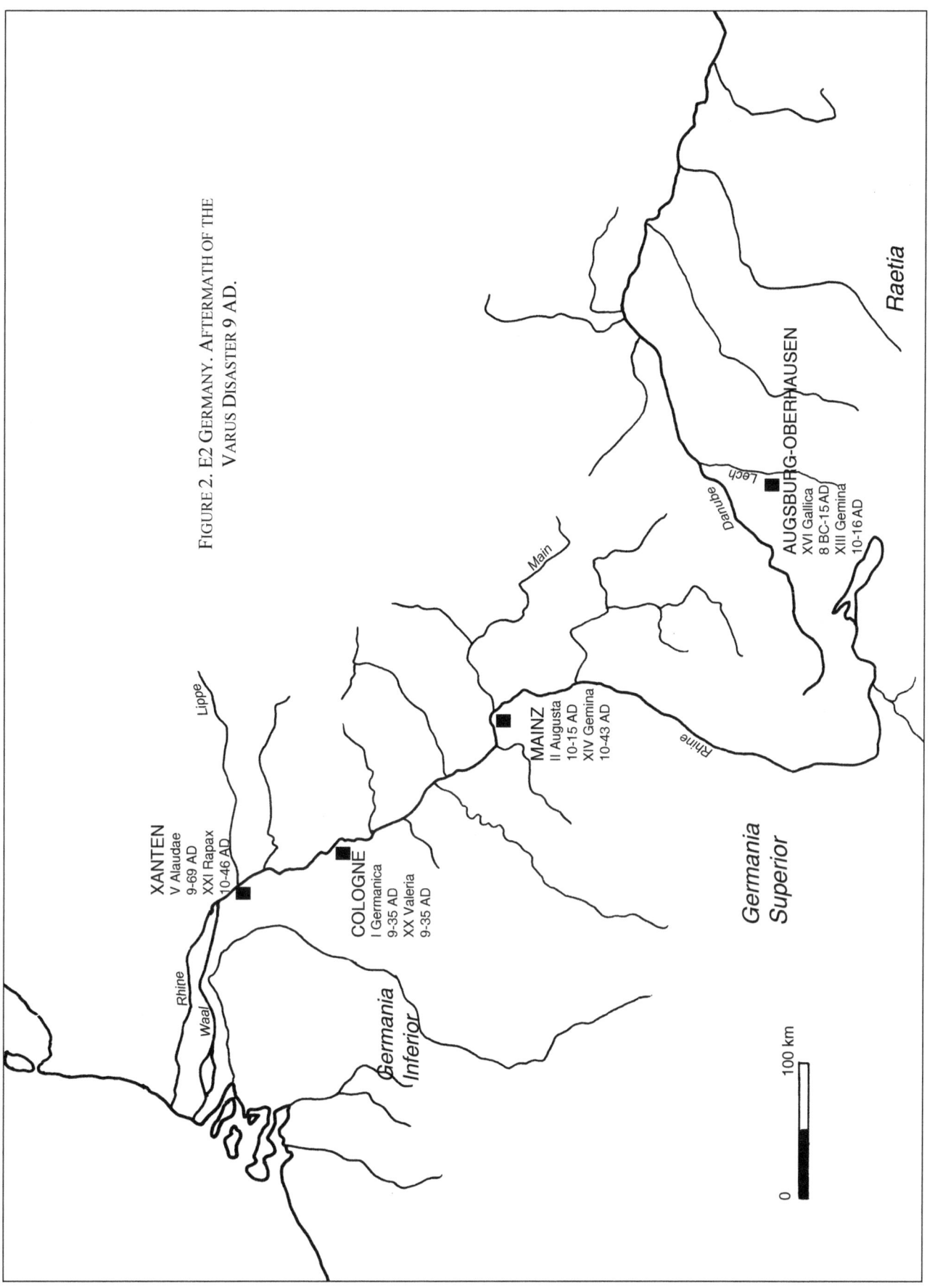

Figure 2. E2 Germany. Aftermath of the Varus Disaster 9 AD.

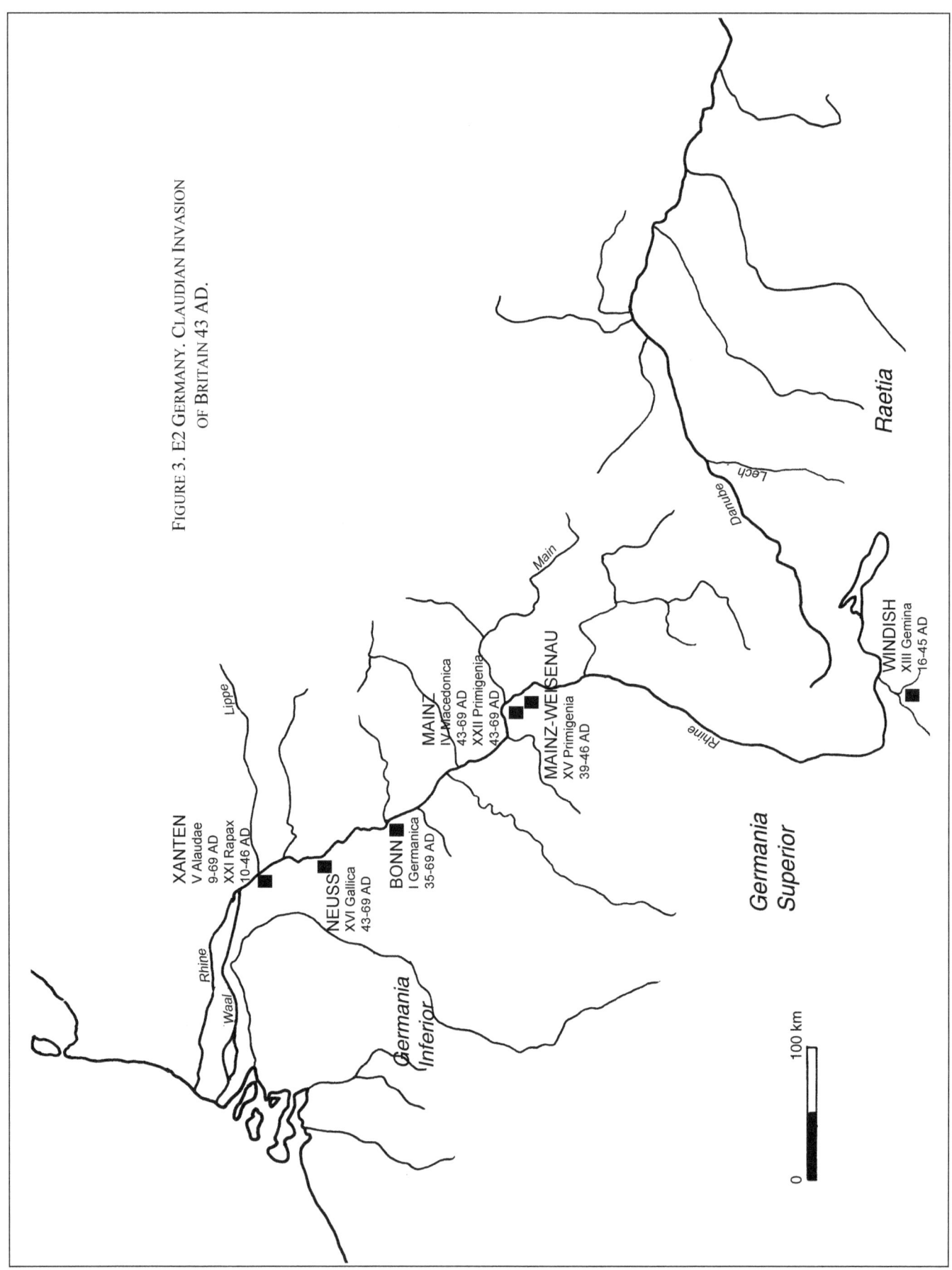

Figure 3. E2 Germany. Claudian Invasion of Britain 43 AD.

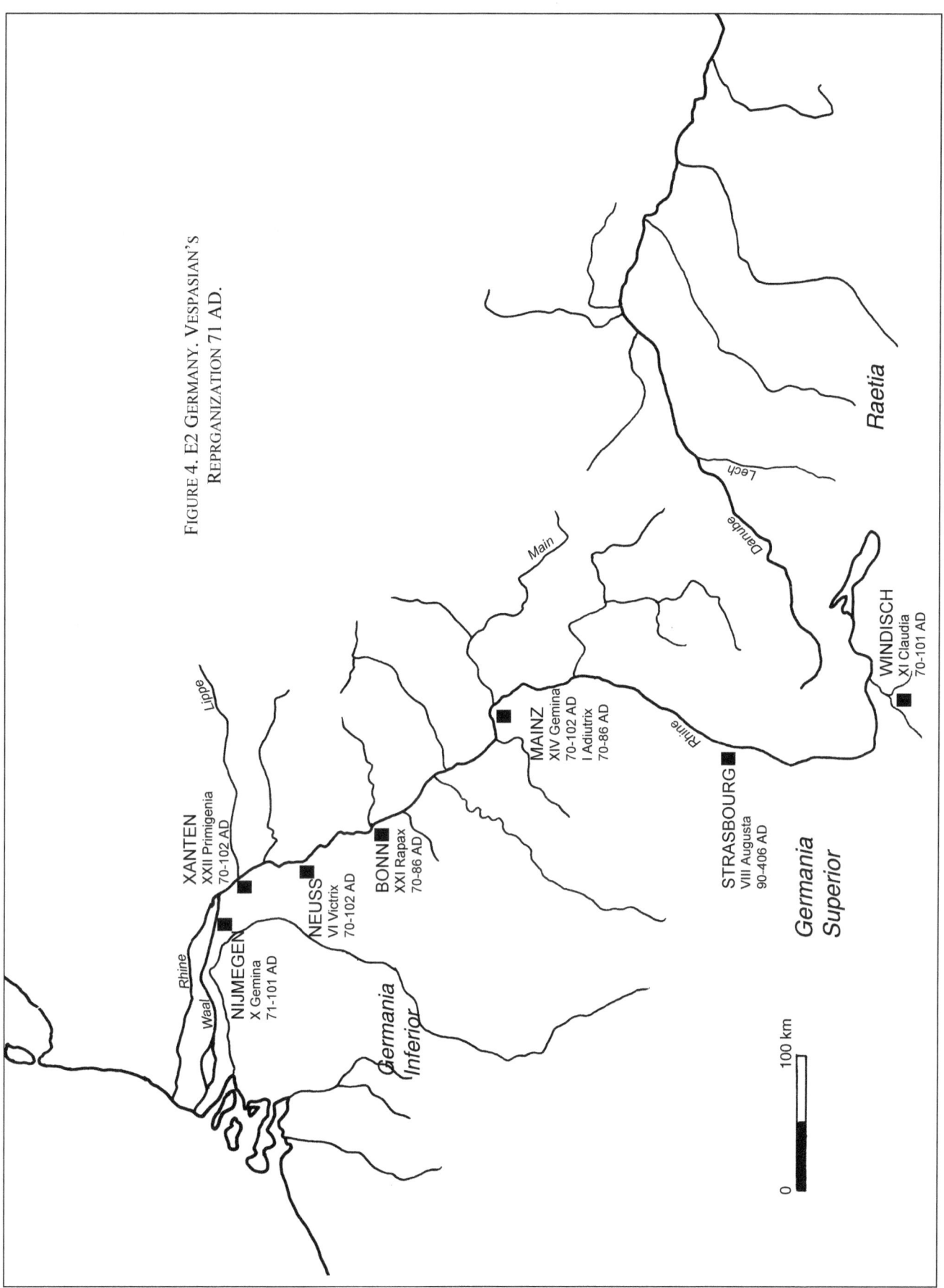

Figure 4. E2 Germany. Vespasian's Reprganization 71 AD.

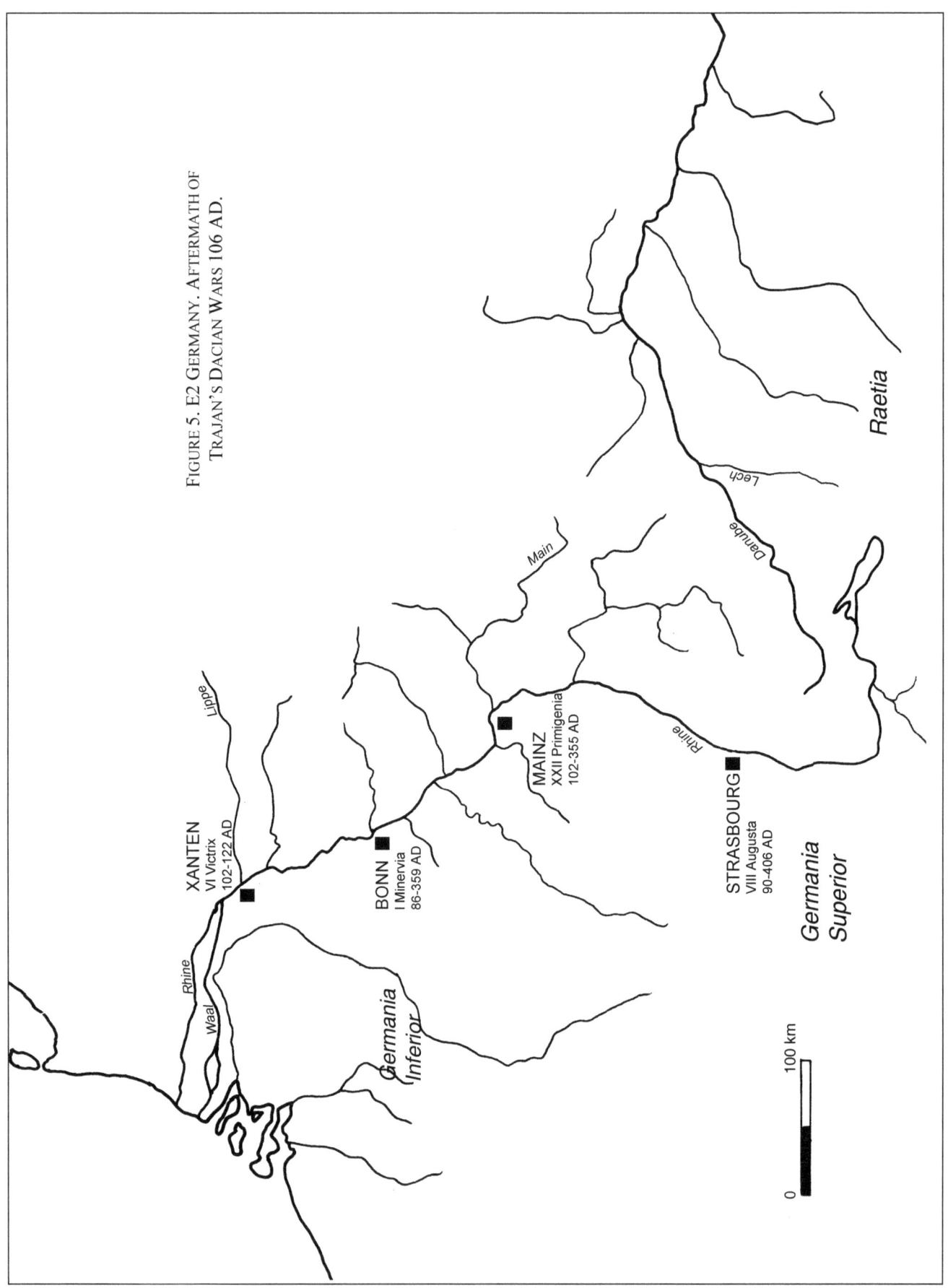

Figure 5. E2 Germany. Aftermath of Trajan's Dacian Wars 106 AD.

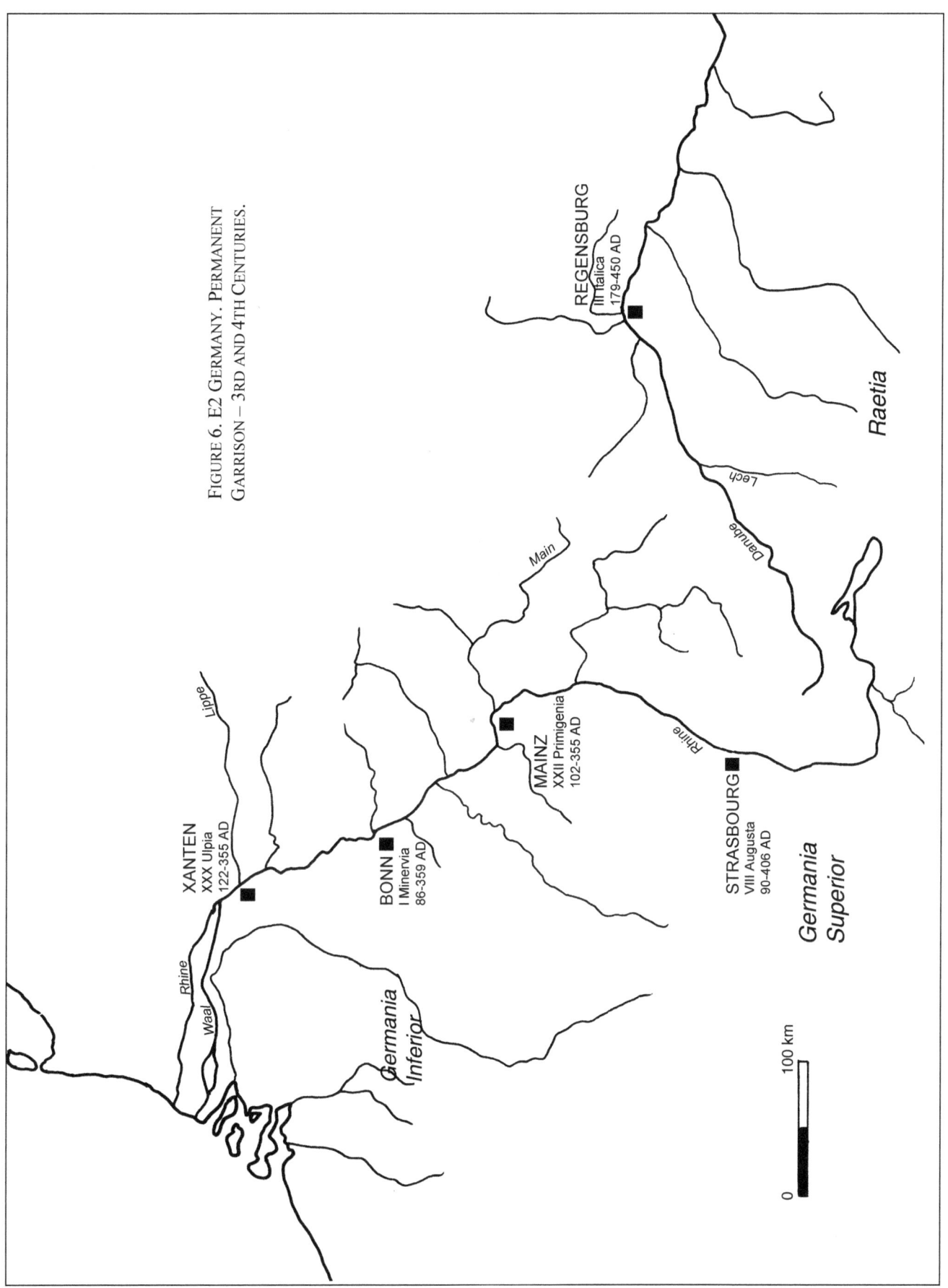

Figure 6. E2 Germany. Permanent Garrison – 3rd and 4th Centuries.

3) Britain

CLAUDIUS (41-54 A.D.)

43 A.D. Invasion with II Augusta, XIV Gemina, and XX Valeria from Germany, and IX Hispana from Pannonia

44-45 A.D. Southeastern Britain conquered
II Augusta opens Chichester
IX Hispana opens Newton-on-Trent
XIV Gemina opens Towcester
XX Valeria opens Colchester

46 A.D. II Augusta closes Chichester to open Silchester

48-49 A.D. Campaigns against Caratacus
II Augusta closes Silchester to open Lake Farm
XIV Gemina closes Towcester to open Mancetter
XX Valeria closes Colchester to open Kingsholm

NERO (54-68 A.D.)

55-56 A.D. Campaign to conquer Wales
II Augusta closes Lake Farm to open Exeter
XIV Gemina closes Mancetter to open Wroxeter
XX Valeria closes Kingsholm to open Usk

66-67 A.D. Aftermath of the Boudiccan uprising
IX Hispana closes Newton-on-Trent to open Lincoln
XIV Gemina from Wroxeter to Italy for Nero's Eastern campaign
XX Valeria closes Usk to Wroxeter to replace XIV Gemina
II Augusta closes Exeter to open Gloucester

69 A.D. Vitellius sends XIV Gemina back to Britain

VESPASIAN (69-79 A.D.)

71-74 A.D. Reinforcement of Britain
XIV Gemina to Germany
IX Hispana from Lincoln opens York
II Adiutrix from Germany to Lincoln to replace IX Hispana
II Augusta closes Gloucester to open Caerleon

78 A.D. Agricola's campaign to conquer the rest of Britain
II Adiutrix closes Lincoln to open Chester

DOMITIAN (81-96 A.D.)

85 A.D. Scottish Lowlands conquered
XX Valeria closes Wroxeter to open Inchtuthill

86 A.D. Sarmatian War on the Danube
II Adiutrix from Chester to Pannonia
XX Valeria abandons Inchtuthill to Chester to replace II Adiutrix

HADRIAN (117-138 A.D.)

121-122 A.D. Tribal uprising in north Britain
IX Hispana, defeated or disgraced, from York to Lower Germany and is disbanded
VI Victrix from Lower Germany to York to replace IX Hispana

SEPTIMIUS SEVERUS (193-211 A.D.)

198 A.D.   After the revolt of Clodius Albinus, Septimius Severus divides Britain. York becomes part of Lower Britain

DIOCLETIAN (284-305 A.D.)

296 A.D.   Carausius transfers II Augusta from Caerleon to Richborough

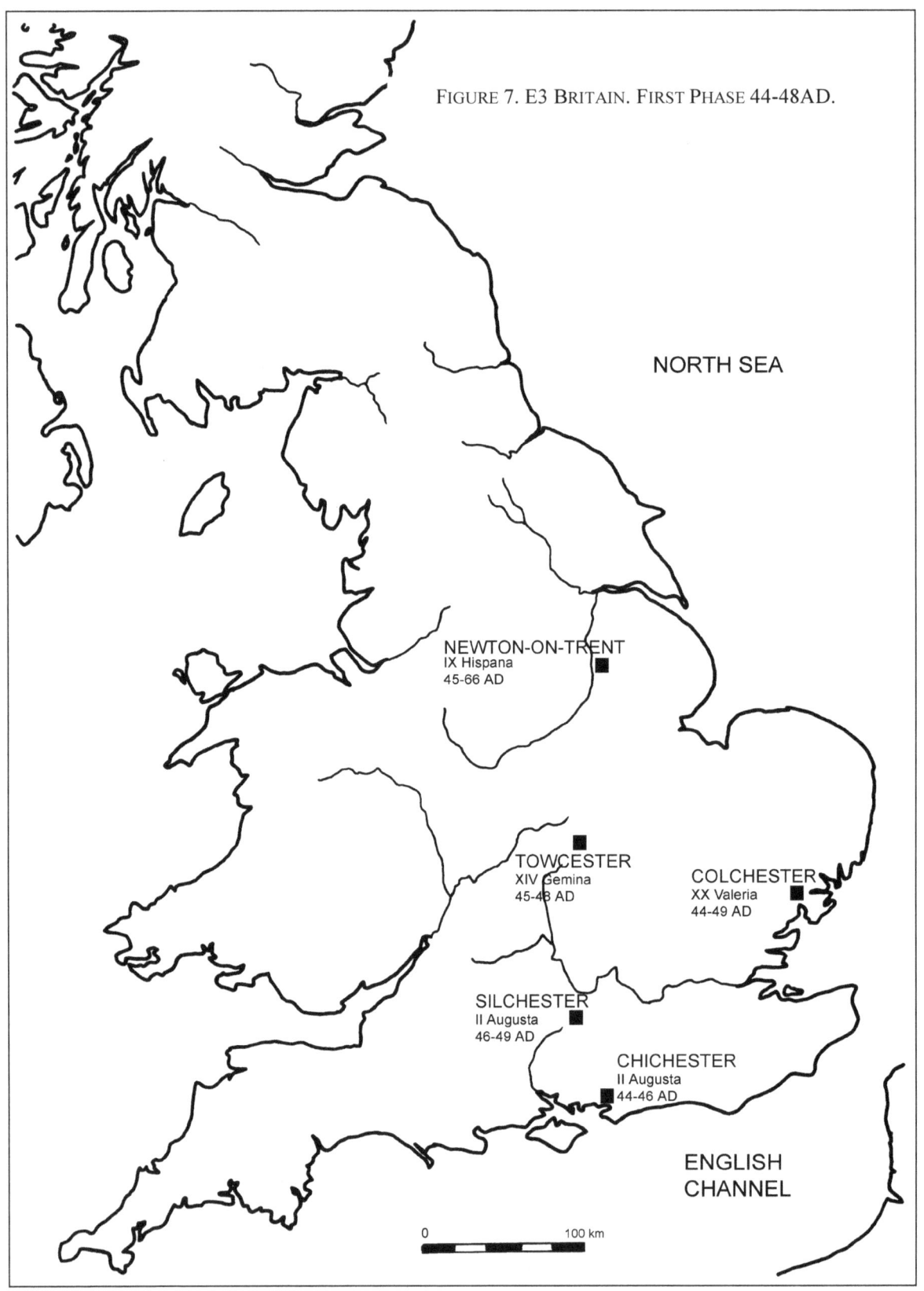

FIGURE 7. E3 BRITAIN. FIRST PHASE 44-48AD.

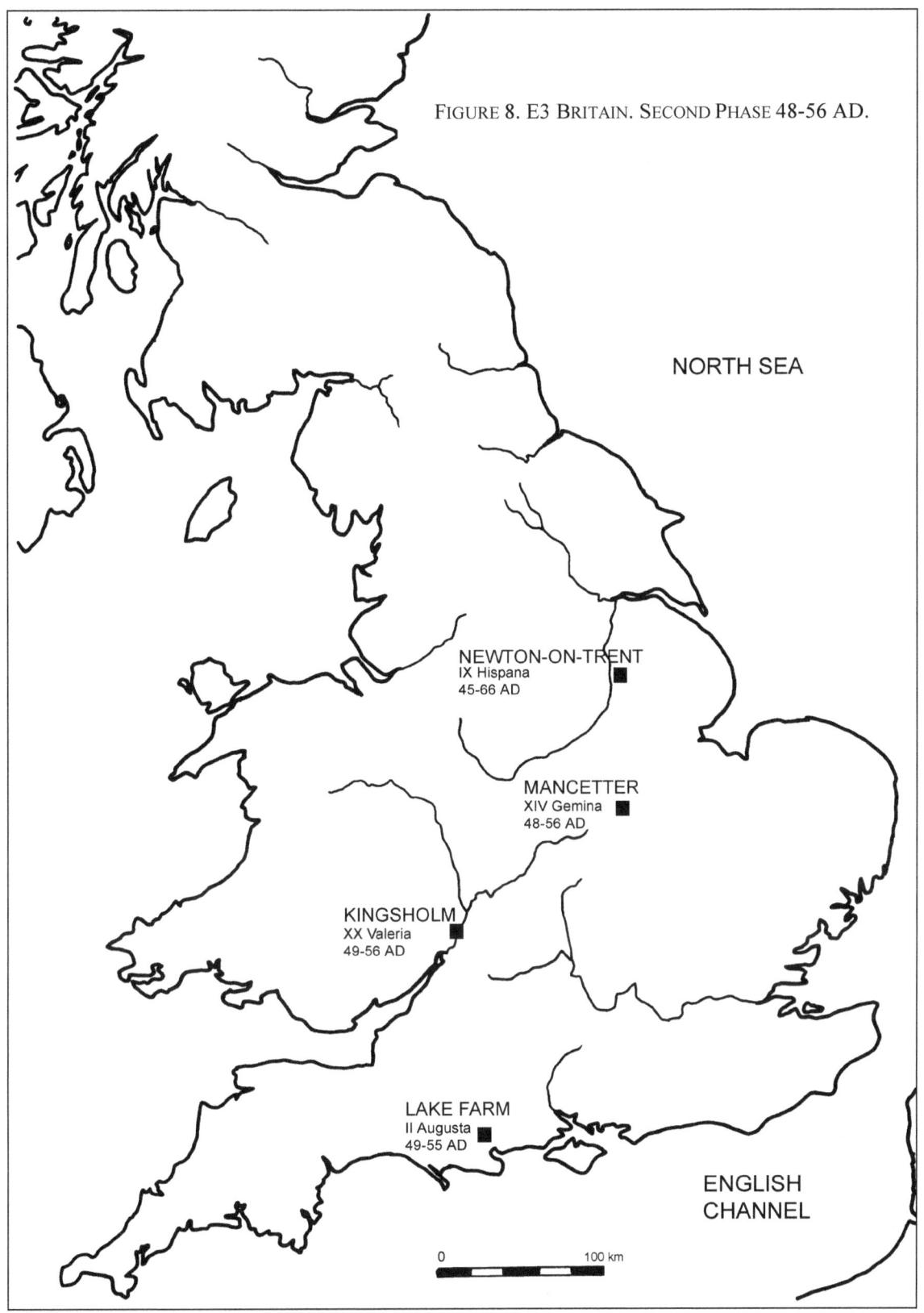

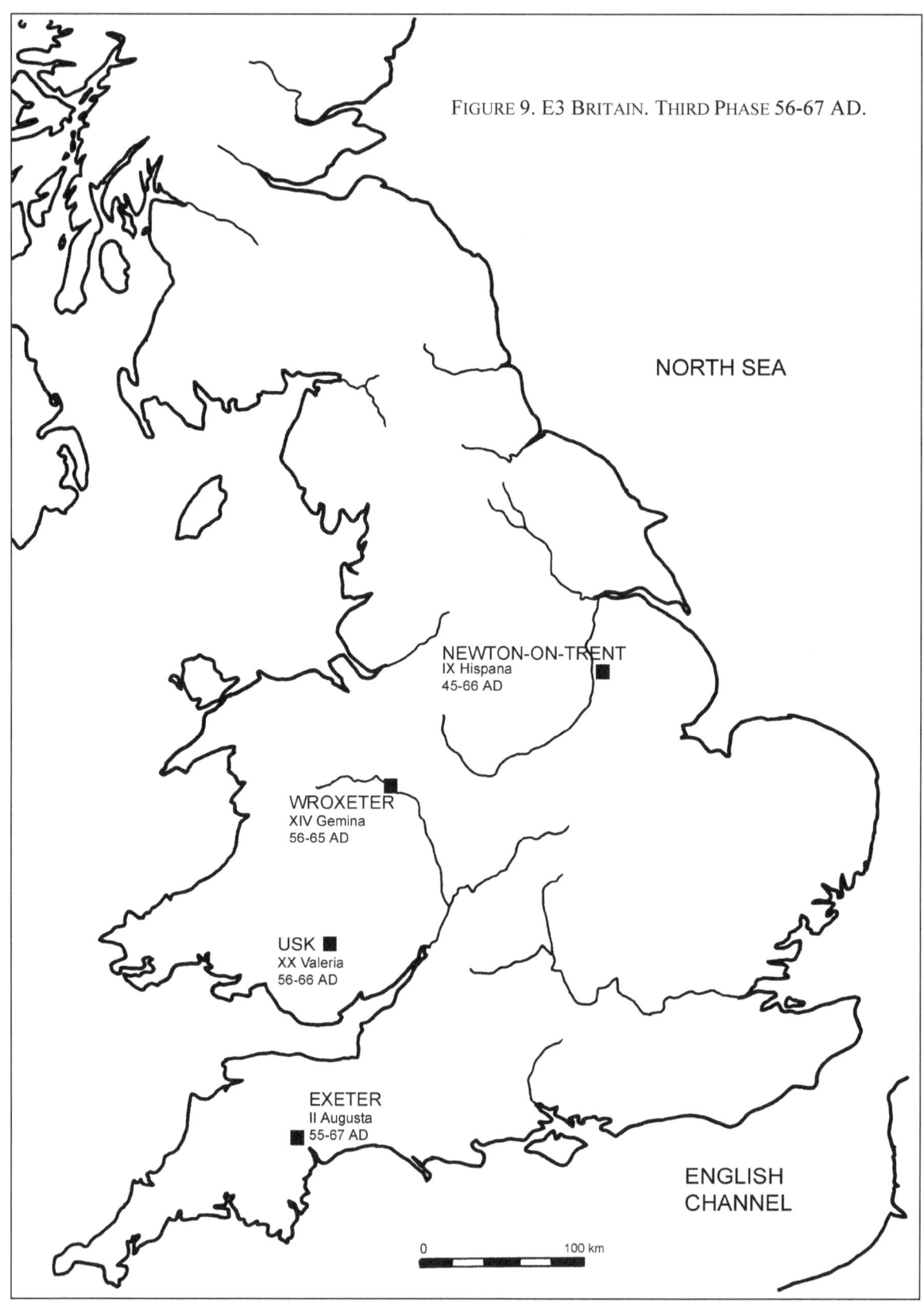

Figure 9. E3 Britain. Third Phase 56-67 AD.

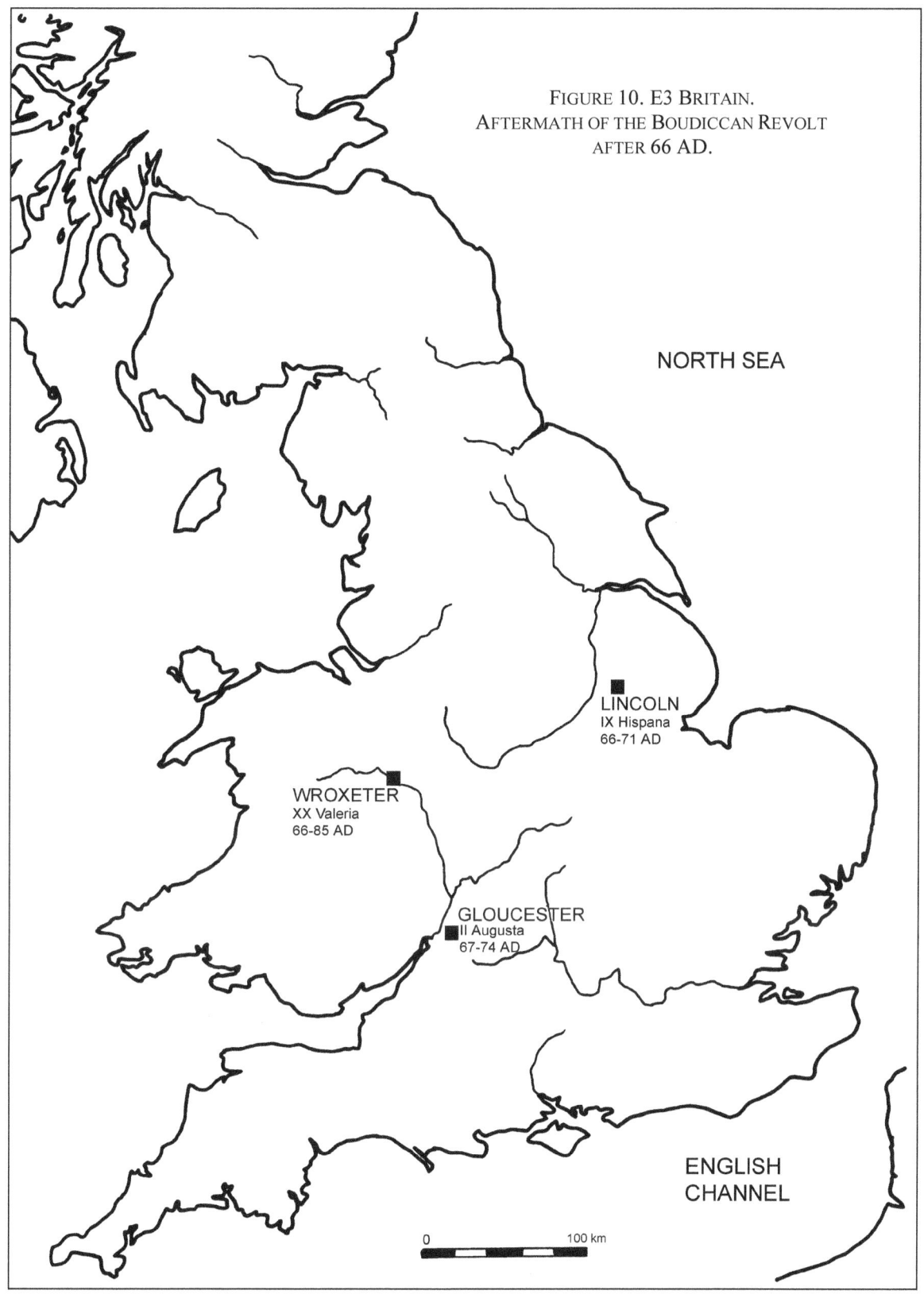

FIGURE 10. E3 BRITAIN. AFTERMATH OF THE BOUDICCAN REVOLT AFTER 66 AD.

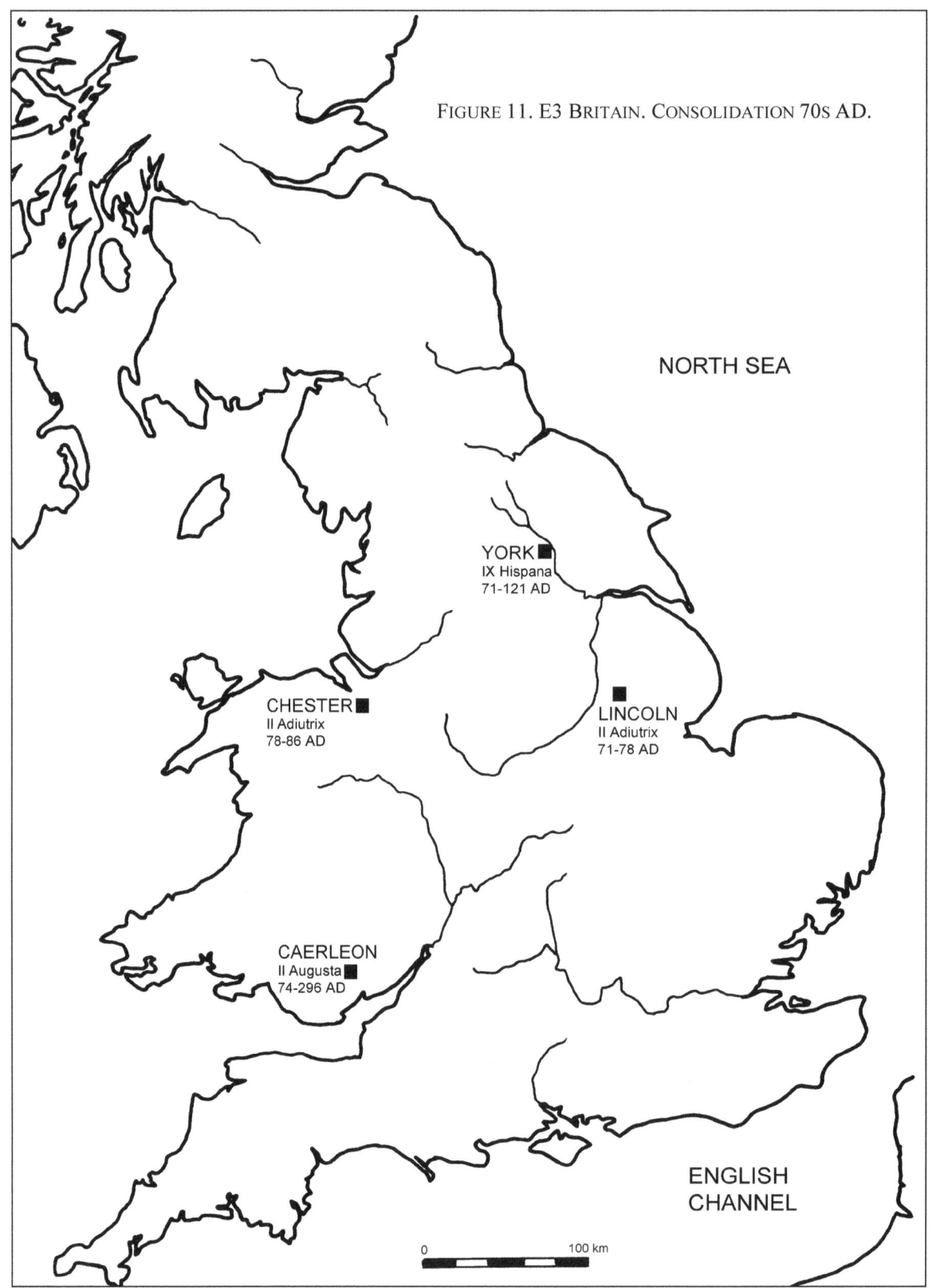

Figure 11. E3 Britain. Consolidation 70s AD.

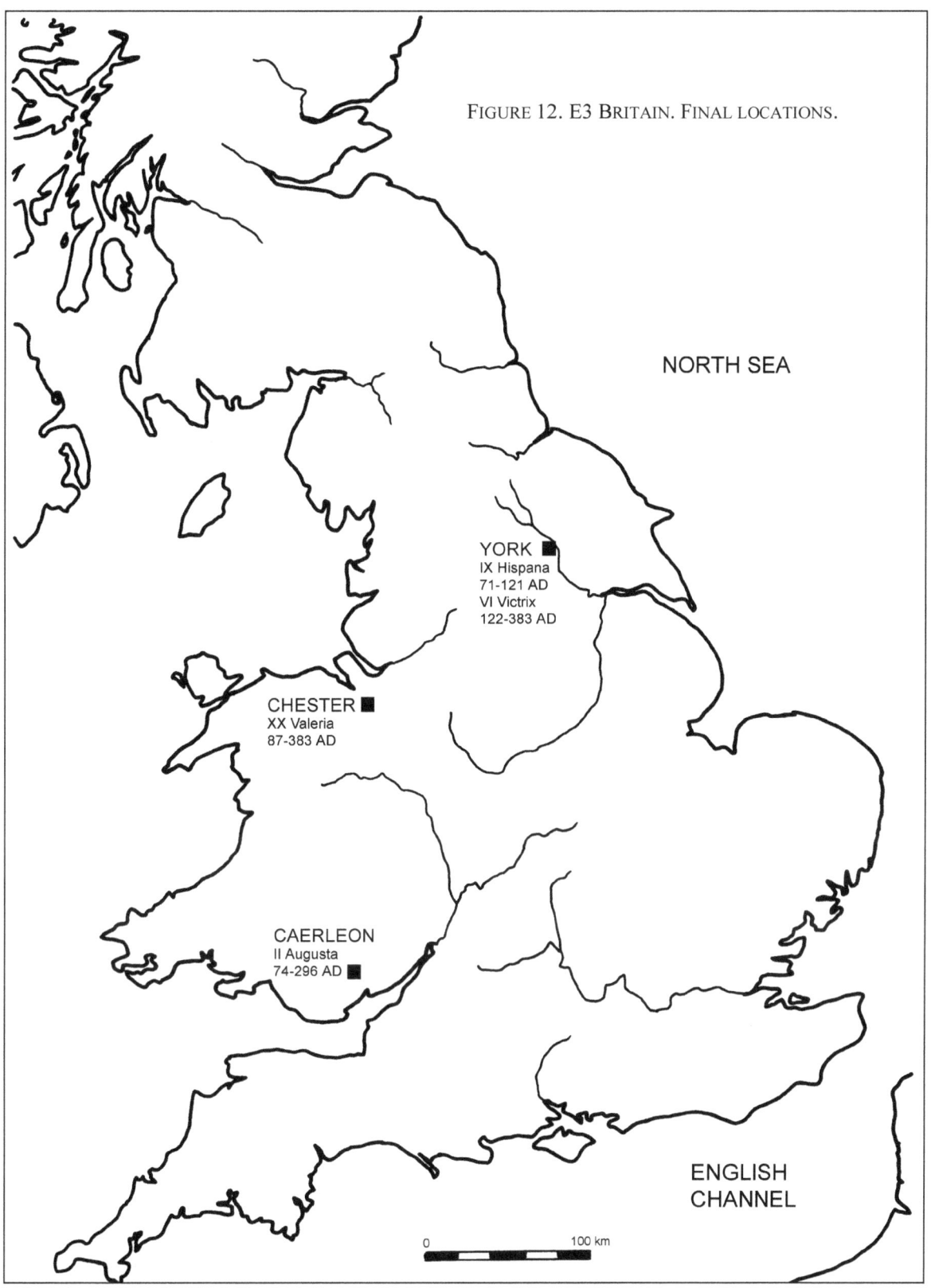

FIGURE 12. E3 BRITAIN. FINAL LOCATIONS.

JEROME H. FARNUM

4) Illyricum, Dalmatia, Pannonia, Dacia, Macedonia, Moesia

    OCTAVIAN AUGUSTUS (31 B.C.-14 A.D.)

27 B.C.   Macedonia subdued and made a client kingdom
        Illyricum 4 legions   Gardun =   XI
                                             Kistanje =   XIII Gemina
                                             Ptuj =   XIV Gemina
                                             Ljubljana = XV Apollinaris

        Macedonia 2 Legions -   Nis = IV Scythica
                                        and   V Macedonica

25 B.C.   Galatia annexed
        V Macedonica from Nis, Macedonia to Galatia

16-15 B.C.   Build-up for the Alpine campaign
        IX Hispana and XX Valeria from Spain to Illyricum

15-14 B.C.   Aftermath of the Drusus War
        XI from Gardun, Illyricum opens Kostolac, Macedonia
        IX Hispana to Gardun to replace XI

        XV Apollinaris from Ljubljana, Illyricum to Raetia
        XIII Gemina from Kistanje, Illyricum to Ljubljana to replace XV Apollinaris
        XX Valeria to Kistanje to replace XIII Gemina

        Illyricum 4, Macedonia 2

6 A.D.   Pannonian uprising
        V Macedonica and VII Macedonica from Galatia to Illyricum
        VIII Augusta from Egypt to Illyricum

9-10 A.D.   Pannonian uprising crushed - Varian Disaster in Germany
        IX Hispana from Gardun, Illyricum opens Sisak, Illyricum
        VII Macedonica to Gardun to replace IX Hispana

        XX Valeria from Kistanje, Illyricum to Germany
        XI from Kostolac, Macedonia to Kistanje to replace XX Valeria
        V Macedonica to Kostolac to replace XI

        XIV Gemina from Ptuj, Illyricum to Germany
        VIII Augusta to Ptuj to replace XIV Gemina

        XIII Gemina from Ljubljana, Illyricum to Raetia
        XV Apollinaris from Raetia to Ljubljana to replace XIII Gemina

        IV Scythica closes Nis, Macedonia to open Silistra, Macedonia on the Danube

        Illyricum 5, Macedonia 2

    TIBERIUS (14-37 A.D.)

40 A.D.   XV Apollinaris closes Ljubljana, Illyricum to open Petronell, Illyricum on the Danube

    CLAUDIUS (41-54 A.D.)

43-45 A.D.   Invasion of Britain - Illyricum divided into Dalmatia and Pannonia; Moesia becomes a province; Client kingdom of Thrace annexed
        IX Hispana closes Sisak, Pannonia to Britain

VIII Augusta from Ptuj, Pannonia opens Svistov, Moesia
XIII Gemina from Germany to Ptuj to replace VIII Augusta

Dalmatia 2, Pannonia 2, Moesia 3

NERO (54-68 A.D.)

55 A.D.   Parthians invade Armenia
IV Scythica closes Silistra, Moesia to Cappadocia

62-63 A.D.   Parthian victory at Rhandia, Armenia
V Macedonica from Kostolac, Moesia to Armenia
VII Claudia closes Gardun, Dalmatia to Kostolac to replace V Macedonica

XV Apollinaris from Petronell, Pannonia to Armenia
X Gemina from Spain to Petronell to replace XV Apollinaris

67 A.D.   III Gallica from Armenia opens Gigen, Moesia

Dalmatia 1, Pannonia 2, Moesia 3

VESPASIAN (69-79 A.D.)

69-71 A.D.   Year of the 4 Emperors - Vespasianic reorganization
XI (now Claudia) from Kistanje, Dalmatia to Germany
IV Flavia (new) to Kistanje to replace XI Claudia

X Gemina from Petronell, Pannonia to Spain
VII Gemina (ex-VII Galbiana, new from Spain) to Petronell to replace X Gemina

V Alaudae from Germany reopens Silistra, Moesia

VIII Augusta from Svistov, Moesia to Gaul
I Italica from Gaul to Svistov to replace VIII Augusta

72 A.D.   III Gallica from Gigen, Moesia returns to Syria
V Macedonica from Syria Palaestina to Gigen to replace III Gallica

74 A.D.   VII Gemina from Petronell, Pannonia to Spain
XV Apollinaris from Syria Palaestina to Petronell to replace VII Gemina

Dalmatia 1, Pannonia 2, Moesia 4

DOMITIAN (81-96 A.D.)

86-88 A.D.   Dacian War - Moesia divided into Upper and Lower provinces
I Adiutrix from Germany opens Szony, Pannonia
II Adiutrix from Britain opens Budapest, Pannonia
IV Flavia closes Kistanje, Dalmatia to open Artschav, Upper Moesia
V Alaudae from Silistra, Lower Moesia, is destroyed. Silistra is closed

89 A.D.   XIII Gemina from Ptuj, Pannonia opens Vienna, Pannonia
XXI Rapax from Germany to Ptuj to replace XIII Gemina

Dalmatia 0, Pannonia 5, Upper Moesia 2, Lower Moesia 2

TRAJAN (98-117 A.D.)

101-102 A.D. 1st Dacian War
I Adiutrix from Szony, Pannonia to the Dacian War

XI Claudia from Germany to Szony to replace I Adiutrix

II Adiutrix from Budapest, Pannonia to the Dacian War
X Gemina from Germany to Budapest to replace II Adiutrix

XXI Rapax from Ptuj, Lower Pannonia disbanded or destroyed
XIV Gemina from Germany to Ptuj to replace XXI Rapax

103 A.D. Pannonia divided into Upper and Lower Provinces
Upper Pannonia – Vienna XIII Gemina, Petronell XV Apollinaris, Szony XI Claudia
Lower Pannonia – Ptuj XIV Gemina, Budapest X Gemina

104 A.D. II Traiana (new) to Svistov, Lower Moesia to join I Italica

106 A.D. Aftermath of the Dacian Wars
IV Flavia closes Artschav, Upper Moesia to open Resita, Dacia

V Macedonica closes Gigen, Lower Moesia to open Iglitza-Turcoaia, Lower Moesia
XI Claudia from Szony, Upper Pannonia reopens Silistra, Lower Moesia
XXX Ulpia (new) to Szony to replace XI Claudia

XIII Gemina from Vienna, Upper Pannonia opens Alba Iulia, Dacia
XIV Gemina closes Ptuj, Lower Pannonia to Vienna to replace XIII Gemina
I Adiutrix joins XIII Gemina at Alba Iulia, Dacia
II Adiutrix opens Varhély, Dacia

Upper Pannonia 3, Lower Pannonia 1, Upper Moesia 1, Lower Moesia 4, Dacia 4

113 A.D. Parthian War
II Traiana from Svistov, Lower Moesia to Syria

HADRIAN (117-138 A.D.)

120 A.D. Frontiers reorganzed – Dacia considered to be pacified and divided into Upper and Lower provinces
XV Apollinaris from Petronell, Upper Pannonia to Cappadocia
XIV Gemina from Vienna, Upper Pannonia to Petronell to replace XV Apollinaris
X Gemina from Budapest, Lower Pannonia to Vienna to replace XIV Gemina
II Adiutrix closes Varhély, Dacia to return to Budapest to replace X Gemina
IV Flavia closes Resita, Dacia to open Belgrade, Upper Moesia

121-122 A.D. Replacement in Germany
XXX Ulpia from Szony, Lower Pannonia to Germany
I Adiutrix from Alba Iulia, Dacia to Szony to replace XXX Ulpia

Upper Pannonia 3, Lower Pannonia 1, Upper Moesia 2, Lower Moesia 3, Dacia 1

MARCUS AURELIUS (161-180 A.D.)

167 A.D. Marcomanni War
V Macedonica closes Iglitza-Turcoaia, Lower Moesia to open Turda, Dacia

CARACALLA (211-217 A.D.)

213 A.D. Szony becomes part of Lower Pannonia

CLAUDIUS GOTHICUS (268-270 A.D.)

268 A.D. Decision made to abandon Dacia
XIII Gemina closes Alba Iulia, Dacia to reopen Ptuj, Lower Pannonia

270 A.D.   XIII Gemina closes Ptuj, Lower Pannonia to reopen Artschav/Arcar, Dacia Ripensis

            AURELIAN (270-275 A.D.)

271 A.D.   Evacuation of Dacia
                  V Macedonica closes Turda, Dacia to reopen Gigen, Lower Moesia

            DIOCLETIAN (284-305 A.D.)

294 A.D.   V Jovia (new) and VI Herculea (new) open Mitronica, Lower Pannonia

300 A.D.   II Herculea (new) opens Iglitza-Turcoaia, Scythica Minor

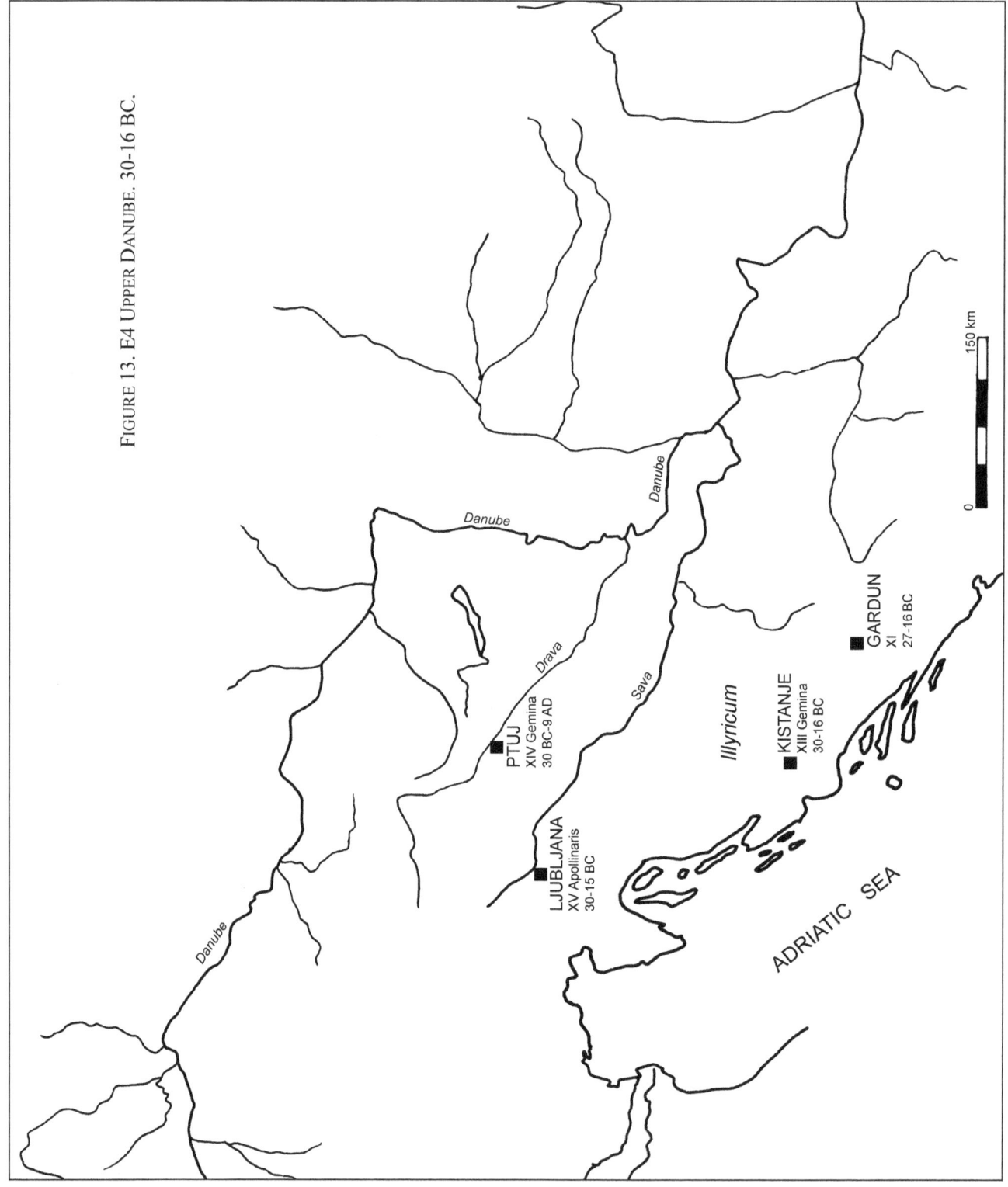

FIGURE 13. E4 UPPER DANUBE. 30-16 BC.

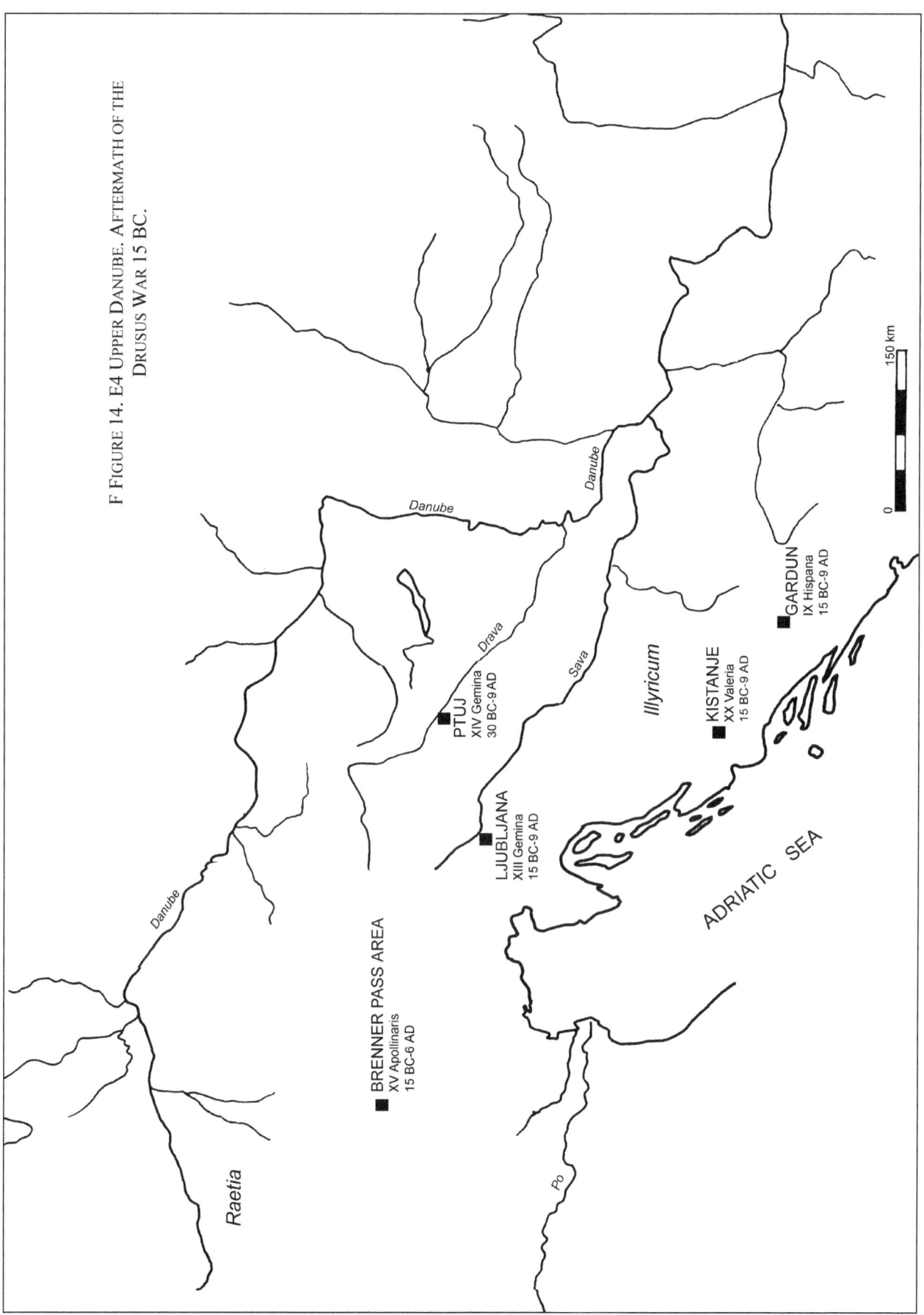
F Figure 14. E4 Upper Danube. Aftermath of the Drusus War 15 BC.

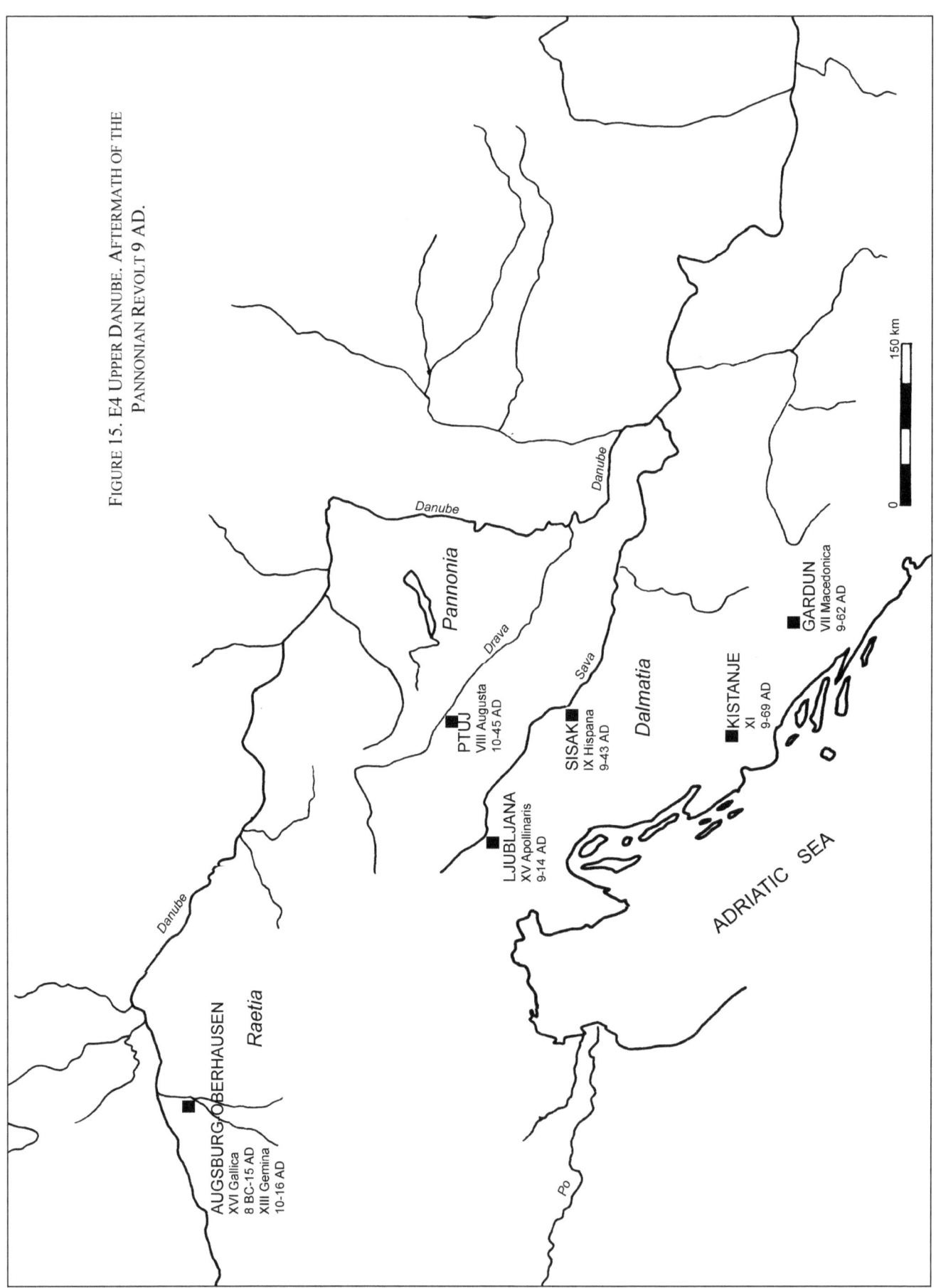

Figure 15. E4 Upper Danube. Aftermath of the Pannonian Revolt 9 AD.

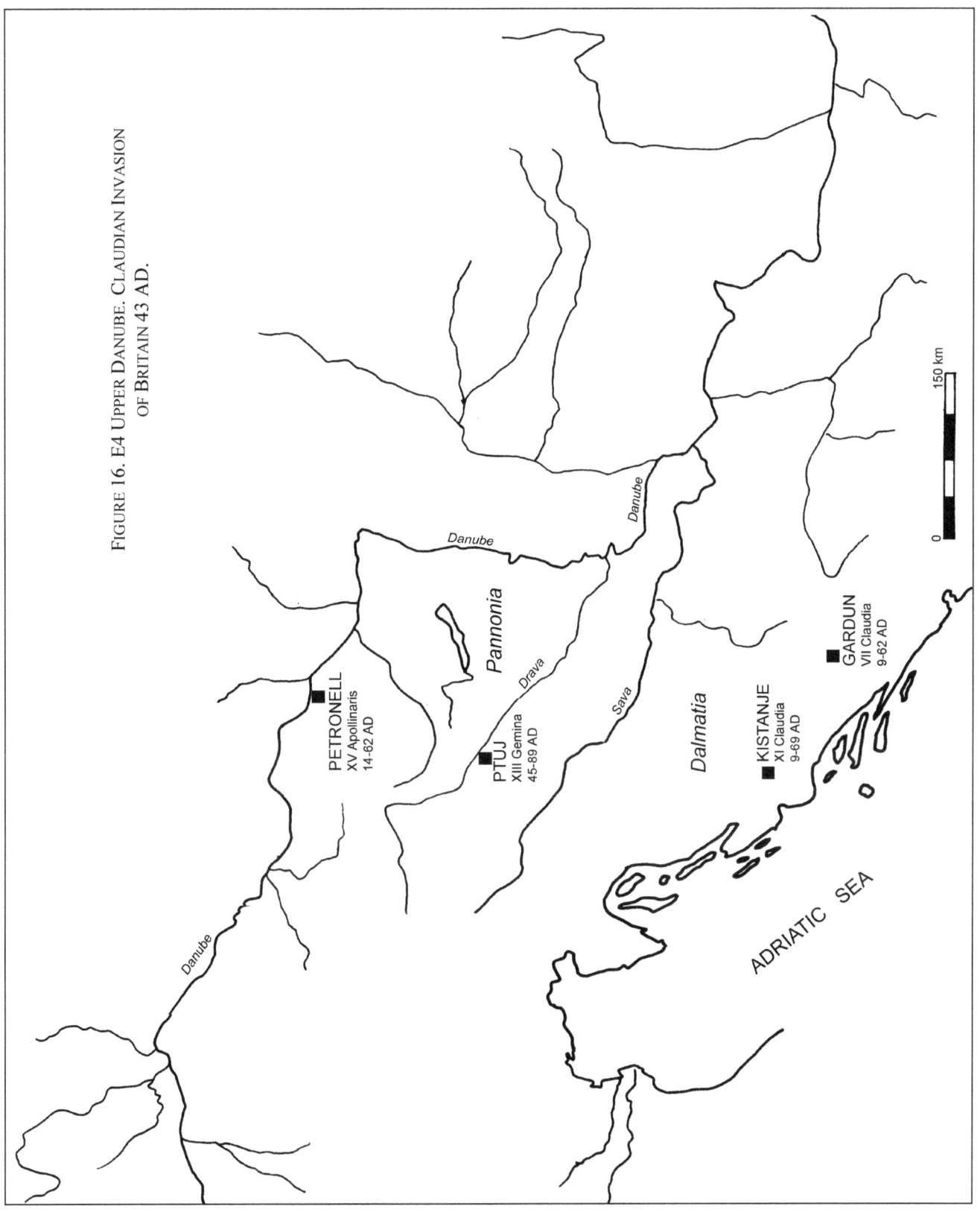

Figure 16. E4 Upper Danube. Claudian Invasion of Britain 43 AD.

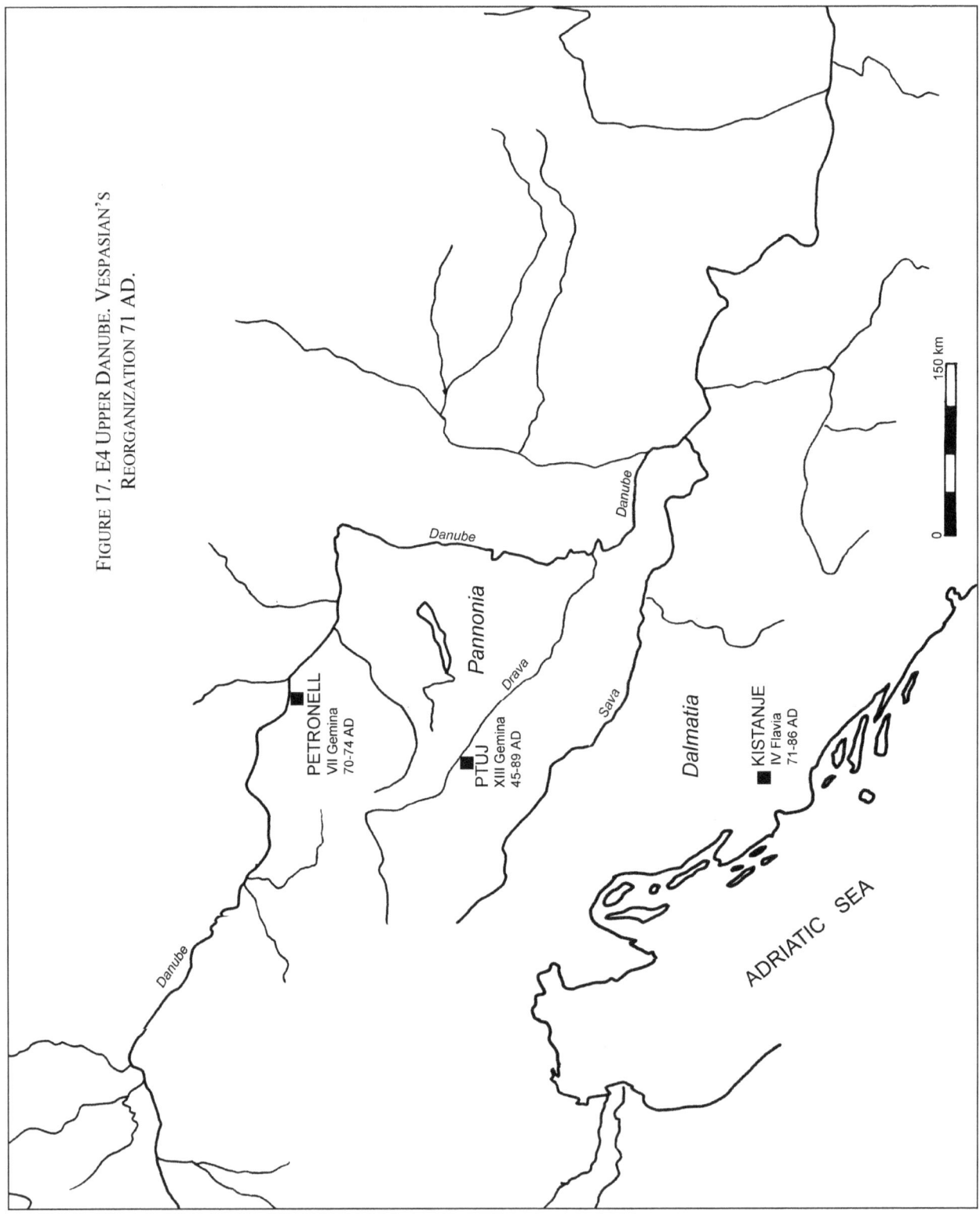

FIGURE 17. E4 UPPER DANUBE. VESPASIAN'S REORGANIZATION 71 AD.

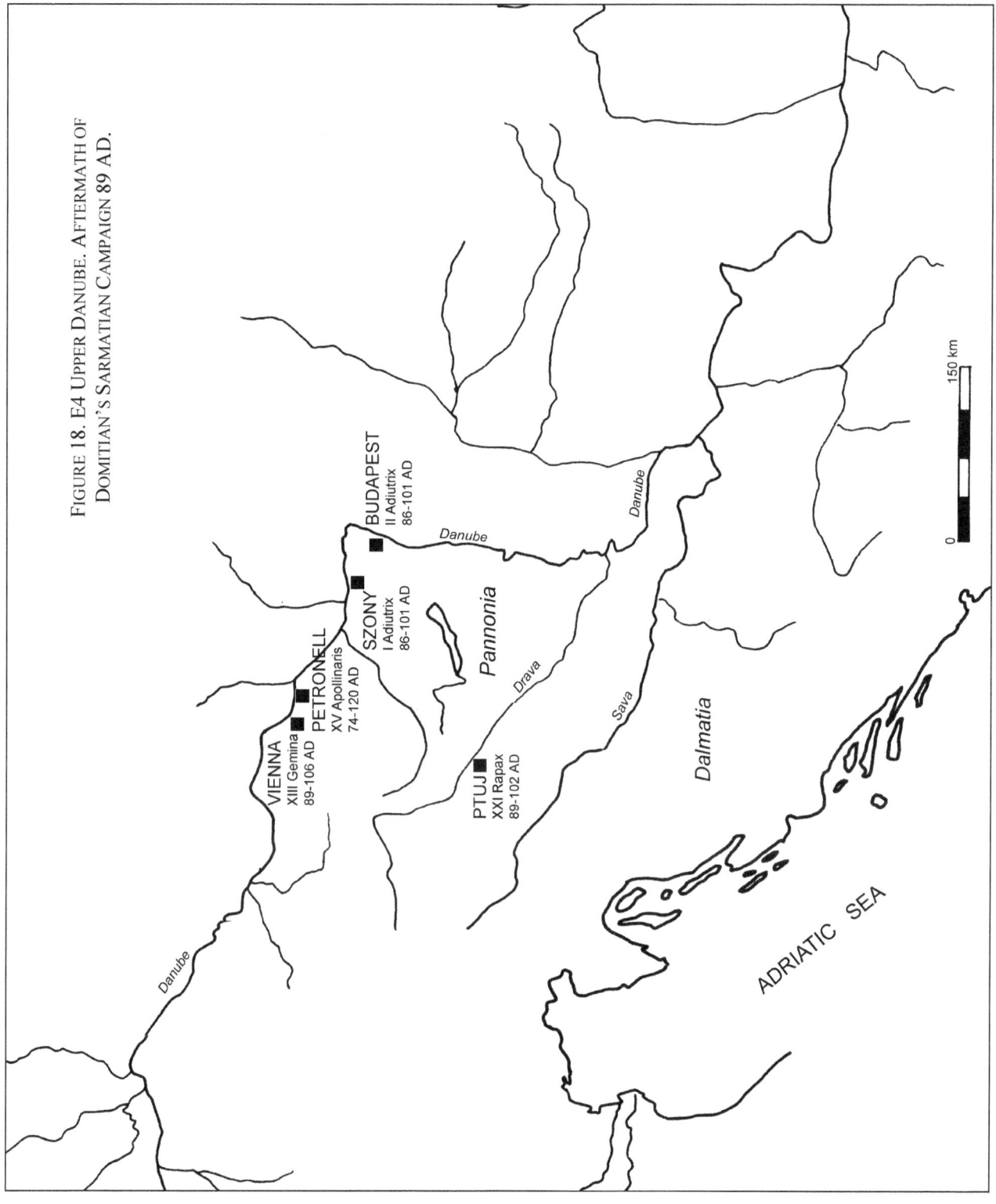

Figure 18. E4 Upper Danube. Aftermath of Domitian's Sarmatian Campaign 89 AD.

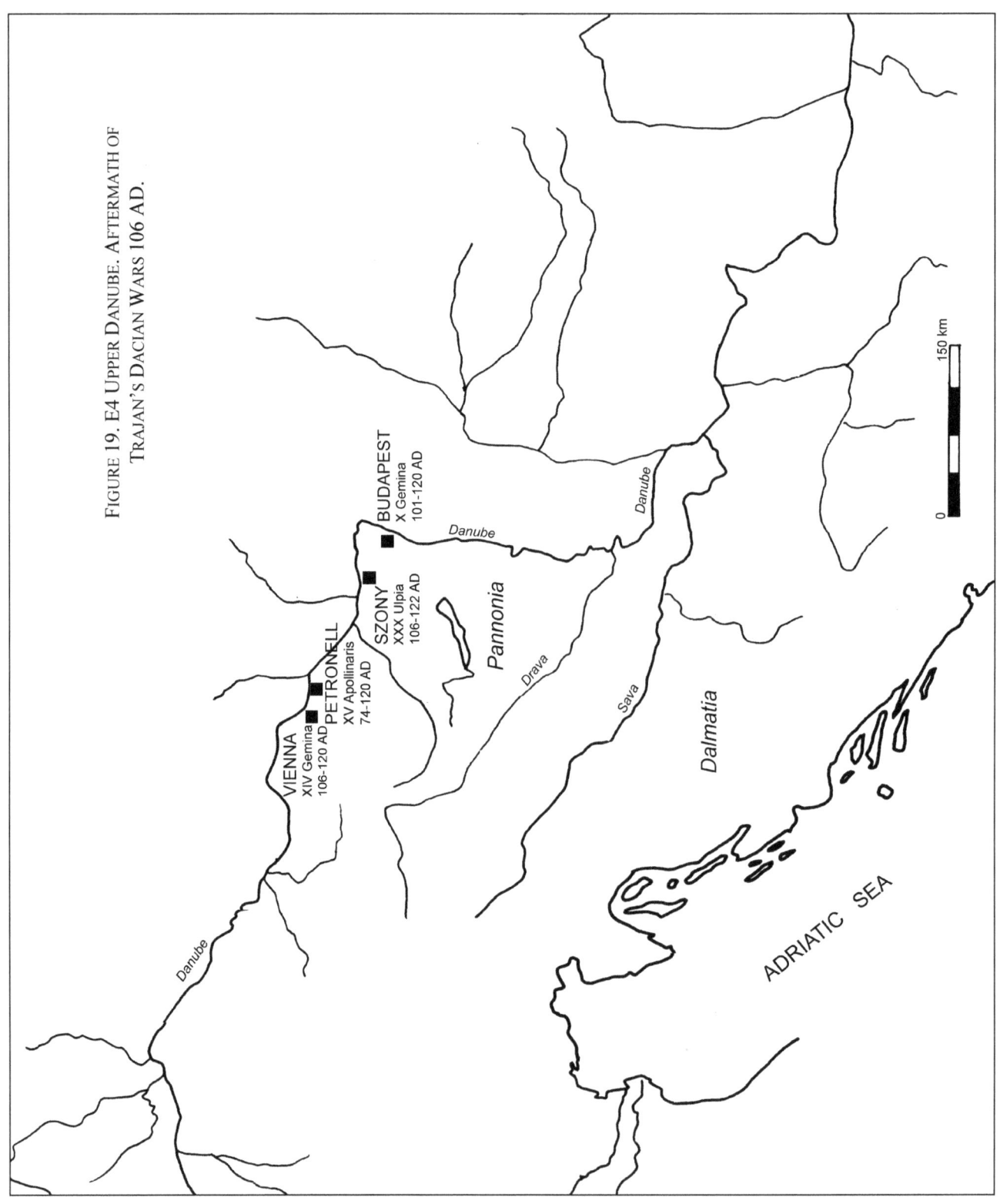

Figure 19. E4 Upper Danube. Aftermath of Trajan's Dacian Wars 106 AD.

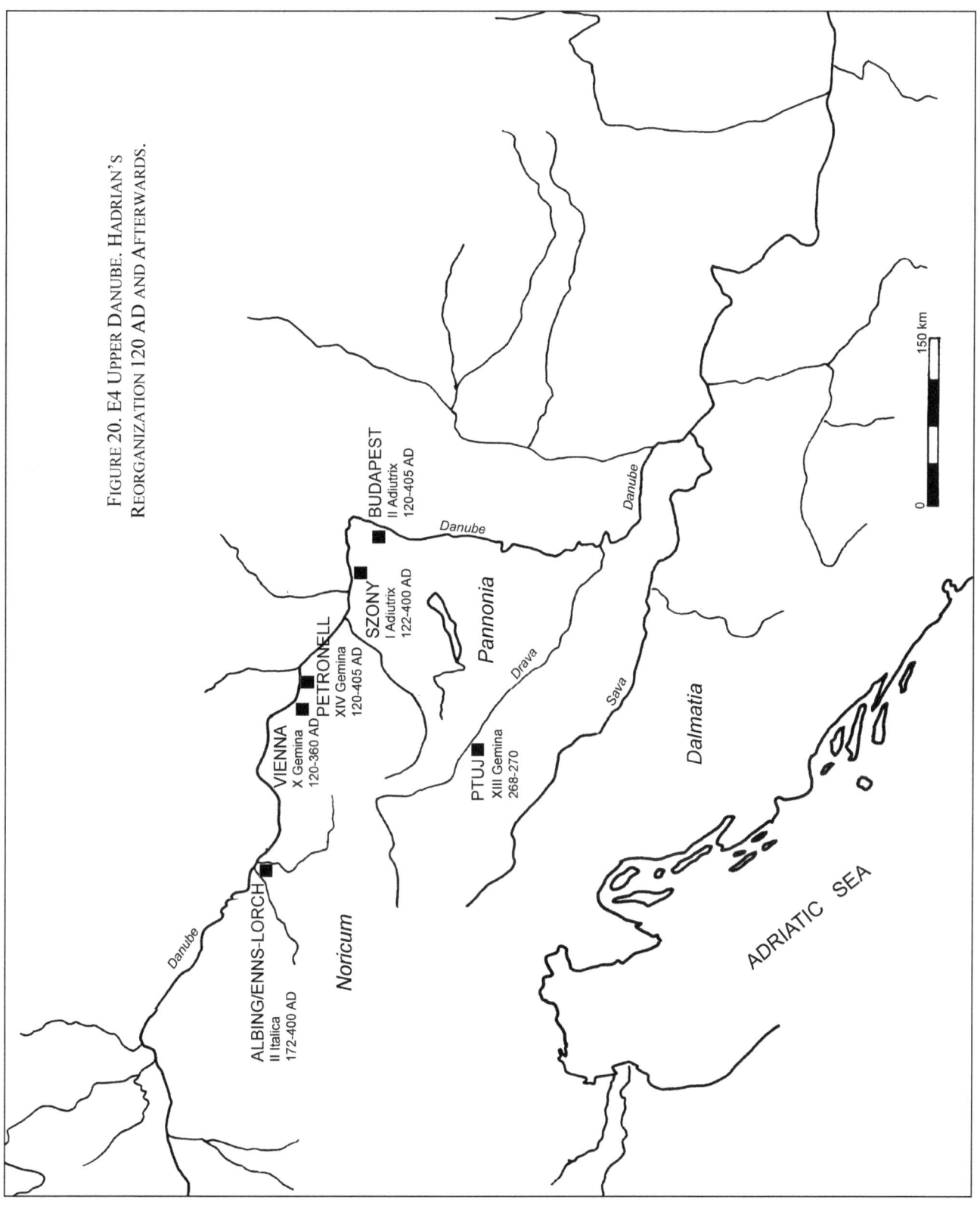

Figure 20. E4 Upper Danube. Hadrian's Reorganization 120 AD and Afterwards.

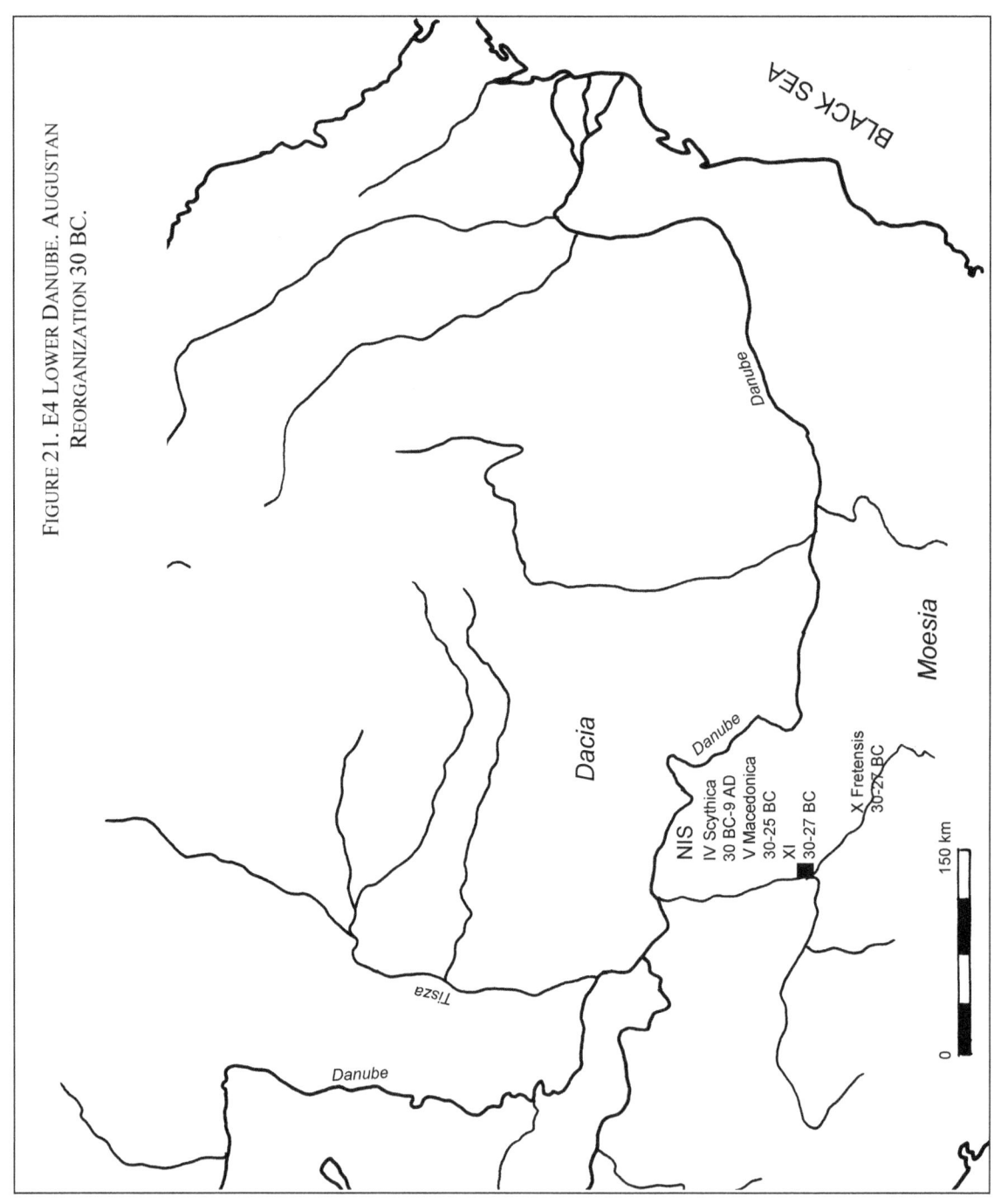

FIGURE 21. E4 LOWER DANUBE. AUGUSTAN REORGANIZATION 30 BC.

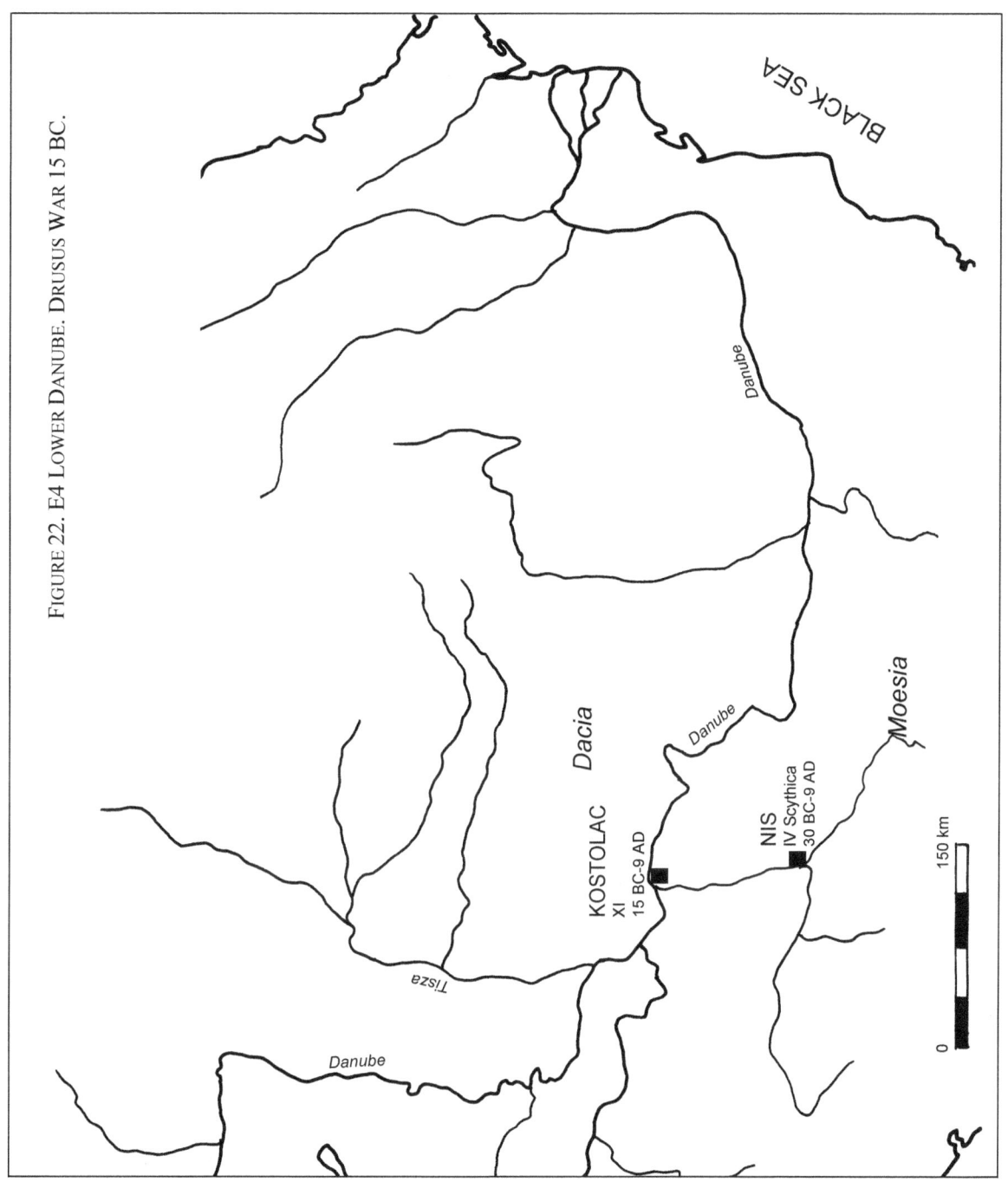

FIGURE 22. E4 LOWER DANUBE. DRUSUS WAR 15 BC.

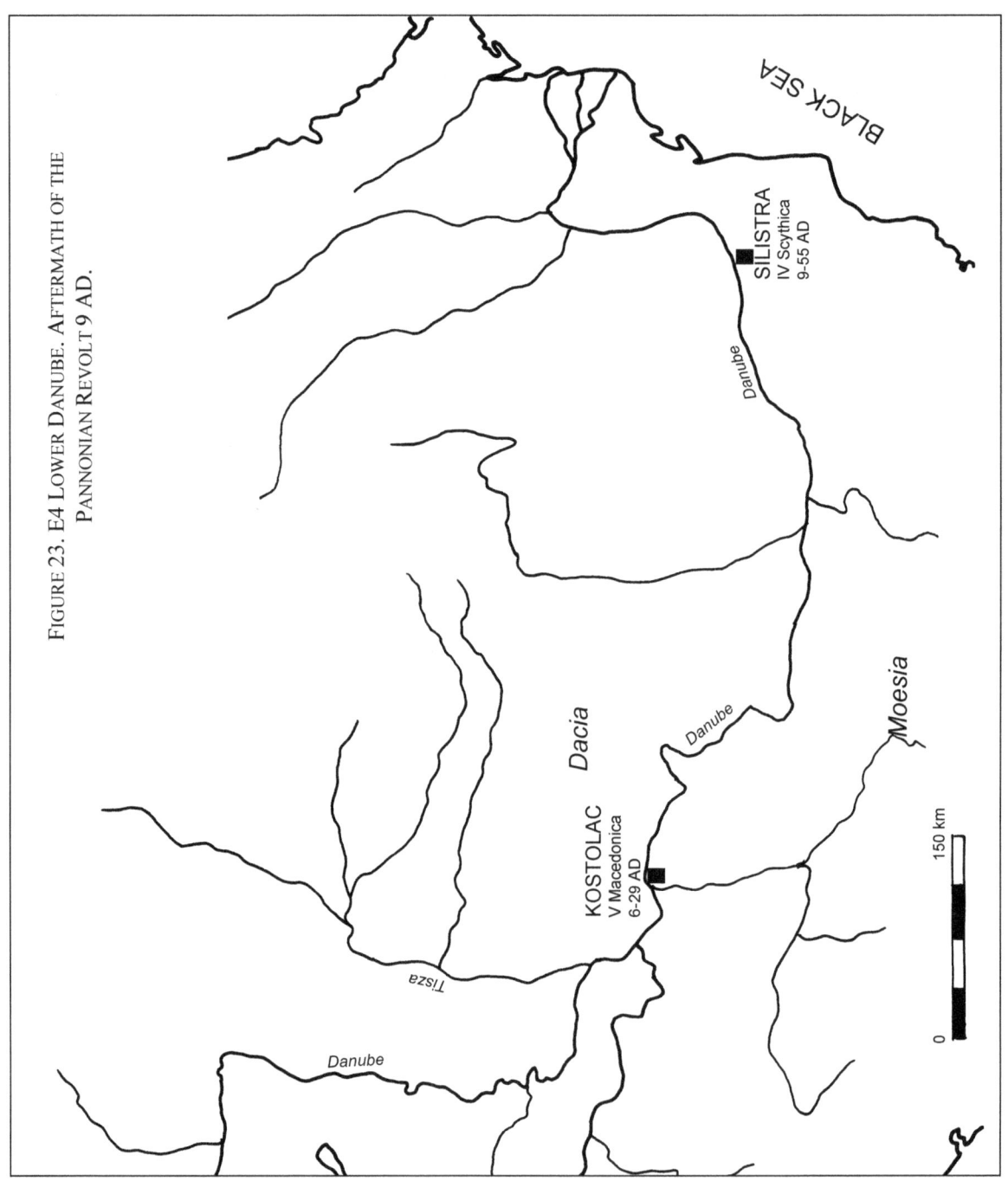

Figure 23. E4 Lower Danube. Aftermath of the Pannonian Revolt 9 AD.

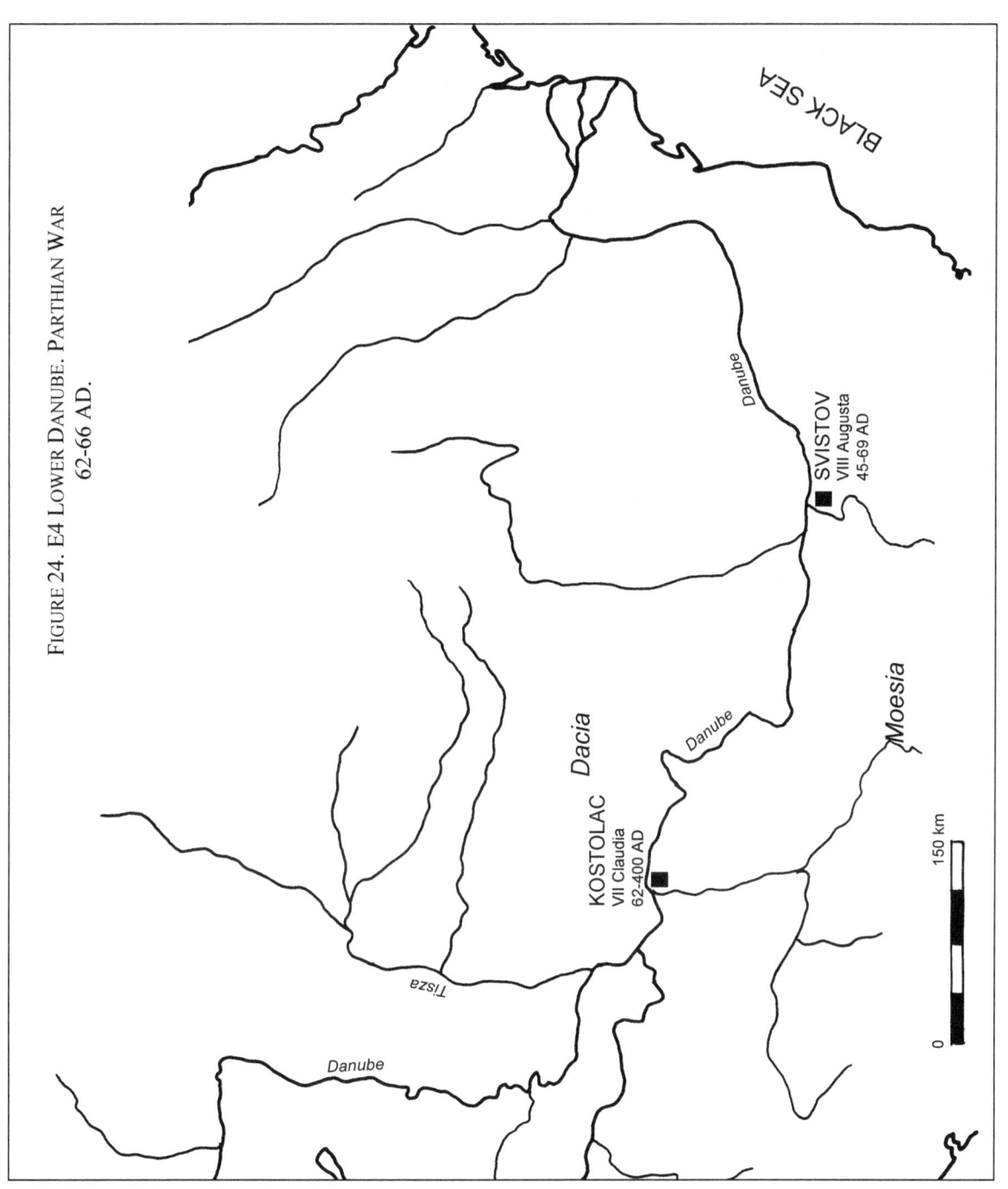

Figure 24. E4 Lower Danube. Parthian War 62-66 AD.

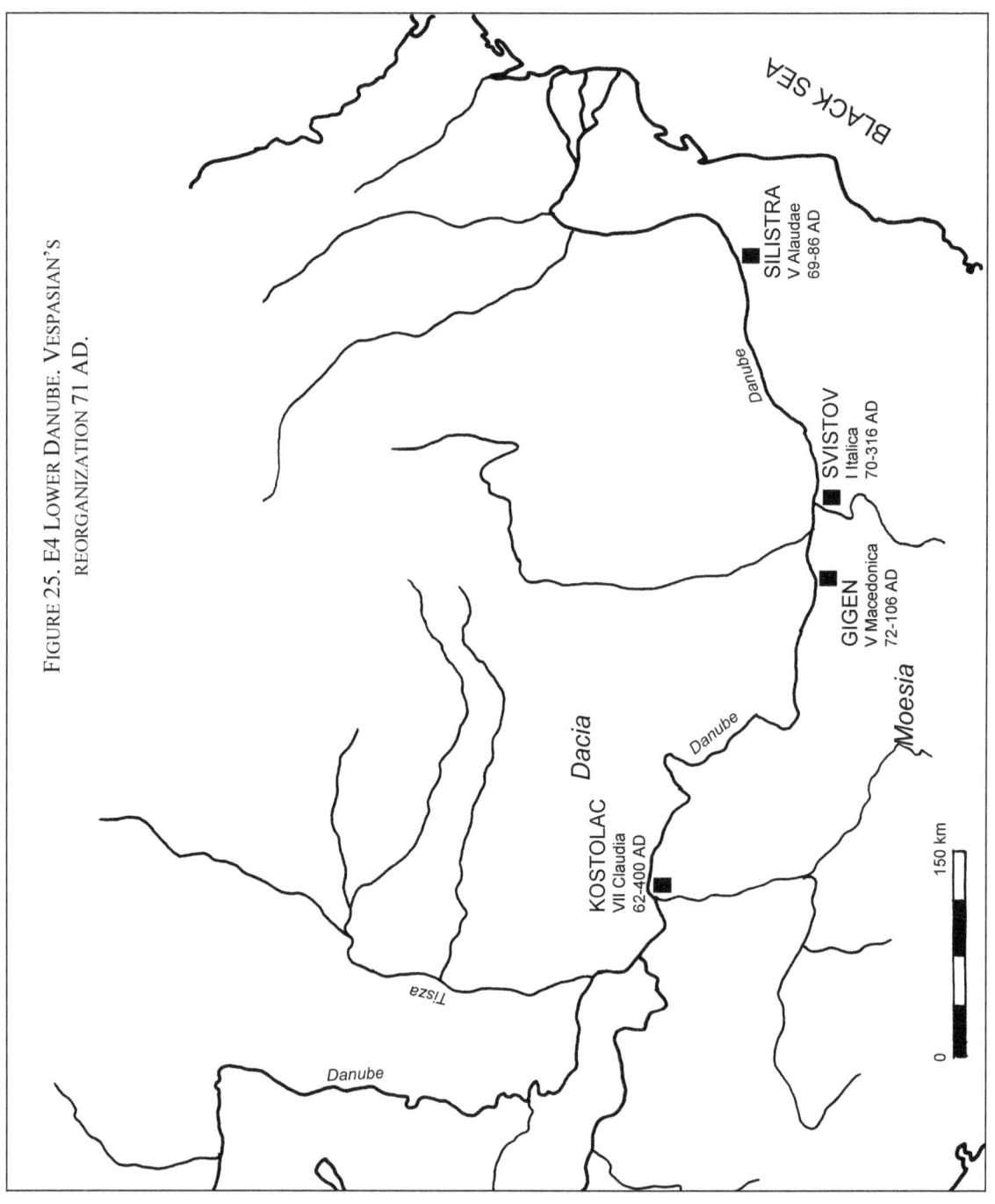

Figure 25. E4 Lower Danube. Vespasian's reorganization 71 AD.

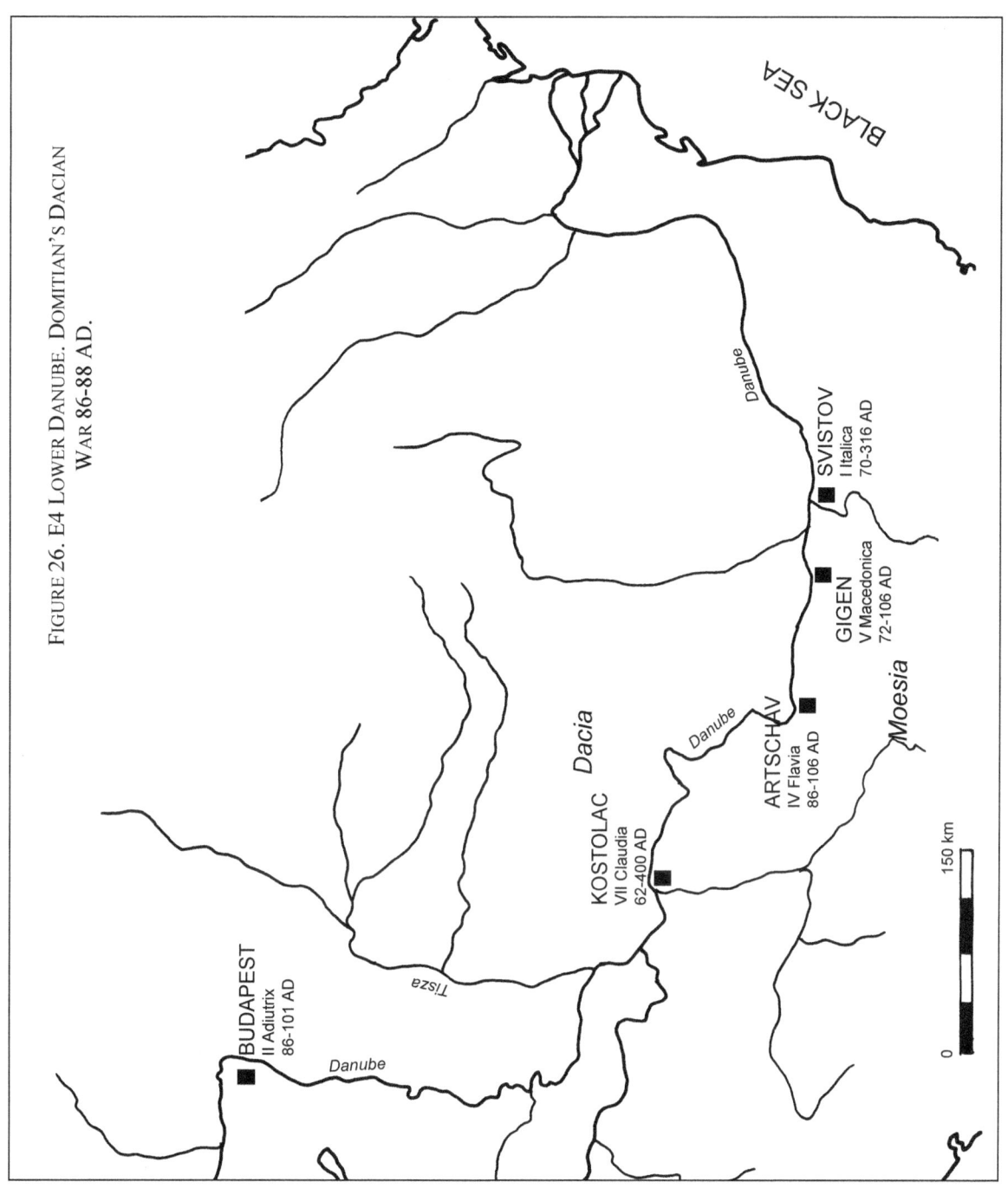

FIGURE 26. E4 LOWER DANUBE. DOMITIAN'S DACIAN WAR 86-88 AD.

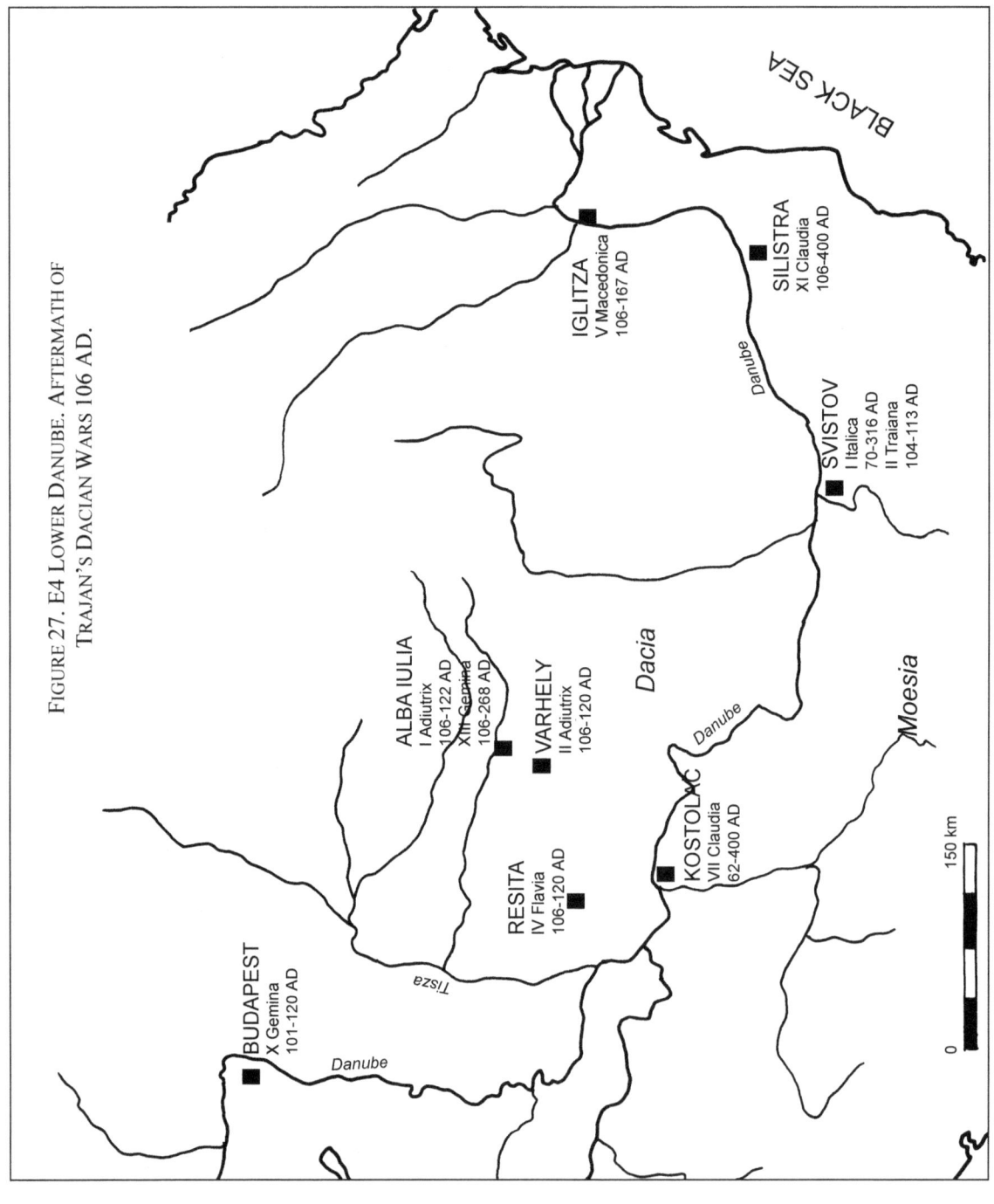

Figure 27. E4 Lower Danube. Aftermath of Trajan's Dacian Wars 106 AD.

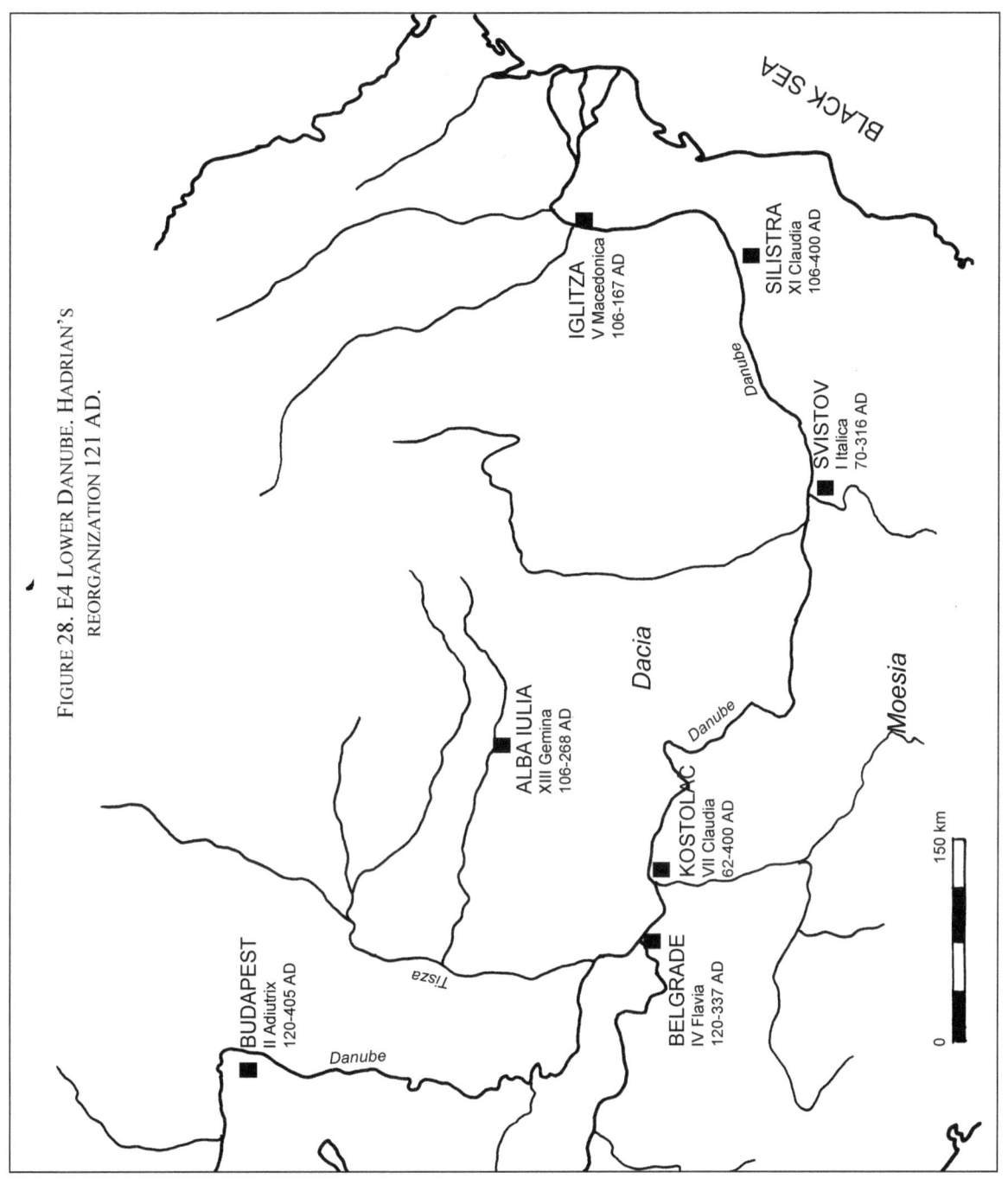

FIGURE 28. E4 LOWER DANUBE. HADRIAN'S REORGANIZATION 121 AD.

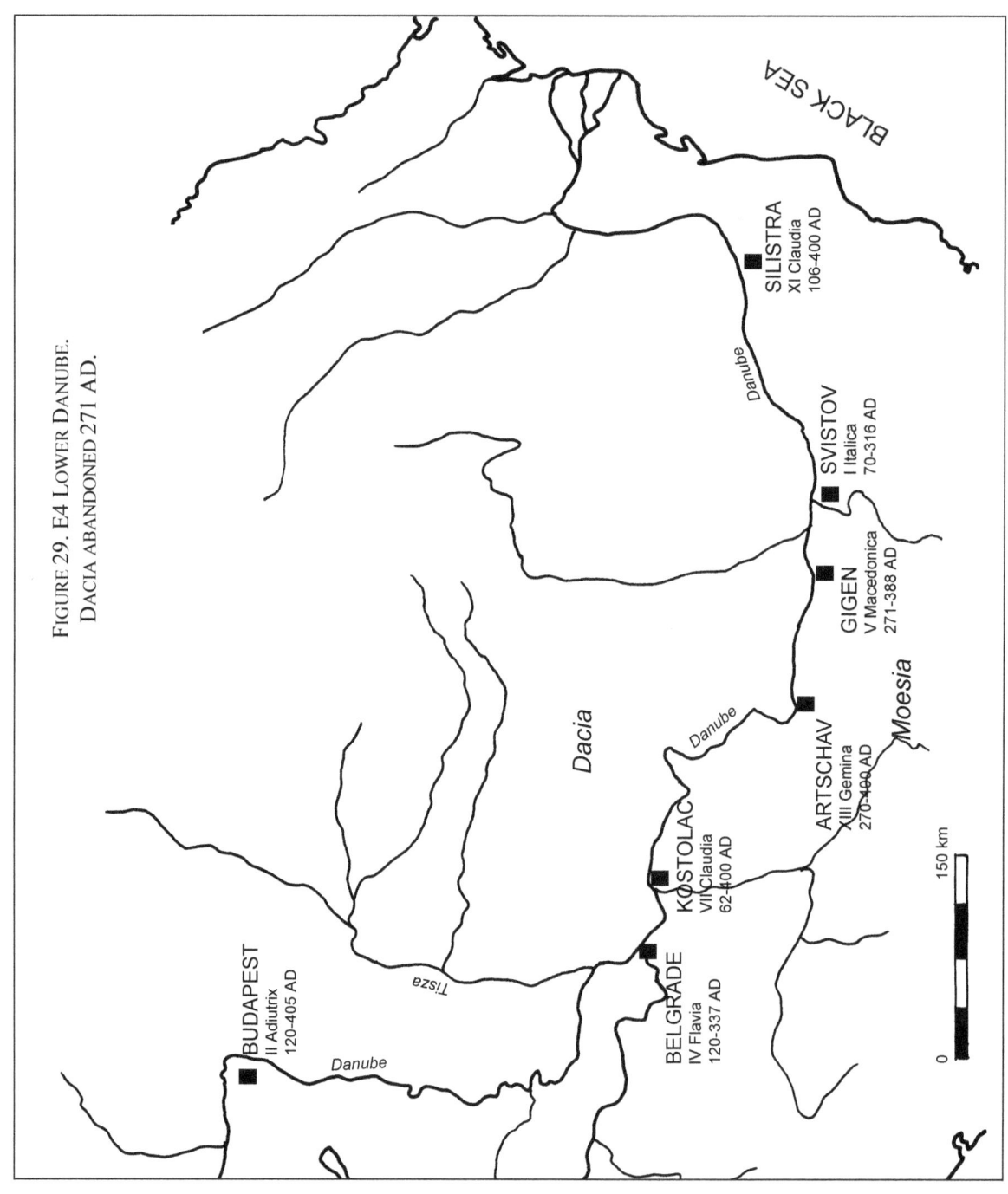

Figure 29. E4 Lower Danube. Dacia abandoned 271 AD.

5) The East

OCTAVIAN AUGUSTUS (31 B.C.-14 A.D.)

30 B.C. Syria had III Gallica at Antioch and VI Ferrata at Latakia

27 B.C. Macedonia conquered
X Fretensis from Macedonia opens Kuros, Syria

25 B.C. Galatia annexed; Syria becomes a 4-legion province
V Macedonica from Macedonia opens Antakya, Galatia
VII Macedonica from Mauritania to Antalya, Galatia to join V Macedonica
XII Fulminata from Egypt opens Rafniyeh, Syria

6 A.D. Galatia pacified; Pannonian uprising
V Macedonica from Antakya, Galatia to Macedonia
VII Macedonica from Antakya, Galatea to Illyricum
Antakya closed

TIBERIUS (14-37 A.D.)

18 A.D. Belkis separated from Commagene and attached to Syria
X Fretensis closes Kuros, Syria to open Belkis, Syria on the Euphrates

NERO (54-68 A.D.)

55 A.D. Parthians invade of Armenia
IV Scythica from Moesia to Cappadocia

62 A.D. Defeat by the Parthians at Rhandeia, Armenia
III Gallica closes Antioch, Syria to Armenia
V Macedonica from Moesia to Armenia
X Fretensis from Belkis, Syria to Armenia
IV Scythica defeated at Rhandeia to Belkis to replace X Fretensis
XV Apollinaris from Pannonia to Armenia

65/66 A.D. Parthian threat contained; Nero's proposed campaign in the East
V Macedonica, X Fretensis and XV Apollinaris from Armenia to Alexandria, Egypt

66 A.D. Jewish uprising
V Macedonica, X Fretensis and XV Apollinaris from Alexandria, Egypt to Syria

Syria 6, Armenia 1

67 A.D. III Gallica from Armenia to Moesia

68 A.D. V Macedonica opens Imwas, Syria

VESPASIAN (69-79 A.D.)

72 A.D. Cappadocia and Commagene annexed as Roman provinces
XVI Flavia (new) opens Kelkit, Cappadocia
XII Fulminata from Rafniyeh, Syria opens Malataya, Cappadocia
VI Ferrata from Latakia via Italy to Rafniyeh to replace XII Fulminata

III Gallica returns from Moesia via Italy to open Samsat, Syria on the Euphrates
V Macedonica closes Imwas, Syria to return to Moesia

73 A.D. End of the Jewish uprising – Syria Palaestina separated from Syria

	X Fretensis opens Jerusalem, Syria Palaestina
74 A.D.	XV Apollinaris from Syria Palaestina returns to Pannonia

Syria 3, Syria Palaestina 1, Cappadocia 2

TRAJAN (98-117 A.D.)

106 A.D.	Nabatea annexed as the province of Arabia VI Ferrata from Rafniyeh, Syria opens Bosra, Arabia III Gallica closes Samsat, Syria to Rafniyeh to replace VI Ferrata

Syria 2, Syria Palaestina 1, Cappadocia 2, Arabia 1

113 A.D.	Parthian War II Traiana from Lower Moesia reopens Samsat, Syria

HADRIAN (117-138 A.D.)

120 A.D.	Eastern uprisings crushed; Frontiers reorganized VI Ferrata from Bosra, Arabia opens Legio-Kefar Otnay, Syria Palaestina III Cyrenaica from Egypt to Bosra to replace VI Ferrata II Traiana from Samsat, Syria to Egypt to replace III Cyrenaica XVI Flavia from Kelkit, Cappadocia to Samsat to replace II Traiana XV Apollinaris from Upper Pannonia to Kelkit to replace XVI Flavia

Syria 3, Syria Palaestina 2, Cappadocia 2, Arabia 1

SEPTIMIUS SEVERUS (193-211 A.D.)

198 A.D.	Aftermath of the succession crisis and the Parthian War; Syria divided into Syria Coele and Syria Phoenice; Osrhoene and Mesopotamia become provinces I Parthica (new) opens Balad Sinjar, Mesopotamia III Parthica (new) opens Constantina, Osrhoene IV Scythica closes Belkis, Syria Coele to open Tayibeh, Syria Coele XVI Flavia closes Samsat, Syria Coele to open Souriya, Syria Coele

Syria Phoenice 1, Syria Coele 2, Syria Palaestina 2 Cappadocia 2,
Arabia 1, Mesopotamia 1, Osrhoene 1

ELAGABALUS (218-222 A.D.)

218 A.D.	Gannys defeats Macrinus and IV Scythica at Inmae, Syria III Gallica closes Rafniyeh, Syria Phoenice to open Damascus, Syria Phoenice
219 A.D.	III Parthica closes Constantina, Osrhoene to open Rhesenae, Osrhoene
238 A.D.	Gordian III disbands III Augusta in Numidia III Gallica closes Damascus, Syria Phoenice to Numidia

VALERIAN (253-260 A.D.)

253 A.D.	III Gallica from Numidia reopens Damascus, Syria Phoenice
260 A.D.	Valerian defeated by the Parthians at Edessa, Osrhoene VI Ferrata probably destroyed. Legio Kefar-Otnay, Syria Palaestina is closed

AURELIAN (270-275 A.D.)

274 A.D.   Aftermath of the defeat of Zenobia of Palmyra
I Illyriacorum (new) opens Palmyra, Syria Phoenice
IV Martia (new) joins to Bosra, Arabia following Zenobia's defeat of III Cyrenaica

Syria Phoenice 2, Syria Coele 2, Syria Palaestina 1, Cappadocia 2, Arabia 2, Mesopotamia 1, Osrhoene 1

PROBUS (276-282 A.D.)

278 A.D.   Unrest in Issauria
I Issaurus (new), II Issaurus (new), and III Issaurus (new) garrison Seleucia, Issauria

DIOCLETIAN (284-305 A.D.)

288 A.D.   Defense against the Alans from the North
I Pontica (new) opens Trabzon, Pontus on the Black Sea

IV Martia from Bosra, Arabia opens Al Lejum, Syria Palaestina

290 A.D.   X Fretensis closes Jerusalem, Syria Palaestina and opens Aqaba, Syria Palaestina

300 A.D.   New garrisons on the Tigris
I Armeniaca (new) opens Klaudias, Cappadocia
II Parthica from Italy opens Cefae, Mesopotamia on the Tigris
III Parthica closes Rhesenae, Osrhoene and opens Tel Araban, Osrhoene
IV Parthica (new) opens Beseira, Osrhoene on the Euphrates
V Parthica (new) opens Diarbekir, Mesopotamia on the Tigris

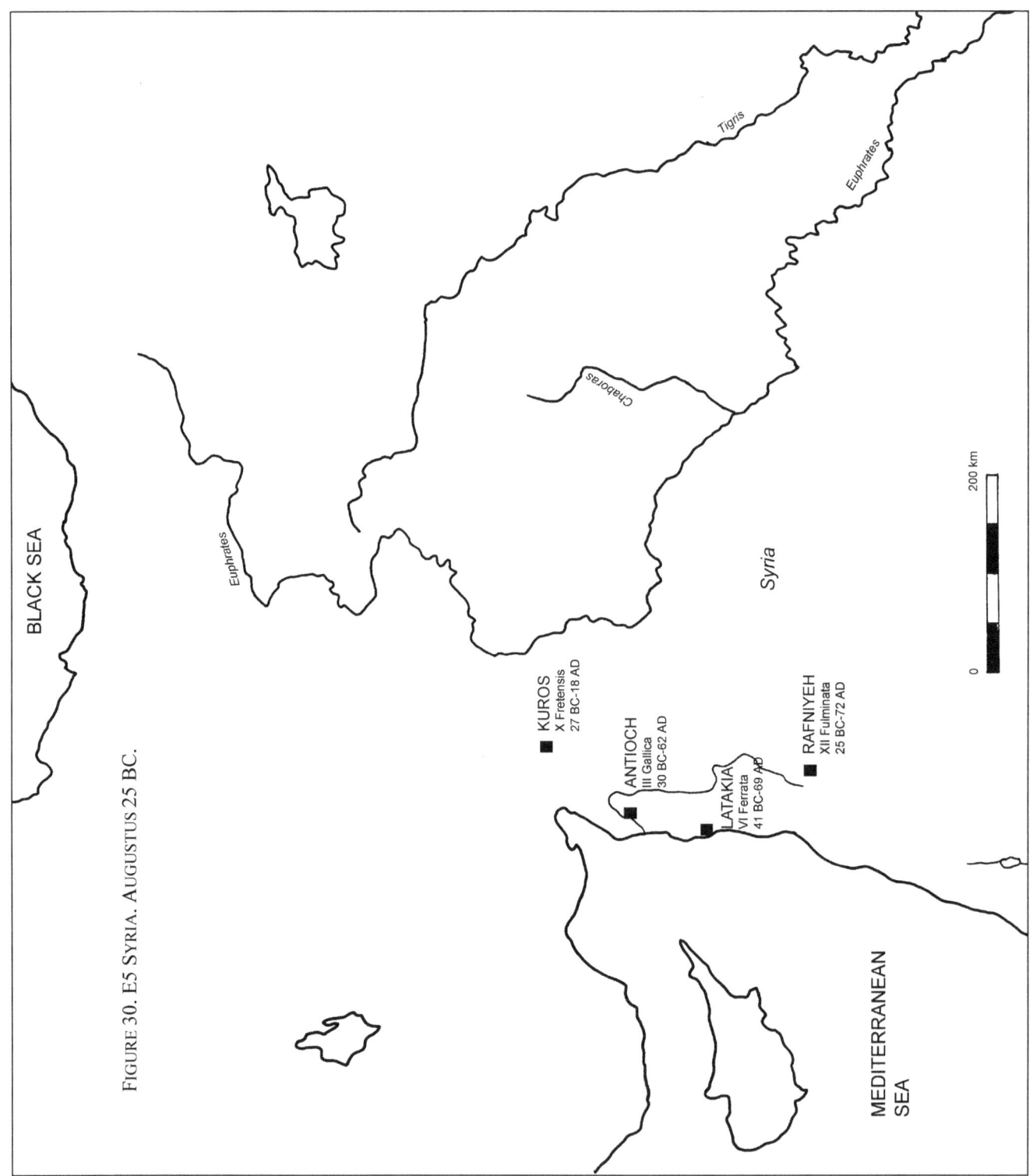

FIGURE 30. E5 SYRIA. AUGUSTUS 25 BC.

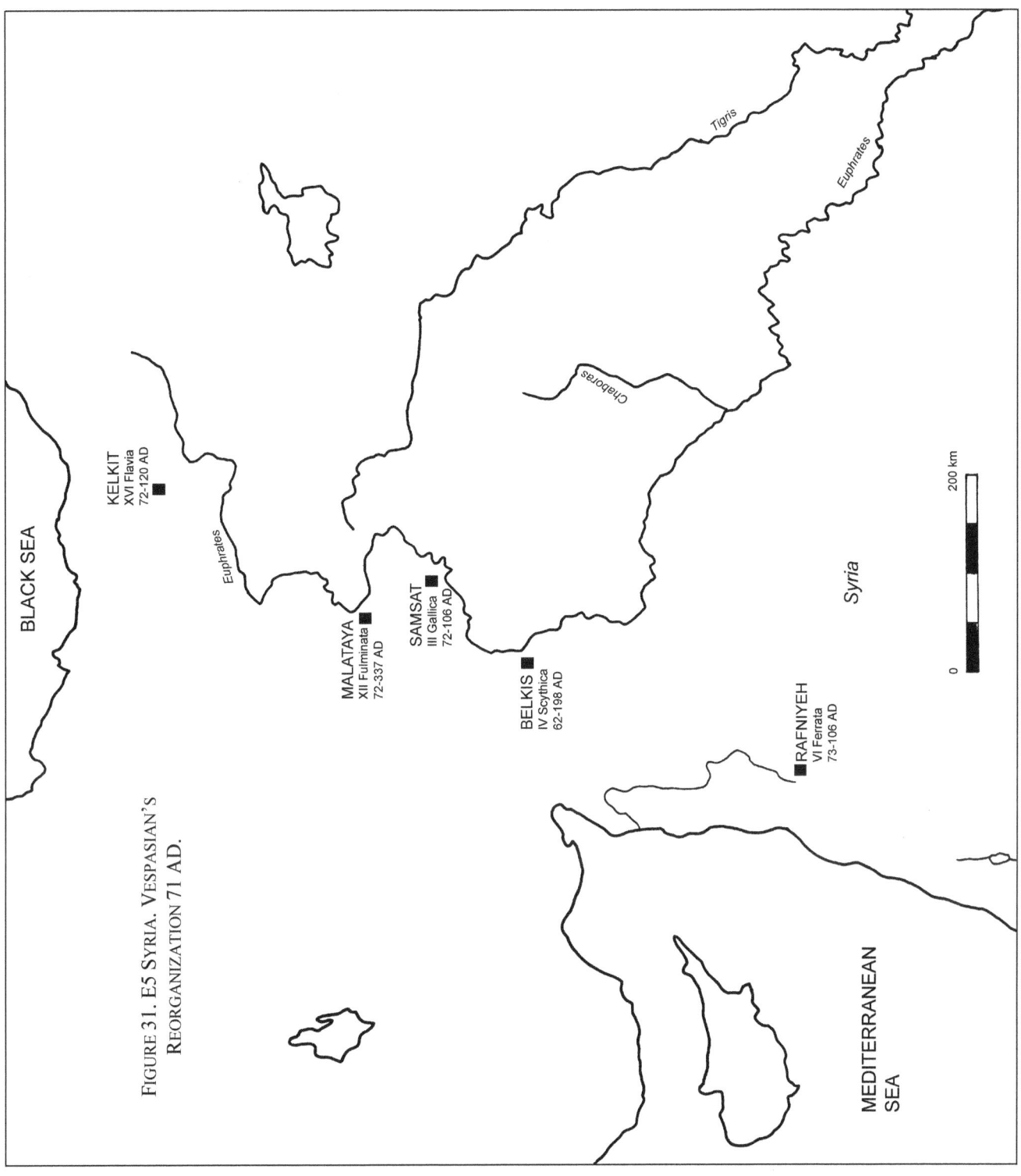

Figure 31. E5 Syria. Vespasian's Reorganization 71 AD.

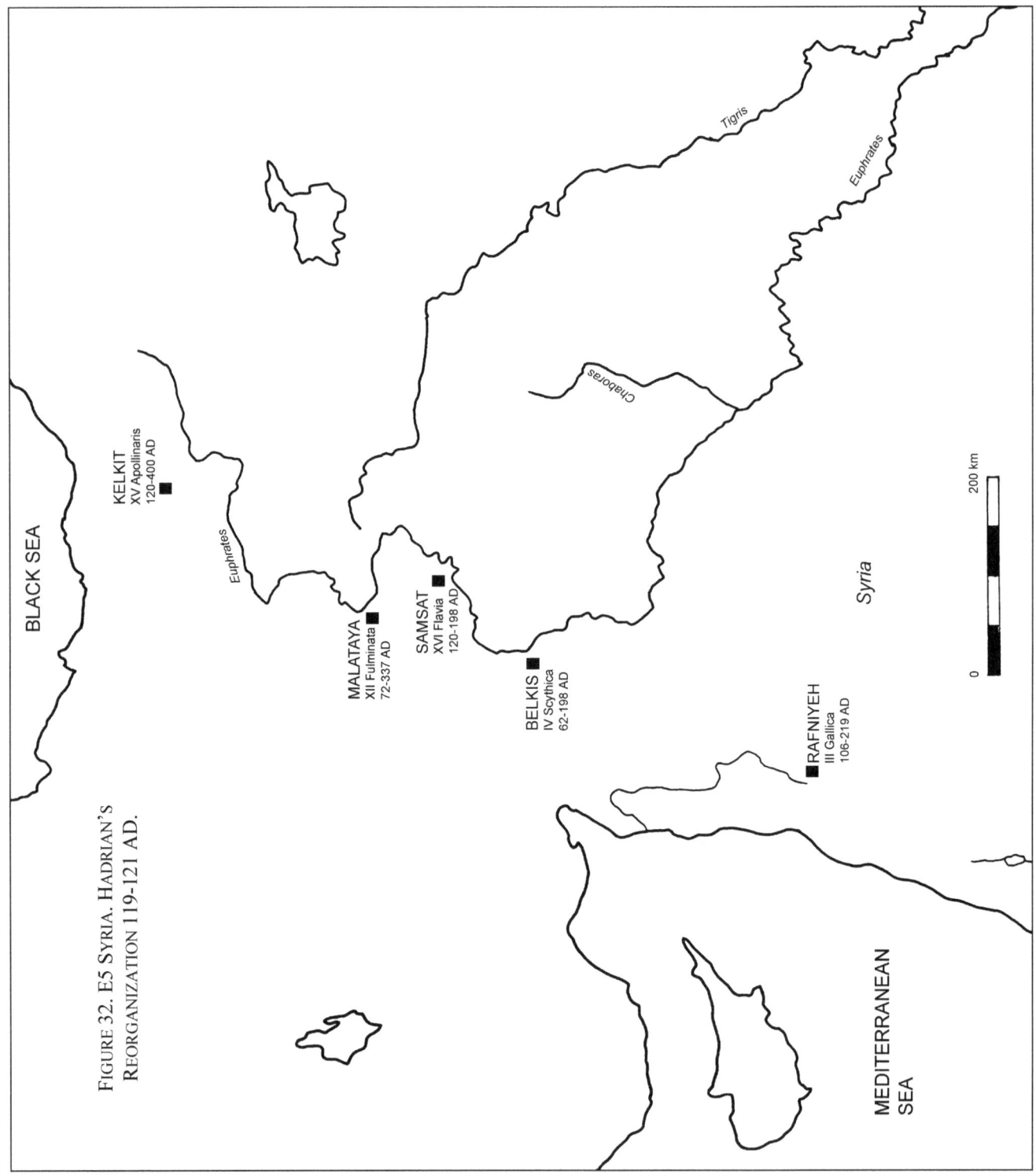

Figure 32. E5 Syria. Hadrian's Reorganization 119-121 AD.

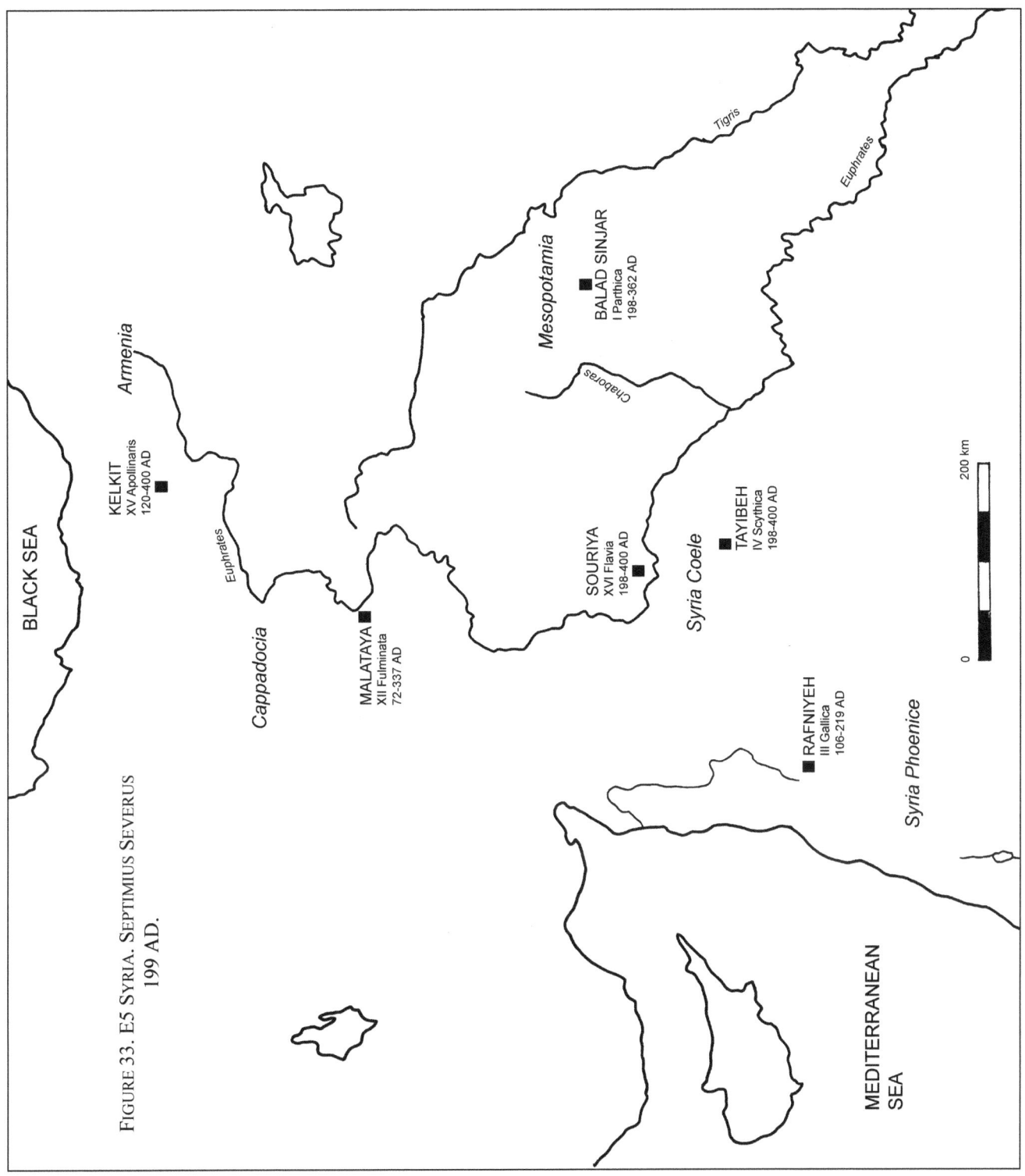

FIGURE 33. E5 SYRIA. SEPTIMIUS SEVERUS 199 AD.

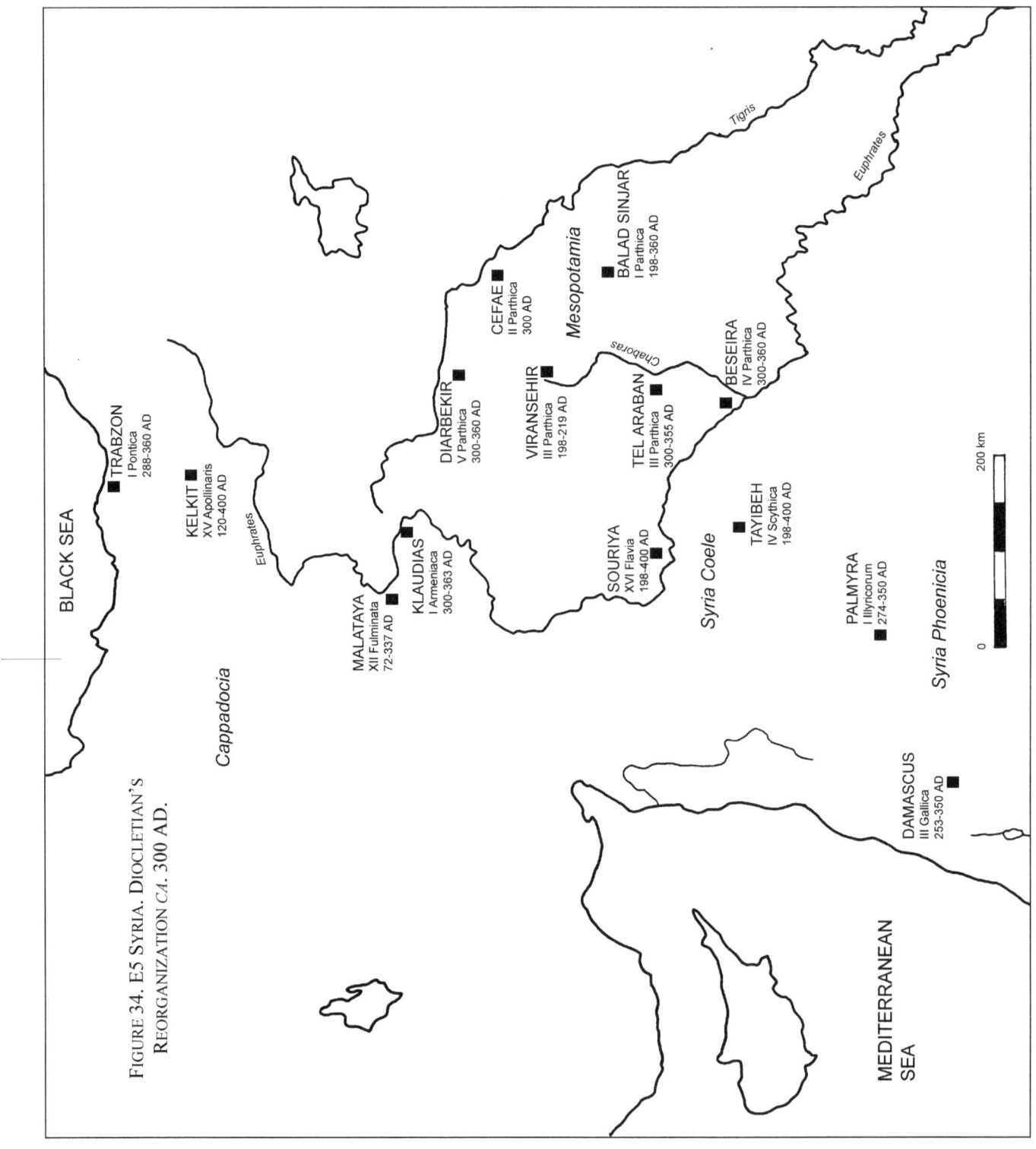

FIGURE 34. E5 SYRIA. DIOCLETIAN'S REORGANIZATION CA. 300 AD.

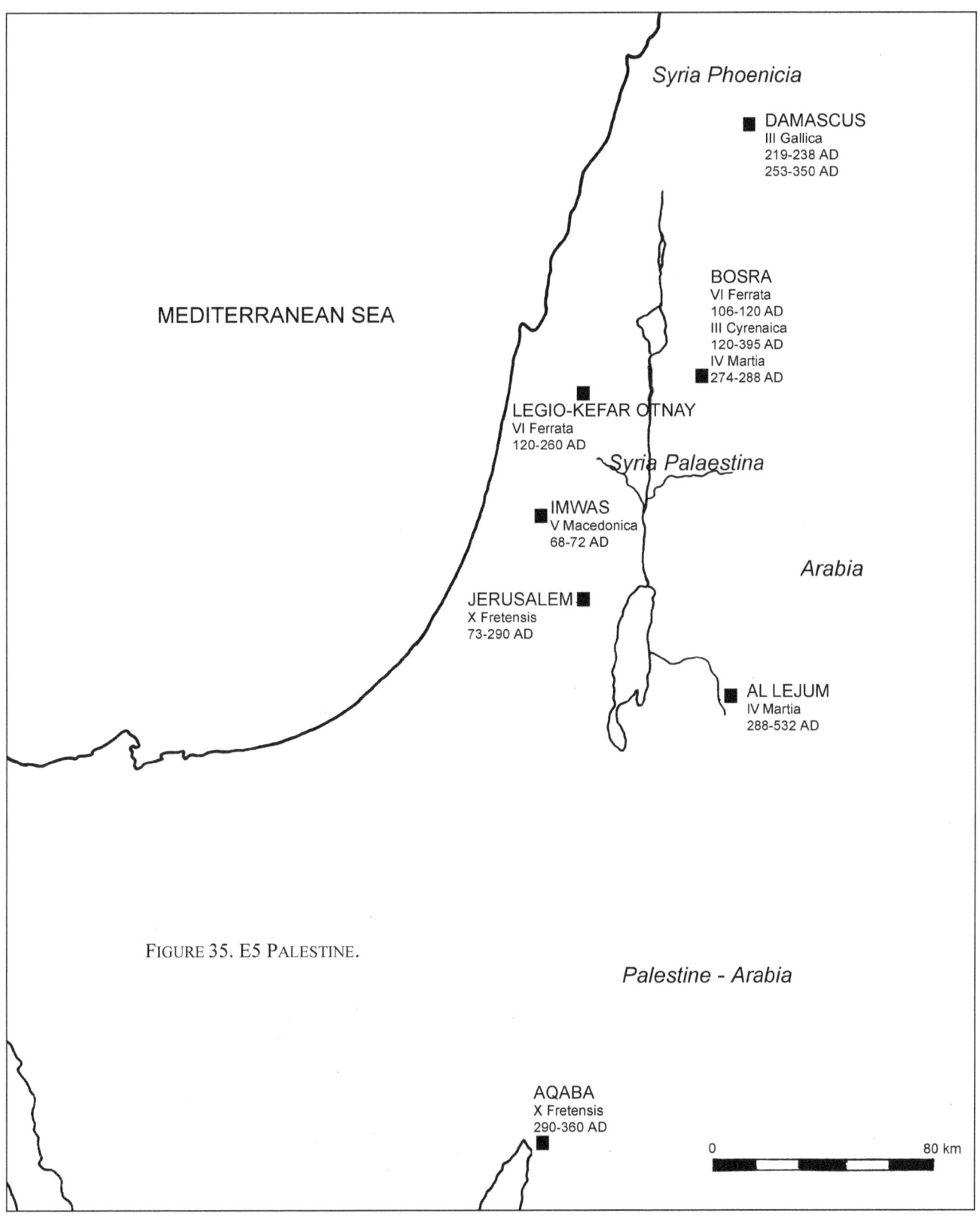

FIGURE 35. E5 PALESTINE.

6) Egypt and Africa

OCTAVIAN AUGUSTUS (31 B.C.-14 A.D.)

30 B.C.	Mauritania	=	VII Macedonica
	Africa Haidra	=	III
	Egypt Alexandria Kasr Kayasire	=	XII Fulminata
	Cairo	=	III Cyrenaica

29 B.C.　　　Uprising in Thebes, Egypt
　　　　　　VIII from Italy opens Thebes

25 B.C.　　　Mauritania pacified and made a client kingdom - Galatia annexed
　　　　　　VII Macedonica from Mauritania to Galatia

　　　　　　XII Fulminata from Alexandria Kasr Kayasire, Egypt to Syria
　　　　　　XXII Deiotariana (new) from Galatia to Alexandria Kasr Kayasire to replace XII Fulminata

24 B.C.　　　Mountain tribes attack Mauritania
　　　　　　IX Hispana from Spain to Mauritania

19 B.C.　　　Mauritania pacified
　　　　　　IX Hispana from Mauritania to Spain

6 A.D.　　　Pannonian uprising
　　　　　　VIII Augusta closes Thebes, Egypt to Illyricum

TIBERIUS (14-37 A.D.)

14 A.D.　　　Concentration of the Egyptian garrison
　　　　　　III Cyrenaica closes Cairo, Egypt to Alexandria Kasr Kayasire to join XXII Deiotariana

VESPASIAN (69-79 A.D.)

75 A.D.　　　III Augusta closes Haidra, Africa to open Tebessa, Africa

HADRIAN (117-138 A.D.)

120 A.D.　　　III Cyrenaica from Alexandria Kasr Kayasire, Egypt to Arabia
　　　　　　II Traiana from Syria to Alexandria Kasr Kayasire to replace III Cyrenaica

128 A.D.　　　III Augusta closes Tebessa, Africa to open Lambese, Africa

132-135 A.D.　Jewish uprising
　　　　　　XXII Deiotariana from Alexandria Kasr Kayasire, Egypt destroyed in Syria Palaestina

238 A.D.　　　Gordian I's revolt is crushed by III Augusta
　　　　　　III Augusta disbanded by Gordian III at Lambese, Numidia
　　　　　　III Gallica from Syria Phoenice to Lambese to replace III Augusta

VALERIAN (253-260 A.D.)

253 A.D.　　　III Augusta reformed at Lambese, Numidia
　　　　　　III Gallica from Lambese returns to Syria Phoenice

DIOCLETIAN (284-305 A.D.)

293 A.D.	I Maximiana Thebaeorum (new) opens Thebes, Egypt
296 A.D.	III Diocletiana Thebaeorum (new) opens Andaro, Egypt
297 A.D.	II Flavia Constantia (new) to Thebes to join I Maximiana Thebaeorum
298 A.D.	III Herculea (new) to Mauritania

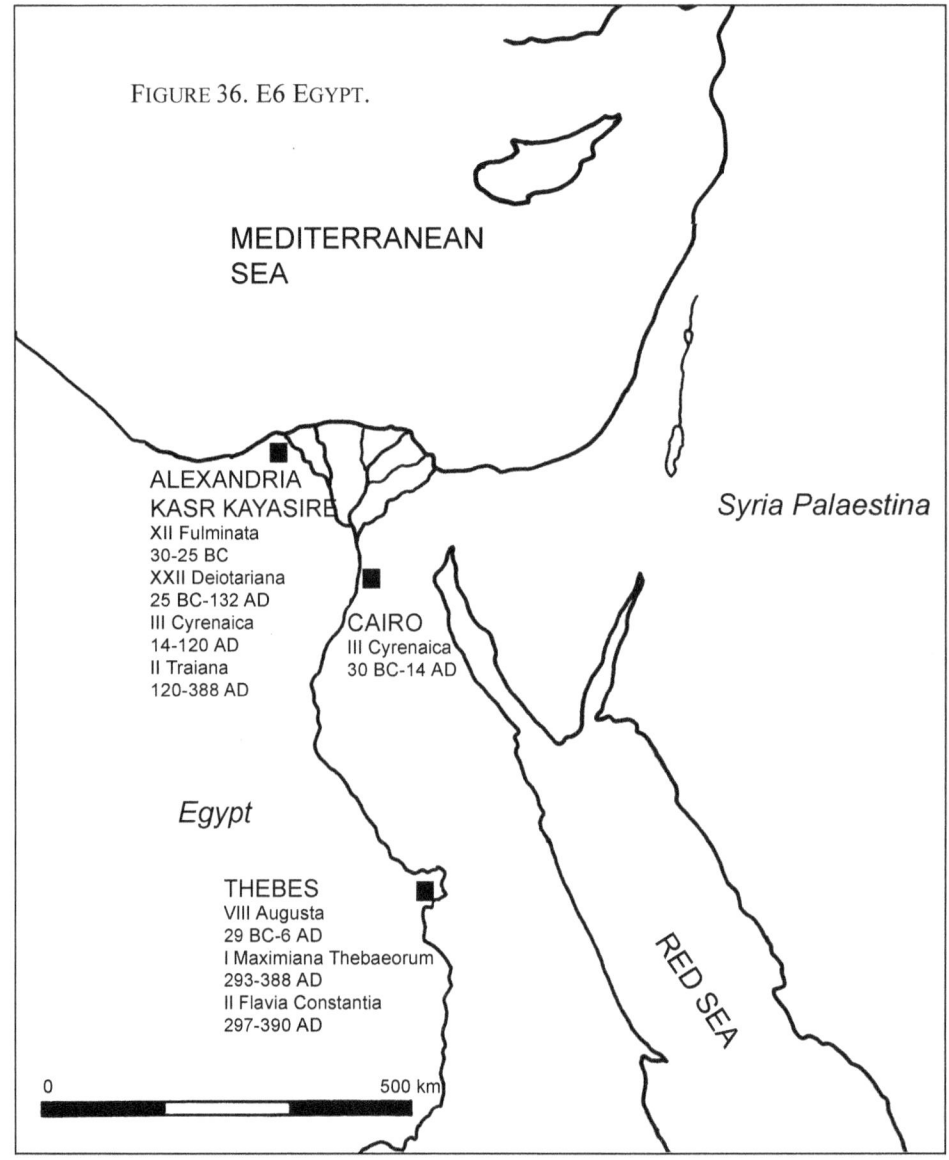

FIGURE 36. E6 EGYPT.

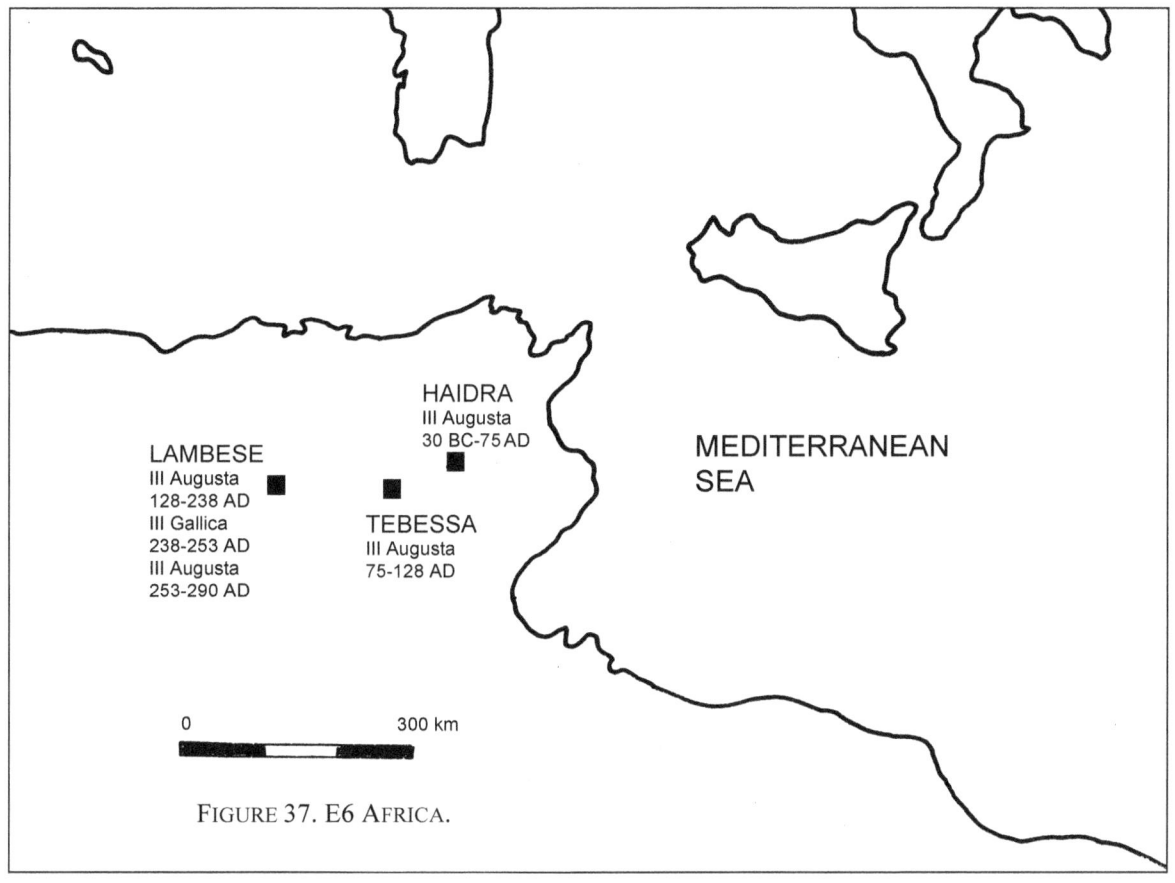

FIGURE 37. E6 AFRICA.

Table F
List of Additions and Deletions to the Legion List
30 B.C. - 250 A.D

I Germanica	Disbanded 70 A.D. after swearing fealty to the New Gallic Empire
Italica	Formed 66 A.D. for Nero's Eastern campaign
Adiutrix	Formed 68 A.D. by Nero
Macriana Liberatrix	Formed 68 A.D. in Africa to support the Vindex revolt. Disbanded 69 A.D. by Vespasian
Minervia	Formed 83 A.D. for Domitian's German campaign
Parthica	Formed 196 A.D. for Septimius Severus' Parthian campaign
II Adiutrix	Formed 70 A.D. by Mucianus to support Vespasian
Traiana	Formed 102 A.D. for Trajan's 2nd Dacian War
Italica	Formed 165 A.D. for Marcus Aurelius' northern campaign
Parthica	Formed 196 A.D. for Septimius Severus' Parthian campaign
III Italica Felix	Formed 166 A.D. for Marcus Aurelius Danube campaign
Parthica	Formed 196 A.D. for Septimius Severus' Parthian campaign
IV Macedonica	Disbanded 70 A.D. after swearing fealty to the New Gallic Empire
Flavia	Formed 70 A.D. probably as a reconstituted IV Macedonica
V Alaudae	Destroyed 86 A.D. by the Dacians
VI Ferrata	Probably destroyed 260 A.D. by the Parthians
VII Galbiana	Formed 68 A.D. to support Galba's accession
IX Hispana	Disbanded 121 A.D. after a disaster in Britain
XV Primigenia	Formed 39 A.D. for Caligula's German campaign - Destroyed 69 A.D. in the Civilis uprising
XVI Gallica	Disbanded 70 A.D. after swearing fealty to the New Gallic Empire
Flavia	Formed 70 A.D. in the East to replace XVI Gallica
XVII Classica	Destroyed 9 A.D. by the Cherusci
XVIII Libyca	Destroyed 9 A.D. by the Cherusci
XIX Paterna	Destroyed 9 A.D. by the Cherusci
XXI Rapax	Destroyed or disbanded ca. 102 A.D. after the 1st Dacian War
XXII Primigenia	Formed 39 A.D. for Caligula's German campaign
Deiotariana	Into Roman service 25 B.C. - Destroyed 132-135 A.D. in the Bar-Kochba uprising
XXX Ulpia	Formed 99 A.D. for Trajan's 1st Dacian War

TABLE G
DISTRIBUTION OF THE LEGIONS BY REGION AT VARIOUS DATES
(L) = LOWER PROVINCE   (U) = UPPER PROVINCE

	30 B.C.	25 B.C.	15 B.C.	10 A.D.
Spain	I Augusta II Augusta IV Macedonica V Alaudae VI Victrix IX Hispana X Gemina XX Valeria	I Augusta II Augusta IV Macedonica V Alaudae VI Victrix IX Hispana X Gemina XX Valeria	II Augusta IV Macedonica VI Victrix X Gemina	IV Macedonica VI Victrix X Gemina
Germany/Gaul	XVII Classica XVIII Libyca XIX Paterna XXI Rapax	XVI Gallica XVII Classica XVIII Libyca XIX Paterna XXI Rapax	I Germanica V Alaudae XVI Gallica XVII Classica XVIII Libyca XIX Paterna XXI Rapax	I Germanica II Augusta V Alaudae XIV Gemina XX Valeria XXI Rapax
Raetia			XV Apollinaris	XIII Gemina XVI Gallica
Illyricum	XIII Gemina XIV Gemina XV Apollinaris	XI XIII Gemina XIV Gemina XV Apollinaris	IX Hispana XIII Gemina XIV Gemina XX Valeria	VII Macedonica VIII Augusta IX Hispana XI XV Apollinaris
Macedonia	IV Scythica V Macedonica X Fretensis XI	IV Scythica	IV Scythica XI	IV Scythica V Macedonica
Galatia		V Macedonica VII Macedonica	V Macedonica VII Macedonica	
Syria	III Gallica VI Ferrata	III Gallica VI Ferrata X Fretensis XII Fulminata	III Gallica VI Ferrata X Fretensis XII Fulminata	III Gallica VI Ferrata X Fretensis XII Fulminata
Egypt	III Cyrenaica XII Fulminata	III Cyrenaica VIII Augusta XXII Deiotariana	III Cyrenaica VIII Augusta XXII Deiotariana	III Cyrenaica XXII Deiotariana
Africa	III Augusta VII Macedonica	III Augusta	III Augusta	III Augusta
Italy	VIII Augusta XVI Gallica			

JEROME H. FARNUM

	44 A.D.	**66 A.D.**	**73 A.D.**	**89 A.D.**
Spain	VI Victrix X Gemina	VI Victrix		VII Gemina
Germany/ Gaul	I Germanica IV Macedonica V Alaudae XIII Gemina XV Primigenia XVI Gallica XXI Rapax XXII Primigenia	I Germanica IV Macedonica V Alaudae XV Primigenia XVI Gallica XXI Rapax XXII Primigenia	I Adiutrix VI Victrix VIII Augusta X Gemina XI Claudia XIV Gemina XXI Rapax XXII Primigenia	I Minervia (L) VI Victrix (L) X Gemina (L) XXII Primigenia (L) VIII Augusta (U) XI Claudia (U) XIV Gemina (U)
Britain	II Augusta IX Hispana XIV Gemina XX Valeria	II Augusta IX Hispana XX Valeria	II Adiutrix II Augusta IX Hispana XX Valeria	II Augusta IX Hispana XX Valeria
Dalmatia	VII Claudia XI Claudia	XI Claudia	IV Flavia	
Pannonia	VIII Augusta XV Apollinaris	X Gemina XIII Gemina	VII Gemina XIII Gemina	I Adiutrix II Adiutrix XIII Gemina XV Apollinaris XXI Rapax
Moesia	IV Scythica V Macedonica	VII Claudia VIII Augusta	I Italica V Alaudae V Macedonica VII Claudia	I Italica (L) V Macedonica (L) IV Flavia (U) VII Claudia (U)
Cappadocia/ Armenia		III Gallica	XII Fulminata XVI Flavia	XII Fulminata XVI Flavia
Syria	III Gallica VI Ferrata X Fretensis XII Fulminata	IV Scythica V Macedonica VI Ferrata X Fretensis XII Fulminata XV Apollinaris	III Gallica IV Scythica VI Ferrata XV Apollinaris	III Gallica IV Scythica VI Ferrata
Syria Palaestina			X Fretensis	X Fretensis
Egypt	III Cyrenaica XXII Deiotariana	III Cyrenaica XXII Deiotariana	III Cyrenaica XXII Deiotariana	III Cyrenaica XXII Deiotariana
Africa	III Augusta	III Augusta	III Augusta	III Augusta
Italy		I Italica XIV Gemina		

The Positioning of the Roman Imperial Legions

	106 A.D.	122 A.D.	198 A.D.	273 A.D.
Spain	VII Gemina	VII Gemina	VII Gemina	VII Gemina
Germany	I Minervia (L) VI Victrix (L) VIII Augusta (U) XXII Primigenia (U)	I Minervia (L) XXX Ulpia (L) VIII Augusta (U) XXII Primigenia (U)	I Minervia (L) XXX Ulpia (L) VIII Augusta (U) XXII Primigenia (U)	I Minervia (L) XXX Ulpia (L) VIII Augusta (U) XXII Primigenia (U)
Britain	II Augusta IX Hispana XX Valeria	II Augusta VI Victrix XX Valeria	II Augusta (U) XX Valeria (U) VI Victrix (L)	II Augusta (U) XX Valeria (U) VI Victrix (L)
Raetia			III Italica	III Italica
Noricum			II Italica	II Italica
Pannonia	X Gemina (L) XIV Gemina (U) XV Apollinaris (U) XXX Ulpia (U)	II Adiutrix (L) I Adiutrix (U) X Gemina (U) XIV Gemina (U)	II Adiutrix (L) I Adiutrix (U) X Gemina (U) XIV Gemina (U)	I Adiutrix (L) II Adiutrix (L) X Gemina (U) XIV Gemina (U)
Moesia	I Italica (L) II Traiana (L) V Macedonica (L) XI Claudia (L) VII Claudia (U)	I Italica (L) V Macedonica (L) XI Claudia (L) IV Flavia (U) VII Claudia (U)	I Italica (L) XI Claudia (L) IV Flavia (U) VII Claudia (U)	I Italica (L) V Macedonica (L) XI Claudia (L) IV Flavia (U) VII Claudia (U)
Dacia	I Adiutrix II Adiutrix IV Flavia XIII Gemina	XIII Gemina (U)	V Macedonica (L) XIII Gemina (U)	XIII Gemina (U)
Cappadocia	XII Fulminata XVI Flavia	XII Fulminata XV Apollinaris	XII Fulminata XV Apollinaris	XII Fulminata XV Apollinaris
Syria	III Gallica IV Scythica	III Gallica IV Scythica XVI Flavia	III Gallica (Ph) IV Scythica (C) XVI Flavia (C)	III Gallica (Ph) IV Scythica (C) XVI Flavia (C)
Syria Palaestina	X Fretensis	VI Ferrata X Fretensis	VI Ferrata X Fretensis	X Fretensis
Mesopotamia			I Parthica	I Parthica
Osrhoene			III Parthica	III Parthica
Arabia	VI Ferrata	III Cyrenaica	III Cyrenaica	III Cyrenaica
Egypt	III Cyrenaica XXII Deiotariana	II Traiana XXII Deiotariana	II Traiana	II Traiana
Africa/Numidia	III Augusta	III Augusta	III Augusta	III Augusta
Italy			II Parthica	II Parthica

TABLE H
CAMPAIGNS AND BATTLES 30 B.C. - 300 A.D.

OCTAVIAN AUGUSTUS (31 B.C.-14 A.D.)

29 B.C.	Cornelius Gallus suppresses an uprising at Thebes, Egypt - VIII Augusta M. Statilius Taurus campaigns against the Cantabri, Astures and Vaccaei in Spain C. Carinas suppresses an uprising of the Morini in Gaul
29-28 B.C.	Marcus Licinius Crassus conquers the Geto-Dacians and Bastarnae in Macedonia - IV Scythica, V Macedonica, X Fretensis, XI
28 B.C.	Lucius Apronius defeated by the Frisians in Germany
28-27 B.C.	Suebi attack across the Rhine in Germany
28-26 B.C.	Marcus Valerius Mesalla Corvinus pacifies Aquitania – XVII Classica, XVIII Libyaca, XIX Paterna, XXI Rapax
26-25 B.C.	Caius Antistius Vetus campaigns against the Cantabri and Astures in Spain - I Augusta, II Augusta, IV Macedonica, VI Victrix, IX Hispana, XX Valeria, supported from Farther Spain by Publius Carisius with V Alaudae and X Gemina
25 B.C.	Marcus Terrentius Varro Murena conquers the Salassi in Northern Italy – XVI Gallica Aelius Gallus campaigns in the Arabian Peninsula – III Cyrenaica, XXII Deiotariana
24 B.C.	Lucius Aemilius Lamia suppresses an uprising in Spain by the Cantabri and Astures Caius Petronius campaigns against the Ethiopians in Upper Egypt – VIII Augusta
23 B.C.	Marcus Primus campaigns in Thrace against the Odryse - IV Scythica Marcus Terrentius Varro Murena suppresses brigands in Trachonitis, Syria
22 B.C.	Caius Furnius suppresses an uprising of the Cantabri in Farther Spain Campaigns against the Berbers in North Africa - III Augusta, IX Hispana
21 B.C.	Marcus Vipsanius Agrippa repels a German raid into Gaul
19 B.C.	Lucius Cornelius Balbus defeats the Garamates in North Africa - III Augusta, IX Hispana Marcus Vipsanius Agrippa crushes an uprising of the Cantabri in Farther Spain
17 B.C.	Sugambri, Tenteri and Usibi defeat Marcus Lollius in Gaul - V Alaudae
16 B.C.	Last uprising in Farther Spain P. Silius Nerva conquers the Vennones, Leponti and Camunni in Illyricum Attacks against Macedonia
15-14 B.C.	Tiberius/Drusus War conquers Raetia and Vindelica Tiberius and Lucius Calpurnius Piso - I Germanica, V Alaudae, XVI Gallica, XVII Classica, XVIII Libyaca, XIX Paterna, XXI Rapax Nero Claudius Drusus and Publius Silius Nerva - IV Scythica, IX Hispana, XI, XIII Gemina, XIV Gemina, XV Apollinaris, XX Valeria
14 B.C.	M. Vinicius quells an uprising in the Sava Valley in Illyricum - XIII Gemina Marcus Vipsanius Agrippa campaigns in the Maritime Alps against the Cotti
13 B.C.	Marcus Vipsanius Agrippa campaigns in Illyricum against the Pannonian Breuci and Amantini - IX Hispana, XX Valeria Lucius Calpurnius Piso defeats the Bessi in Thrace - IV Scythica, V Macedonica, VII Macedonica, XI

12 B.C.	Tiberius campaigns in Illyricum against the Breuci Nero Claudius Drusus conquers lower Germany and attacks the Usipetes, Chauci and Sugambri
11 B.C.	M. Vinicius campaigns in Thrace against the Dacians and Basternae – IV Scythica Nero Claudius Drusus campaigns along the Lippe in lower Germany against the Marsi, Cherusci, Usipets, and Sugambri - XVI Gallica, XVIII Libyaca
10 B.C.	Tiberius suppresses an uprising in Illyricum - IX Hispana, XX Valeria Nero Claudius Drusus defeats the Chatti and Cherusci at Arbalo in upper Germany - I Germanica, V Alaudae, XVIII Libyaca
9 B.C.	Tiberius defeats the Dacians - IV Scythica, XI Nero Claudius Drusus marches to the Elbe in Germany, attacks the Chatti, Cherusci, Marcomanni and Suebi - I Germanica, V Alaudae, XVII Classica, XVIII Libyca
8 B.C.	Tiberius defeats the Sugambri in lower Germany
6 B.C.- 4 A.D.	Tiberius campaigns against the Dacians on the Danube - IV Scythica, XI
5 B.C.	Lucius Domitius Ahenobarbus campaigns against the Chatti and Bructeri in lower Germany
4-3 B.C.	Lucius Calpurnius Piso campaigns in Galatia against the Homonadenses - V Macedonica, VII Macedonica
3 B.C.	Publius Quinctilius Varus suppresses a Jewish uprising in Palestine - III Gallica, VI Ferrata, XII Fulminata
1 B.C.- 3 A.D.	Gaius Caesar campaigns against the Parthians in Armenia - V Macedonica, VII Macedonica M. Vinicius campaigns in Germany
2-6 A.D.	Cossus Cornelius conquers the Getules in Mauritania - III Augusta P. Sulpicius Quirinius conquers the Marmaridae in Mauritania – III Augusta
5 A.D.	Tiberius campaigns against the Marcomanni in Bohemia Gaius Sentius Saturninus campaigns into Germany
6 A.D.	M. Plautius Silvanus suppresses an Isaurian uprising in Galatia - V Macedonica, VII Macedonica Q. Aemilius Secundus campaigns against the Itrurii in Lebanon - X Fretensis Cossus Cornelius Lentulus subdues the Gaetuli in Mauritania - III Augusta The Dacians attack Moesia
6-9 A.D.	Bato uprising in Illyricum - IV Scythica, VII Macedonica, VIII Augusta, IX Hispana, XI, XIII Gemina, XIV Gemina, XV Apollinaris, XVI Gallica, XX Valeria, XXI Rapax
7 A.D.	M. Plautius Silvanus and Aulus Caecina Severus defeat the Pannonian tribes at the Volcaean Marshes
9 A.D.	Publius Quinctilius Varus and 3 legions destroyed by the Cherusci in the Teutoberger Forest in lower Germany - XVII Classica, XVIII Libyca, XIX Paterna
10 A.D.	Gnaeus Lentulus defeats the Dacians and Sarmatians
12 A.D.	Didius Gallus repels a Dacian attack on Macedonia - IV Scythica, V Macedonica
14 A.D.	Germanicus campaigns against the Marsi, Bructeri, Tubantes and Usipetes on the Lippe in lower Germany - V Alaudae, XXI Rapax

TIBERIUS (14-37 A.D.)

	Augustus dies - Western legions mutiny - I Germanica, II Augusta, V Alaudae, VIII Augusta, IX Hispana, XV Apollinaris, XX Valeria, XXI Rapax
15 A.D.	Germanicus campaigns against the Marsi, Cherusci, and Bructeri in lower Germany Aulus Caecina Severus campaigns against the Chatti in upper Germany Barbarians attack Troesmi, Macedonia - IV Scythica
16 A.D.	Germanicus defeats the Cherusci - C. Silius Caecina campaigns against the Chatti in upper Germany under Arminius at Idistaviso in Germany – II Augusta, XIV Gemina
17-24 A.D.	Tacfarinas uprising in North Africa - III Augusta
19 A.D.	C. Poppaeus Sabinus suppresses an uprising in Thrace - IV Scythica, V Macedonica
20 A.D.	L. Cornelius Scipio campaigns against Tacfarinas in North Africa - III Augusta, IX Hispana
21 A.D.	Gaius Silius subdues an uprising of the Aedui and Treveri under Sacrovir and Florus in Gaul - II Augusta Publius Vallaius subdues an uprising in Thrace
24 A.D.	Publius Cornelius Dolabella defeats Tacfarinas at Auzea in Mauritania - III Augusta, IX Hispana
26 A.D.	Uprising in Thrace
28 A.D.	Lucius Apronius quells a Frisian uprising in lower Germany - V Alaudae
35 A.D.	Lucius Vitellius campaigns against the Parthians in Armenia
36 A.D.	M Trebellius subdues an uprising in Cilicia

CALIGULA (37-41 A.D.)

38 A.D.	Riots in Alexandria, Egypt - III Cyrenaica, XXII Deiotariana
40 A.D.	Mauritanian uprising – III Augusta

CLAUDIUS (41-54 A.D.)

41 A.D.	Gabinius Secundus defeats the Chauci in lower Germany
41-42 A.D.	Servius Sulpicius Galba defeats the Chatti in upper Germany
42 A.D.	The revolt by Lucius Arruntius Camillus Scribonianus in Dalmatia with VII Macedonica and XI fizzles out Gaius Suetonius Paulinus subdues an uprising in Mauritania led by Aedemon - III Augusta
43 A.D.	Tiberius Aelianus invades Britain - II Augusta, IX Hispana, XIV Gemina, XX Valeria
47-49 A.D.	Gnaeus Domitius Corbulo campaigns against the Chauci and Frisians in lower Germany - V Alaudae, XV Primigenia Publius Ostorius Scapula campaigns against Caratacus in Britain
50 A.D.	Publius Ostorius Scapula subdues an uprising of the Iceni and defeats Caratacus in Britain - XIV Gemina, XX Valeria Publius Pomponius Secundus campaigns against the Chatti in lower Germany
52-56 A.D.	Aulus Didius Gallus campaigns against the Silures in Wales, Britain
53 A.D.	G. Manilius Valens is defeated in Wales, Britain - XX Valeria

NERO (54-68 A.D.)

58-59 A.D.	Gnaeus Domitius Corbulo drives the Parthians from Armenia - III Gallica, IV Scythica, VI Ferrata, X Fretensis T. Curtilius Mancia campaigns against the Chatti in lower Germany
58-60 A.D.	Gaius Suetonius Paulinus campaigns in Wales, Britain against the Silures and Ordovices
60 A.D.	Quintus Petilius Cerialis Caesius Rufus is defeated by Boudicca near Colchester, Britain - IX Hispana Gnaeus Domitius Corbulo defeats the Parthian Monobazus in Adiabene
61 A.D.	Gaius Suetonius Paulinus crushes the Boudiccan revolt in Britain – XIV Gemina, XX Valeria
62 A.D.	Lucius Caesennius Paetus is defeated by the Parthians at Rhandeia and withdraws from Armenia - IV Scythica, XII Fulminata
62-64 A.D.	Tiberius Plautius Silvanus Aelianus campaigns against the Scythians in the Crimea
66 A.D.	Tiberius Julius Alexander suppresses Jewish riots in Alexandria – III Cyrenaica, XXII Deiotariana C. Cestius Gallus is defeated at the Beth Horon Pass in a Jewish uprisng in Palestine - XII Fulminata
66-70 A.D.	Jewish uprising in Palestine suppressed by Vespasian and Titus - V Macedonica, X Fretensis, XV Apollinaris
68 A.D.	Lucius Verginius Rufus crushes revolt of Julius Vindex at Besancon, Gaul - XXI Rapax M. Plautius Sylvanus suppresses an uprising of the Issaurians in Turkey M. Aponius Saturninus defeats the Rhoxalani on the Danube
69 A.D.	Year of the 4 Emperors - 2 legionary battles at Bedriacum in Italy Caecina Alienus – I Italica, XXI Rapax and parts of IV Macedonica, V Alaudae, XV Primigenia, XVI Gallica, XXII Primigenia Otho - I Adiutrix, XIII Gemina, and part of XIV Gemina Antonius Primus - III Gallica, VII Claudia, VII Hispana, VIII Augusta, XIII Gemina Titus captures Jerusalem - V Macedonica, X Fretensis Aurelius Fulvus defeats a Rhoxoloni raid in Moesia - III Gallica Julius Civilis besieges Xanten in lower Germany and destroys XV Primigenia Publius Petronius Turpilianus suppresses a Brigantian uprising in Britain - IX Hispana Valerius Festus defeats the Garamantes in North Africa - III Augusta Fonteius Agrippa defeated by the Dacians and Sarmatians in Moesia

VESPASIAN (69-79 A.D.)

70 A.D.	Gaius Licinius Mucianus defeats the Dacians Rubrius Gallus defeats the Sarmatians in Moesia
70-71 A.D.	Quintus Petilius Cerialis Caesius Rufus suppresses the Civilis uprising in lower Germany - I Adiutrix, II Adiutrix, VI Victrix, VIII Augusta, X Gemina, XI Claudia, XIII Gemina, XIV Gemina, XXI Rapax
71 A.D.	Quintus Petilius Cerialis Cassius Rufus campaigns against the Brigantes, Silures and Ordovices in Britain
72 A.D.	Alans attack Armenia – XVI Flavia Lucillus Bassus captures Machaerus in Palestine – X Fretensis
73 A.D.	Flavius Silva captures Masada to end the 1st Jewish uprising - X Fretensis Quintus Petilius Cerialis Caesius Rufus defeats the Brigantes at Stanwick, Britain - IX Hispana, XX Valeria The Parthians defeat A. Marius Celsus in Syria and are, in turn, defeated by Marcus Ulpius Traianus

73-74 A.D.	Gn. Pinarius Cornelius Clemens conquers the Agri Decumates in Germany -I Adiutrix, VII Gemina, VIII Augusta, XI Claudia, XIV Gemina
75-77 A.D.	Sextus Julius Frontinus campaigns in Wales, Britain - II Augusta, XX Valeria
76 A.D.	Marcus Ulpius Traianus defeats the Parthians
77-78 A.D.	C. Rutilius Gallicus campaigns against the Bructeri in lower Germany
78-84 A.D.	Gnaeus Julius Agricola conquers the Ordovices and Brigantes in Britain and campaigns into Scotland - IX Hispana, XX Valeria

DOMITIAN (81-96 A.D.)

83-85 A.D.	Sextus Julius Frontinus campaigns against the Chatti in Germany - I Adiutrix, XI Claudia, XXI Rapax
85 A.D.	Dacians under Decebalus defeat Oppius Sabinus in Moesia - I Italica, V Alaudae, V Macedonica
86 A.D.	Gn. Suellius Flaccus destroys the Nasamones in the Syrtic Gulf of Libya - III Augusta Dacians defeat Cornelius Fuscus above the Danube with I Italica, I Adiutrix V Alaudae, V Macedonica, and VII Claudia and destroy V Alaudae
88 A.D.	Tettius Julianus defeats the Dacians at Tapae, Dacia - I Italica, I Adiutrix, II Adiutrix, IV Flavia, V Macedonica, VII Claudia
88-89 A.D.	A. Bucius Lappius Maximus and Norbanus with I Minervia, VI Victrix, X Gemina, XI Claudia and XXII Primigenia crush the revolt of Lucius Antonius Saturninus with XIV Gemina and XXI Rapax near Koblenz, Lower Germany
89 A.D.	A. Bucius Lappius Maximus campaigns against the Chatti in Lower Germany
92 A.D.	Sarmatian Jazyges attack Pannonia - I Italica, I Adiutrix, II Adiutrix, IV Flavia, V Macedonica, VII Claudia, XIII Gemina, XV Apollinaris, XXI Rapax

NERVA (96-98 A.D.)

97 A.D.	Trajan repels a German attack on the Lower Rhine - VIII Augusta, XXII Primigenia
98 A.D.	Trajan campaigns against the Suebi on the Danube

TRAJAN (98-117 A.D.)

101-102 A.D.	1st Dacian War - I Italica, I Adiutrix, I Minervia, II Adiutrix, IV Flavia, V Macedonica, VI Victrix, VII Claudia, X Gemina, XI Claudia, XIII Gemina, XV Apollinaris, XXX Ulpia. XXI Rapax destroyed or disbanded
105-106 A.D.	2nd Dacian War - I Adiutrix, I Italica, I Minervia, II Adiutrix, II Traiana, IV Flavia, V Macedonica, X Gemina, XI Claudia, XIII Gemina, XIV Gemina, XV Apollinaris, XXX Ulpia British Northern frontier attacked by the Caledonians
106 A.D.	Aulus Cornelius Palma annexes the Nabataean Kingdom in Arabia – III Cyrenaica, VI Ferrata, X Fretensis
107 A.D.	Hadrian defeats the Jazyges in Lower Pannonia - X Gemina, XXX Ulpia
111 A.D.	Lucius Quietus pacifies Osrhoene and destroys Edessa

114-116 A.D.	Trajan overruns Armenia and Mesopotamia but withdraws - I Adiutrix, II Adiutrix, II Traiana, III Gallica, III Cyrenaica, IV Scythica, VI Ferrata, X Fretensis, XII Fulminata, XIII Gemina, XV Apollinaris, XVI Flavia, XXX Ulpia
116 A.D.	Jewish riots in Alexandria and Cairo, Egypt, Cyprus, and Cyrenaica, North Africa Uprising in Mesopotamia

HADRIAN (117-138 A.D.)

117-118 A.D.	Q. Marcius Turbo crushes uprisings in Egypt and Cyrenaica - III Cyrenaica, XXII Deiotariana Lucius Quietus crushes the uprising in Mesopotamia
119 A.D.	Quintus Pompeius Falco suppresses a Brigantian uprising in Britain – IX Hispana defeated or is disgraced Hadrian defeats the Rhoxolani in Pannonia – II Adiutrix, XXX Ulpia
121 A.D.	Q. Marcius Turbo defeats the Rhoxolani and Jazyges on the Danube - II Adiutrix, XXX Ulpia
132-135 A.D.	Sextus Julius Severus suppresses a Jewish uprising under Simon Bar Kochba in Palestine followed by the Diaspora – II Adiutrix, II Traiana, III Gallica, III Cyrenaica, V Macedonica, VI Ferrata, X Fretensis, XI Claudia, XII Fulminata – XXII Deiotariana is destroyed
136 A.D.	Flavius Arrianus defeats the Alans in Cappadocia - XII Fulminata, XV Apollinaris
138 A.D.	T. Haterius Nepos defeats the Quadi on the Danube

ANTONINUS PIUS (138-161 A.D.)

141-142 A.D.	Quintus Lollius Urbicus defeats the Caledones in Britain
143 A.D.	Alans attack Armenia - XV Apollinaris
145-148 A.D.	Uttedius Honoratus and Flavius Priscus suppress an uprising in Mauretania - III Augusta, VI Ferrata, X Fretensis
155 A.D.	Parthians invade Armenia but are driven out - XII Fulminata, XV Apollinaris
155-157 A.D.	Gnaeus Julius Verus suppresses uprising of the Brigantes and Selgovae in Britain
158 A.D.	Campaign against the Berbers in Numidia - VII Gemina
160 A.D.	Costobocci invade Upper Dacia - XIII Gemina

MARCUS AURELIUS - LUCIUS VERUS (161-169 A.D.)

161 A.D.	Parthians defeat M. Sedatius Severianus at Elegeia, Armenia - XV Apollinaris Vologaises I defeats L. Attidius Cornelianus in Syria - IV Scythica, XVI Flavia Chatti attack in Germany and defeat Gaius Aufidius Victorinus – XXII Primigenia
162 A.D.	Gaius Aufidius Victorinus repels the Chatti from Upper Germany Publius Helvius Pertinax clears Raetia and Noricum of Alemanni – I Adiutrix
163 A.D.	M. Statius Prixus recaptures Armenia including Artaxata from the Parthians
162-165 A.D.	Gaius Avidius Cassius captures the Euphrates line from the Parthians – Nisibis and Ctesiphon captured - Osrhoene conquered - I Minervia, II Adiutrix, III Gallica, IV Scythica, V Macedonica, XVI Flavia
167 A.D.	Eastern armies bring plague to the West Marcomanni under Balomar, and Jazyges attack Pannonia, Raetia, Noricum and reach Northern Italy

167-172 A.D.	Marcomanni War along the Danube - I Adiutrix, II Adiutrix, II Italica, III Italica, V Macedonica, XII Fulminata, XIII Gemina

MARCUS AURELIUS (169-180 A.D.)

169 A.D.	Didius Julianus campaigns against the Chatti in Lower Germany
170 A.D.	Chatti invade Italy and burn Opitergium Costobocci and Ostrogoths defeat and kill Marcus Claudius Fronto, destroy Serdica, Moesia and reach Athens - I Italica, IV Flavia, XI Claudia
171 A.D.	Moors invade Mauritania Tingitania and Baetica Marcomanni and Quadi invade Italy, attack Aquilea, Italy, kill Macrinus Vindex and are defeated in retreat by Tiberius Claudius Pompeianus – II Italica, III Italica, V Macedonica Gratus Julianus defeats the Costobocci in Thessaly
172 A.D.	Chauci attack the coast of Gaul but are defeated by Didius Julianus Marcus Aurelius defeats the Quadi and Cotini in Pannonia - V Macedonica, XII Fulminata Gaius Avidius Cassius crushes an uprising in Egypt by the Boucoloi – II Traiana
173 A.D.	Marcus Aurelius campaigns against the Marcomanni, Quadi and Sarmatians in Pannonia - V Macedonica
174 A.D.	Gaius Avidius Cassius revolts in Egypt and defeats II Traiana Quadi and Sarmatians attack Raetia, Noricum and Pannonia but are defeated by Didius Julianus and Pertinax - V Macedonica
175 A.D.	Gaius Avidius Cassius captures Antioch, Syria but is assassinated Marcus Aurelius defeats the Sarmatians and Jazyges in Pannonia - III Augusta, V Macedonica
177 A.D.	Suebi invade Pannonia - Bassaeus Rufus killed
179 A.D.	Taruttienus Paternus defeats the Marcomanni and Quadi in Pannonia - V Macedonica

COMMODUS (180-192 A.D.)

180 A.D.	Commodus defeats the Quadi in Pannonia
180-182 A.D.	Berber campaign in Mauritania - III Augusta
184 A.D.	Ulpius Marcellus defeats the Maeatae in Lowland Scotland Bruttius Praesens campaigns against Sarmatians and Jazyges in Pannonia
185 A.D.	Maternus revolt in Gaul. His deserters invade Spain
188-189 A.D.	Campaigns against the Quadi and Marcomanni in Pannonia

SEPTIMIUS SEVERUS (193-211 A.D.)

194 A.D.	Septimius Severus with I Italica, I Adiutrix, II Adiutrrix, II Italica, III Italica, IV Flavia, V Macedonica, VII Claudia, X Gemina, XI Claudia, and XIV Gemina defeats Gaius Pescennius Niger with III Gallica, IV Scythica, X Fretensis, XII Fulminata, and XV Apollinaris at Nicaea and Issos, Syria
194-195 A.D.	Septimius Severus campaigns against the Parthians in Mesopotamia
196 A.D.	Septimius Severus captures Byzantium in Thrace

197 A.D.	Septimius Severus with I Minervia, III Italica, VIII Augusta, XXII Primigenia and XXX Ulpia defeats Decimus Clodius Albinus with II Augusta, VI Victrix, VII Gemina and XX Valeria at Lyon, Gaul Maeatae attack Northern Britain Parthians under Vologaises V invade Mesopotamia
197-202 A.D.	Septimius Severus recaptures Mesopotamia, captures Ctesiphon from the Parthians but cannot capture Hatra in southern Mesopotamia. Northern Mesopotamia annexed – II Adiutrix, II Parthica
203 A.D.	Scotti attack Britain
206 A.D.	Alfenus Senecio campaigns against the Scotti in Britain
209-210 A.D.	Septimius Severus defeats the Caledonians in Scotland - II Augusta, VI Victrix, XX Valeria

CARACALLA (211-217 A.D.)

213 A.D.	Marcomanni attack Dacia - II Augusta, II Adiutrix, V Macedonica, VI Victrix, XIII Gemina Caracalla defeats the Alemanni and Chatti near Mainz, Upper Germany – II Adiutrix, II Traiana, II Parthica, III Italica
214 A.D.	Caracalla defeats the Goths, Quadi, Jazyges and Carpi in Dacia and on the Danube – I Adiutrix
215 A.D.	Caracalla suppresses riots in Alexandria, Egypt - II Traiana
216 A.D.	Caracalla annexes Osrhoene, Armenia invaded, Arbela and Assur in Parthia captured - I Adiutrix, I Parthica, II Adiutrix, II Parthica, III Italica, III Parthica, IV Scythica

MACRINUS (217-218 A.D.)

217 A.D.	Macrinus is defeated by the Parthians at Nisibis, Mesopotamia - I Adiutrix, II Parthica, IV Scythica
218 A.D.	Gannys defeats Macrinus and III Gallica and IV Scythica at Inmae near Antioch, Syria – II Parthica

SEVERUS ALEXANDER (222-235 A.D.)

223 A.D.	The Parthian Ardashir defeats Severus Alexander
231-233 A.D.	Parthian invasion of Mesopotamia under Ardashir repulsed - I Italica, I Parthica, II Parthica, III Parthica, IV Scythica
233-234 A.D.	Alemanni, Chatti and Hermundure overwhelm part of the German Limes and attack Raetia

MAXIMINUS THRAX (235-238 A.D.)

235 A.D.	Parthians conquer Mesopotamia
235-236 A.D.	Maximinus Thrax defeats the Alemanni in Germany - II Parthica
237 A.D.	Maximinus Thrax campaigns against the Sarmatians and Dacians on the Danube – I Adiutrix, II Adiutrix, II Italica
238 A.D.	Capellianus suppresses the revolt of Marcus Antonius Gordianus Sempronianus in Numidia - III Augusta Goths attack Moesia Maximinus with I Adiutrix defeated at Aquileia

GORDIAN III (238-244 A.D.)

240 A.D.	Parthians under Schapur capture Hatra, Carrhae and Nisibus, Mesopotamia - II Parthica, III Parthica Baquates attack Mauritania Menophilus defeats the Carpi and Goths in Moesia
242 A.D.	Gaius Furius Sabinus Aquila Timesitheus defeats an invasion of Thrace by Alans, Ostrogoths, Sarmatians - I Italica, XI Claudia Alemanni attack Noricum
243 A.D.	Gaius Furius Sabinus Aquila Timesitheus defeats the Parthians at Mesopo, Mesopotamia and recovers the province - II Parthica
244 A.D.	Alemanni invade Gaul Parthians defeat Gordian III at Misikhe near Baghdad on the Euphrates – I Parthica, II Parthica, III Parthica

PHILIPP THE ARAB (244-249 A.D.)

245 A.D.	Philip the Arab defeats the Carpi after they raid Dacia
247 A.D.	Germans attack on the Rhine
249 A.D.	Decius defeats an invasion of Moesia by Goths and Carpi - I Italica, IV Flavia, VII Claudia, XI Claudia Philip the Arab killed at the battle of Beroa, Macedonia by the Moesian and Pannonian armies under Decius

DECIUS (249-251 A.D.)

250 A.D.	Goths under Kniva capture Philippopolis and Beroia in Thrace
251 A.D.	Goths defeat and kill Decius at Abrittus, Scythia - I Italica, IV Flavia, VII Claudia, XI Claudia

TREBONIANUS GALLUS (251-253 A.D.)

252 A.D.	Parthian victory by Schapur at Barbalissos, Mesopotamia on the Euphrates leads to their capture of Antioch and Belkis in Syria – I Parthica, II Parthica Goths attack Turkey and plunder Ephesus and Pessinuntum Alemanni raid Gaul Aemilianus with the Moesian legions defeats and kills Trebonianus Gallus at Terni
253 A.D.	Aemilianus reconquers Illyria from the Goths

VALERIAN AND GALLIENUS (253-260 A.D.)

253 A.D.	Gallienus defeats the Franks and Alemanni raiding Gaul and Raetia Goths advance into Thessaly - I Italica, VII Claudia Berber raids in Numidia, Blemmyes raid Egypt
254 A.D.	Gallienus campaigns against the Marcomanni in Pannonia Alemanni attack Upper Germany and Raetia
255 A.D.	Franks attack across the Rhine Gallienus campaigns against the Goths in Dacia and Moesia – V Macedonica, XIII Gemina
256 A.D.	Gallienus defeats the Alemanni on the Rhine Parts of Dacia conquered by the Carpi - V Macedonica, XIII Gemina Goths destroy Pityus on the Bosporus and Trabzon, Pontus

	Parthians defeat Valerian at Barbalissus and capture Dura Europos, Mesopotamia, Zeugma, and Antioch, Syria - I Adiutrix, I Parthica, II Adiutrix, III Cyrenaica, IV Scythica, X Gemina Gaius Macrinius Decianus suppresses a Berber uprising in Numidia and Mauritania
257 A.D.	Gallienus defeats the Alemanni in Gaul Goths cross the Bosporus into Turkey Parthians invade Armenia and are defeated - XV Apollinaris
258 A.D.	Ingenuus revolts in Pannonia and is opposed by Gallienus and the Rhine legions + II Parthica Franks invade Gaul and march toward Spain Goths capture Chalcedon, Nicomedia and Nicea in Bythynia on the Sea of Marmorera
260 A.D.	Alemanni under Chrocus cross the Rhine between Mainz and Basel, Germany, invade Italy and are defeated by Gallienus near Milan – I Italica, I Minervia, II Italica, II Parthica, III Italica, V Macedonica, VII Claudia, VIII Augusta, XI Claudia, XIII Gemina, XIV Gemina, XXII Primigenia, XXX Ulpia Gallienus defeats the Alemanni and Juthungi near Augsburg, Raetia – I Italica, I Minervia, II Italica, II Parthica, III Italica, IV Flavia, V Macedonica, VII Claudia, VIII Augusta, XI Claudia, XIII Gemina, XIV Gemina, XXX Ulpia M. Aelius Aureolus defeats the Moesian and Pannonian legions of Ingenuus at Mursa, Pannonia P. Cornelius Regalianus defeats the Sarmatians in Upper Pannonia Parthians capture Carrhae and Nisibus, Mesopotamia, overrun Cappadocia, Cilicia, and Syria, and defeat and capture Valerian near Edessa - I Adiutrix, I Parthica, II Adiutrix, III Cyrenaica, VI Ferrata, X Gemina
260-268 A.D.	Franks invade Spain and destroy Tarragona

GALLIENUS (260-268 A.D.)

261 A.D.	M. Aelius Aereolus defeats the Eastern legions of T. Fulvius Junius Macrianus in Illyria
261-265 A.D.	Marcus Cassianius Latinius Postumus defeats the Franks in Lower Germany
262 A.D.	Odenathus of Palmyra captures Carrhae, Nisibus and Mesopotamia from the Parthians Franks invade Baetica in Spain Aurelius Theodotus suppresses the revolt of Mussius Aemilianus in Egypt - XII Fulminata, XV Apollinaris
263 A.D.	Sarmatians burn Callatis, Dacia
264-268 A.D.	Goths overrun Greece and Turkey capturing Athens, Corinth, Argos, Sparta, Olympia, Rhodes, Ephesus and are defeated by M. Aurelius Claudius (Gothicus)
266 A.D.	Odenathus of Palmyra defeats the Parthians at Ctesiphon
267 A.D.	Odenathus of Palmyra defeats the Goths in Armenia
268 A.D.	Claudius Gothicus defeats Marcus Aelius Aureolus at Pontirolo, Italy Claudius Gothicus defeats the Alemanni in Italy near the Garda Lake Franks invade Mauritania Goths and Herules raid through Upper Moesia and plunder Athens, Greece Saxons begin to raid Britain

CLAUDIUS GOTHICUS (268-270 A.D.)

269 A.D.	Claudius Gothicus defeats the Goths at Nis, Moesia L. Messius Aemilianus suppresses raids of the Blemmyes in Egypt Palmyrenes under Zabdas conquer Syria and Egypt - III Cyrenaica defeated Marcus Cassianius Latinius Postumus with I Minervia and XXX Ulpia defeats Ulpius Cornelius Laelianus with VIII Augusta and XXII Primigenia

270 A.D.	Claudius Gothicus destroys the Gothic army at Mount Haemus in Thrace Probus reconquers Egypt – II Traiana, III Cyrenaica

AURELIAN (270-275 A.D.)

270 A.D.	Aurelian defeats an Alemanni raid across the Rhine Marcomanni, Vandals, Sarmatians attack across the Danube
271 A.D.	Aurelian abandons Dacia to the Goths and Vandals Aurelian defeats the Juthungi, Sarmatians, Vandals and Goths in Pannonia and Placentia in Northern Italy Gaius Pius Esuvius Tetricus repels a German attack on Gaul
272 A.D.	Aurelian defeats the Goths on the Danube Aurelian defeats Zenobia of Palmyra at Immae and Emesa in Osrhoene
273 A.D.	Aurelian defeats the Carpi in Lower Moesia Aurelian suppresses an uprising at Palmyra
274 A.D.	Aurelian defeats the army of Tetricus near Châlons-sur-Marne, Gaul Aurelian defeats the Alemanni in Gaul and at Augsburg, Raetia
275 A.D.	Aurelian campaigns against the Juthungi in Pannonia

TACITUS (275-276 A.D.)

275 A.D.	Franks, Burgundians and Vandals destroy 70 cities in Gaul including Bonn
276 A.D.	Juthungi attack Switzerland Tacitus defeats the Herules in Thrace and the Alans in Cappadocia Goths attack Pontus, Cilicia, Galatia and penetrate to Ankara, Anatolia

PROBUS (276-282 A.D.)

277 A.D.	Probus defeats the Alemanni and Franks and pacifies Gaul Probus defeats the Vandals and restores the Danube frontier
278 A.D.	Probus defeats the Burgundians and Vandals in Gaul and pacifies Raetia Terentius Marcianus defeats the Isaurians at Cremna in Turkey
279 A.D.	Probus expels the Goths and Getae from Thrace and Illyria
280 A.D.	Proculus defeats the Alemanni in Gaul Probus pacifies Isauria, Pamphylia and Lycia
281 A.D.	Probus defeats the Blemmyes in upper Egypt

CARUS (282-283 A.D.)

283 A.D.	Carinus campaigns in Germany Carus, Carinus and Numerian defeat the Sarmatians and Quadi on the Danube Carus captures and destroys Ctesiphon, Coche and Seleucia on the Tigris

CARINUS (283-285 A.D.)

284 A.D.	Carinus campaigns in Britain Carinus defeats and kills Marcus Aurelius Sabinus Julianus in Pannonia
285 A.D.	Diocletian with the Eastern army defeats and kills Carinus with the Western army at Margus, Moesia

DIOCLETIAN (284-305 A.D.)

285 A.D.	Diocletian campaigns against the Marcomanni and Sarmatians in Pannonia
286 A.D.	Maximian campaigns against the Bagaudae in Gaul
287 A.D.	Maximian defeats the Heruli, Chaibones, Franks, Alemanni and Burgundians in Gaul
288 A.D.	Alemanni raid Gaul and are defeated by Maximian Diocletian and Maximian campaign in Raetia against the Alemanni – XI Claudia
289 A.D.	Maximian is defeated by Carausius and the mobile army in Gaul
290 A.D.	Diocletian campaigns against the Saracens in Syria Aurelius Litua suppresses a Bavare uprising in Mauretania
291 A.D.	Campaign against the Franks in Gaul Alemanni cross the Rhine in Germany
292-293 A.D.	Diocletian campaigns against the Sarmatians in Pannonia
293 A.D.	Constantius Chlorus defeats the Franks in Gaul Constantius Chlorus captures Boulogne, Gaul, from Carausius and the Gallic mobile army
294 A.D.	Constantius Chlorus campaigns against the Alemanni on the Upper Danube Maximian campaigns against the Chamavi and Frisians in Germany
295 A.D.	Goths destroy Tropaeum Traiani in Dacia Diocletian suppresses an uprising in Egypt
296 A.D.	Asclepiodotus defeats Allectus and II Augusta, XX Valeria in Britain Maeatae and Caledones raid Britain Parthians under Narses I defeat Galerius near Carrhae and capture Mesopotamia and Armenia Maximian defeats the Moors in Africa
297 A.D.	Galerius defeats the Carpi, Bastarni and Goths on the Lower Danube Galerius defeats the Parthian Narses and reconquers Mesopotamia and Armenia Franks attack Spain and North Africa
298 A.D.	Constantius Chlorus defeats the Alemanni at Windisch, Upper Germany and Langres, Gaul Maximian defeats the Baquates, Bavares, Quinquegentanai in North Africa, but is forced to evacuate Mauritania - II Parthica, XI Claudia Diocletian crushes the revolt of Aurelius Achilleus in Alexandria, Egypt
299 A.D.	Constantius Chlorus campaigns across the Rhine in Germany Galerius campaigns against the Marcomanni and Sarmatians along the Danube

Appendices

A. The Origin of the Augustan Legions

It is a matter of controversy as to which of the Augustan legions can trace their origins back to Julius Caesar and which were first formed by the members of the II Triumvirate, Octavian, Antonius and Lepidus. After Julius Caesar had defeated the Pompeians at Pharsalus and Thapsus in 48-45 B.C., the Pompeian legions appear to have been disbanded, although many of their legionaries were incorporated into the Caesarian legions.

Caesar then discharged his older legions VI-XIII and transferred the younger men to the formations that remained. The eagles of the discharged legions were undoubtedly returned to the Aerarium in Rome until they were needed again.

After Caesar's assassination, there was a scramble to recruit new legions to first defeat "the Liberators", Brutus and Cassius, and then to settle the ultimate succession. Octavian remained in Italy and thus was able to reform legions VI-XIII with young Italians stiffened by some of Caesar's retired veterans. The reconstituted legions received back their Caesarian eagles and thought of themselves as successors to the heroes of the Gallic Wars. Other formations which continued to exist on one side or another also pointed toward an ancient connection with Julius Caesar, and therefore a measure of their respectability, by their choice of name or legionary symbol, even though there were few legionaries present who had ever seen Caesar.

Augustus' reorganization of the Roman army after his victory at Actium in 31 B.C. took all of these vanities into account. Of the legions which we believe to have fought at Actium and which were retained in Augustus' new army, almost half had fought for Antonius and lost. The continued use of their numbers and names, even where two or more legions in the new army would bear the same number, seems to support an Augustan policy of reconciliation within the army. This also emphasizes the importance that the Augustan army administration placed on legion tradition. The campaign and retirement losses of the retained legions were made good by transferring citizen soldiers from those Augustan and Antonian legions which were too reduced in strength to be worth rebuilding. The newer legions on both sides made up primarily of non-citizens were disbanded. Where two or more legions were combined, and included contingents large enough to provoke an identity crisis, the name Gemina was used to set a neutral and non-controversial tone. Trained legionaries were too valuable an asset to be wasted for political revenge.

Efforts have been made to trace the antecedents of the Augustan legions by reference to their names or to the symbols they carried. The bull should indicate an association with Caesar, and Capricorn with Augustus. This theory is weakened by the bull legions V Macedonica and VI Victrix, which were not Caesarian, and the Capricorn legion II Augusta which almost certainly was. The Caesarian association enabled certain legions of Antonius which survived the Augustan reorganization, III Gallica, V Alaudae, VI Ferrata, and the famous X and XII, to avoid the political odium of having been stationed in the wrong province at the wrong time.

It is usually argued that a legion which was reconstituted or reorganized should be considered to be a new legion and not a continuation of its predecessor in name or number. This is a mistake. If the 442nd Regimental Combat Team were reformed tomorrow in the American Army, it would proudly carry the battle honors won in Italy in World War II even if none of its new complement had been born when these honors were won. The tradition that soldiers believe in is the heart of a military unit. So, if legionaries fought under the symbol of the Caesarian bull, they would have considered themselves as part of a legion founded by the great Julius. It is worthy of note that most of the names and symbols of the Augustan legions remained until the end of the Empire. It would therefore be wrong to deny antiquity to those legions that were so determined to believe in it.

B. THE IMPORTANCE OF A LEGION'S NAME

Legions had numbers from very early times. During the Republic, Legions were disbanded at the end of each campaigning season and reformed as and when needed. When fighting was due to start again, legionaries would be assigned to newly formed legions. They did not belong to them from one season to the next. Nicknames for legions arose as soon as the legions sensed that they had become part of a permanent army. The name X Equestris appears in the decade of the 50s B.C. when the legion was used to move, but not to fight, on horseback. The name was a pun, so beloved by soldiers, on the equestrian class in Rome. Subsequently, Colonia Julia Equestris Noviodunum received its name prior to Julius Caesar's death in 44 B.C. at Nyon, Switzerland, for veterans of his Legio X Equestris. While the colony, sited to block the Helvetians from further adventures in Gaul, may only have been populated after the Civil Wars, its name was an official recognition of that legion's cognomen before 44 B.C.

Names seem to have been coined by the legions themselves in some cases and officially adopted later to increase élan and to simplify the differentiation between several legions with the same number. A legion's name could be changed when circumstances changed. A number could not. X Equestris became X Gemina Equestris when a block of legionaries from another unit were amalgamated with it, and ultimately simply X Gemina in Octavian's reorganization about 30 B.C. This was the moment when the last of Julius Caesar's veterans would have been retired.

During the decade after the Augustan reorganization, legion names appear less often in inscriptions. The is a consequence of the retirement or discharge of large numbers of legionaries during the reorganization and their replacement by men from legions that had disappeared. The newcomers were less involved in the traditions of their new legions and their indifference is reflected in their inscriptions. As the proportion of a legion's men who had served most of their active lives in the same unit increased, the identity of the legion and thus its name became more important. Toward the end of the decade, many of the old names came back into common use. The loss of Legio I's name in 19 B.C., at the time of its disgrace in Spain, shows that this was a punishment that the legionaries were expected to feel. Interestingly, the old legionary symbols (Bull, Capricorn, etc.) continued to be used even during the period when names seem to have fallen into disuse.

Legion names can be divided into categories. Geographic names (e.g. Gallica, Macedonica, Cyrenaica, Germanica, Scythica, Hispana) came from provinces where the legion was raised or where it had once served with distinction. Another series (Paterna, Antiqua, Veneria, Veterana) testify to the seniority that certain legions wished to project for themselves. A third series commemorated battle honors which the legion had won (Mutinensis, Victrix, Triumphalis). A final group (Ferrata, Equestris, Rapax, Fulminata, Alaudae) were slogans or characteristics which would remind the world that this legion was different. From the time of the Augustan reorganization and afterwards, emperors also granted their personal names to certain legions as a sign of special honor. The legion might drop the name upon the death of an unpopular emperor, such as Domitian, or retain it until the end. From the time of Caracalla about 213 A.D., most if not all legions added the name of the current emperor to their older titles during the time of his reign.

When a legion had performed a particular service to an emperor, for example by electing to join the winning side, it might be awarded additional titles, most often Pia = Loyal and Fidelis = Faithful. Victrix = Victorious was sometimes added when the legion had won a notable battle. There does not seem to have been a serious competition for new names. The rather drab "Gemina" was given to four legions (VII, X, XIII, and XIV) and was never changed although these four gave as good an account of themselves as any other legions.

By the year 20 B.C., each legion would appear to have had a title even if not all can be documented in inscriptions. The only legions for whom we have no certain names at this time are XI, and the ill-fated XVII, XVIII, and XIX which were destroyed in the Varian Disaster of 9 A.D. It seems probable that the latter 3 legions also had names and that they were those they had carried before the Augustan reorganization: Classica, Libyca, and Paterna.

C. THE LEGIONARY EAGLES

The eagle represented and symbolized the legion. It provided a continuity to its foundation. Loss or destruction of a legion's eagle would damage the morale of the unit to an extreme degree. Despite the importance of the eagle to the story of the legions, we know comparatively little about them. It is recorded that Marius made the eagle the paramount symbol of the legions in 106 B.C. When a Republican eagle was not in the field with its legion, it was kept in the Aerarium in Rome. In Caesar's time, the eagle was small enough to carry under the arm, was made of silver, and took the form of an eagle with raised wings holding a thunderbolt. "Later", whenever later was, eagles were made of solid gold. None of the legionary eagles has survived, and the representations on antique monuments are crude.

The story of the legionary eagles in Imperial times is therefore one of surmise and analytic detective work based upon probabilities. For this reason, scholars have tended to avoid too much detail on what would be a fascinating subject.

If the Caesarian eagles were silver and later eagles were gold, then there must have been a changeover at some point. The changeover would have applied to the army as a whole to avoid jealousy between those legions carrying the old and those carrying the new eagles. Augustus is supposed to have inherited the remnants of 60 legions when he had finished disposing of all of his competitors for the throne. It seems unlikely that all of these legions, hurriedly raised by a half dozen different generals, would have been carrying golden eagles prior to Actium in 31 B.C.

Equally, it is probable that legionary eagles carried the number of the legion without names. Names of legions changed, but numbers did not. A legion would want to be certain that it always had "its" eagle and not that of another less honorable unit. In a melée on the battlefield or an administrative mistake before or after a parade, unnecessary mix-ups were possible. It would have been equally important that there was no competition between legions to have larger or heavier eagles than the others.

Consequently, we can surmise that the legionary eagles were fabricated in Rome in an imperial workshop according to a standard specification. They would have been presented personally by the ruling emperor on the "natalis aquilae" or official birth date of the legion. This birthday was celebrated annually by each legion. It is tempting to believe that the first series of golden eagles were given to the legions which Augustus formed or reformed in his new army about 30 B.C. It is likely that subsequent emperors copied the Augustan eagles when they formed new legions.

The eagle, carried by the aquilifer in his bearskin, led the legion whenever it moved as an entire unit. When the legion was in its base, the eagle was kept on display in the Aedes Signorum, a special chamber for it and other less important standards, in the heart of the Principia, the legion's headquarters building. Eagles without legions, those recovered from the enemy after a legion had been destroyed, or those from disbanded legions which had not been reconstituted, were probably stored at the Aerarium in Rome.

It is tantalizing to speculate whether a legionary eagle will ever be found. Being gold, it is far more probable that a Dark Age goldsmith turned the eagle into jewelry for a barbarian chief. It is harder to believe that the last legionary in a base on an abandoned frontier would sell his eagle to the metal dealer for his back pay.

D. THE TACTICS OF EXPANSION

From time to time, orders would go out from Rome, signed by the emperor of the time, for a combined force of legions and auxiliaries to cross an existing frontier to seize new territory for the Empire. Such decisions were anything but impulsive. Passive intelligence about the targeted region from Roman traders and native refugees would have been accumulating in Rome for years. Maps, estimates of the amount of resistance to be expected, lists of enemies and of friends and sympathizers, all would be sent to the commander of the invasion force.

Upon receipt of the orders, detailed planning began. The Roman army was a masterpiece of organization. Its numbers could never match those of the tribes around the Empire's rim. The army used its experience and discipline to compensate for its lack of size. The general information pack from Rome would be supplemented by up to date active intelligence provided by special scouting parties, legionaries dressed like tribesmen, who spoke the local dialect and who could infiltrate the target region to discover the mood of the inhabitants and their preparations for war.

From Mauritania to Moesia, the barbarians outside the Empire had a similar organizational handicap. Their social and political structures were based on the family or the clan. Various clans could make up a tribe, of allies and enemies, which had no central authority to organize a defence. A war leader could be named, but his power was consensual and his ability to discipline the warriors around him limited to the length of his sword. The invading legions could rely on having to fight, but they would be fighting against a mob of warriors rather than against a planned defense.

Based upon the intelligence he was able to gather, the legate or general who would lead the invasion began his preparations. The legions and auxiliary units who would march were alerted. Parts of them might remain behind to keep order on the old frontier, and to control the flow of supplies up to the front. Supply dumps were established up to the frontier, and beyond it wherever feasible. Reinforcements were requested - and usually denied. Guides were hired or bribed who could find their way through a wilderness that had no need for roads. The campaigning season started when the winter rains had stopped and the ground had dried enough to permit movement. Obviously, the season was much longer in Spain and Portugal than it was in Britain. Plans were written and distributed to each unit describing the route of march, expected resistance points, sites to be occupied, the timetable to be followed, and the maximum number of acceptable casualties.

Although each campaign required variations, there was a basic plan which was common to all of the conquests from Spain in 29 B.C. to the end of the Dacian Wars in 106 A.D. The legions marched as single units screened by auxiliaries, non-citizen units trained to find an enemy and pin him down until enough power came up to settle the issue. Ahead of the legions, units prepared a way over which the legionaries could march and maintain their formations. Behind the army, the way was improved into a road that could carry supplies up from the rear. Every night, a fortified marching camp of earth and wood was built in which the legionaries could erect their leather tents without concern about a surprise attack.

The immediate goal of the army was to bait the tribesmen into gathering for a major battle. Roman campaigns were directed against political entities, not to seize territory. A legion, fighting on ground of its own choice, was virtually invincible against any number of tribesmen. A set piece battle would end with the destruction of organized resistance to the Roman conquest. The job of mopping up could then begin.

The tribesmen might avoid a battle and retreat into the prehistoric earthworks scattered over most of Europe. With their cattle and families behind massive earthen walls, they might hope that the Roman army would go another way, or avoid a frontal assault. This was the second best outcome for the Roman army. Although casualties might be somewhat higher, the tribesmen were trapped and could be overcome at leisure. Field artillery, catapaults and spear throwers were brought forward, the enemy's will to fight was softened up, and then the legionaries went in with their swords to kill everything that moved until resistance stopped.

The third, and least desireable, form of conquest was when the tribesmen scattered into the forests and up into the high valleys. The Roman army could control the ground it stood on but, as long as significant numbers of armed warriors were wandering about, not more. The legions were dependent upon being supplied from far back to the rear over the military road they had built. Armed convoys could reach them, but there would never be enough convoy guards to protect their food from a serious attack. The will of the native population to resist needed to be broken before it resulted in a long guerilla war.

In hilly terrain, the army controlled the valley floors solely by its presence. At the mouth of each side valley, a fortlet would be built to protect a garrison of one or more centuries of auxiliaries. The garrison in its fortlet was large enough to protect itself from any natives who might spill out of the side valley until reinforcements could arrive. At the same time, the garrison could hunt down small parties of tribesmen who filtered into the main valley for food or shelter. The fugitives would surrender before winter or starve. The garrison could then move on to blockade another valley.

In the forests which stretched over most of Europe, the strategy of pacification was based upon logistics and attrition. If the Romans controlled the cleared land, they could requisition and seize whatever was grown there and transport the rest of their needs from bases in the rear. The tribesmen who had fled to the forests had a more difficult existence. They could raid the settled and Roman controlled regions for food, but that announced their presence and location. They could not support themselves with wild game alone. And they were hunted through the forest by auxiliaries and those of their own tribesmen who had inevitably been suborned by Roman gold and attention. Soon, they also would come out from between the trees and accept the Roman peace.

Having eliminated armed resistance, at least for the time being, the army would have had to then pacify a helpless but still hostile population. The legions could not leave soldiers in every settlement in newly conquered territory. The locals would outnumber the army by 50 100 to one. And the legions were wanted back at their winter bases for training and to prepare themselves for still another mission. Prisoners who had been taken in the fighting, or who were present where fighting had taken place, were collected. The disabled were killed, quickly and cleanly in the Roman manner with a single sword thrust. Warriors, 12-50 years old, were sold to the slave dealers who followed the army, and were marched off to another part of the Empire. They could not be permitted to remain in the territory. Tribal elders were often spared. There would never be enough Romans in the newly conquered territory to administer every village. Local leaders, who would be obeyed by the general population, would be an essential asset in 'Romanizing' the countryside. The aged, and mothers with children, were allowed to pick up the pieces of their lives and to rebuild the economy of the region. A generation later, it was hoped that only distant memories would remain of their former feral freedom. Often, the remaining population would be forcibly resettled away from their hilltop fortifications. The Roman Pax would now protect them from the need to defend themselves. To keep order, auxiliaries were scattered across the territory in forts to keep order. The legions would then move forward as single units from the old frontiers to build new bases at strategically important points. Settlements of veterans were often established in newly conquered territories to increase the Roman influence over the local population.

Except in Germany across the Rhine and in northern Britain, the Roman ability to conquer new lands in Europe was successful. These two areas may well have been too back-ward in social and political development for their to be an indigenous authority. Without this authority, Romanization could hardly take hold. There would be no one in authority to control the local population in their day-to-day activity. The pacification process worked less certainly. Local uprisings broke out periodically in every province. Some were caused by incomplete pacification. The army left too quickly, and too many unregenerate warriors were left behind. Others were caused by overreaching on the part of a new Roman civil administration which saw too many opportunities to become rich on the backs of a seemingly supine population. These uprisings were suppressed with the same pacification techniques used when the region was first conquered: execution, enslavement, and resettlement. Eventually, either hopelessness, or the material benefits brought by the Empire, "civilized" the remainder of the population.

In the East, the situation was quite different. City- and nation-states had existed there as long as Rome had. They were ruled by dynastic monarchs and a mature system of civil administration. The expansion of the Roman Empire to the East took a different form. The preferred tactic was to threaten the local ruler into becoming a "client king" of Rome. Rome granted him his crown for his lifetime and his good behavior. He could retain all of the trappings of monarchy except that he reigned rather than ruled. Units of the Roman army were stationed in his kingdom to ensure that his foreign and financial policies were compatible with what Rome wished. His children were invited to Rome to receive a classical education and would serve as hostages lest he forget who he really was. At his death, it was Rome who decided on his successor or whether the kingdom was to become a normal province ruled by a Roman governor. The advantage of this system for the Romans was that the client king would defend his territory with his own resources, human and material. Some of his assets would also undoubtedly end up in Rome.

This approach of peaceful annexation was possible because the population was already conditioned to be ordered in most aspects of their lives. The traditional ruler was now only being supplanted by another authority and, as long as their individual circumstances were not markedly worse, the general population did not care who occupied the palace. If the ruler was difficult and refused the Roman offer, the army could be sent in. Because these states were organized and politically developed, the legions would then be opposed by the military forces of the ruler, and not by a national resistance. When the local army had been defeated, the issue would be settled permanently. Moreover, survivors of the defeated forces could be retrained as auxiliaries in the Roman army and sent to another part of the Empire.

There were, of course, later uprisings against Roman rule in the East as in the West, in particular the various Jewish revolts of the 1st and 2nd Centuries. Such uprisings, however, had also occurred under the rulers before the Romans came and probably would have broken out under any other authority. These uprisings were suppressed with the same ruthlessness as those in the West. One refinement in the East, however, was the use of exemplary punishment, such as crucifixion. Because the East was so much more civilized than the West, a public demonstration of suffering made a more lasting impression on would be troublemakers. In the West, a death was a death and sent no particular message to anyone not directly affected.

Although the Roman army succeeded in conquering populations many times larger than its own, the price in human terms was enormous. It is estimated that half of the population of what is modern France died or was enslaved in the 10 years that it took Julius Caesar to conquer and reconquer that region. It is probable that similar statistics held true for the campaigns to conquer northwestern Spain and Portugal, the reconquest of Illyricum in 6-9 A.D., and in the two wars in Dacia. At the same time, those portions of the native populations left free maintained their original cultures and rebuilt their economies within a few decades.

One cannot speak of genocide. Those who accepted the new state of things were allowed and encouraged to maximize their quality of life. Taxes and requisitions burdened their lives, but did not destroy them. Scattered uprisings in the future would be suppressed quickly and decisively in police actions against those who were considered to be disturbing the peace. Once conquered, the tribes were no longer treated as enemies. The seeming brutality of the pacification process by modern standards must be measured in the context of what the Romans intended to accomplish, and what means they had available to them. The disparity of numbers between the Roman military and the peoples they conquered required radical solutions. Romans considered themselves to be bringers of civilization to barbarians, much like the Europeans in Africa in the 19th Century. They sincerely believed that Rome had a Manifest Destiny to 'civilize' the known world under her leadership. By the standards of the time, the Romans probably used a minimum of force to reach these ends. The killing was not a sport, but a necessity to successfully effect a preplanned policy. Enslavement was not considered evil. It was a fact of everyday life in every civilization inside and outside the Empire. The Romans used enslavement or resettlement, as in the case of the Diaspora, as a way to remove a problem before it became one. A comparison of the differences between the development of Ireland, which the Romans never reached, and England where they conquered a very similar Celtic population leads one to wonder whether the cure was not worth the pain.

JEROME H. FARNUM

E. WHEN AND WHY WERE LEGIONS DISBANDED?

It is something of a mystery as to why certain legions disappeared in a crisis, and others, in the face of a similar disaster, did not. Some legions suffered defeats with heavy casualties and even lost their eagles, but were rebuilt and served on for another century. Others disappeared leaving no evidence as to why. No legion was ever totally annihilated. There were always some survivors as well as base troops from even the XVII, XVIII and XIX legions that were overrun in the Teutoberger Forest with Varus in 9 A.D. It was therefore an administrative decision whether a legion that had failed was rebuilt or disbanded.

To understand how this decision might have been made, it is useful to compare those situations where a choice arose to either rebuild or disband during the 200 years from Augustus to Diocletian.

1) In 17 B.C., the German Sugambri raided across the Rhine into northeastern Gaul. The Roman governor, Marcus Lollius, led V Alaudae, just transferred from Spain, against the raiders. The bulk of the legion must have left its base at Neuss because the legionary eagle was on the scene. The Germans attacked and the legion did not hold. In the ensuing flight, V Alaudae's eagle was lost to the enemy. Casualties, on the other hand, do not seem to have been severe. The legion was laughed at throughout the army for the "Clades Lolliana", but was not cashiered. Presumably, the missing eagle was soon recaptured or ransomed as there were none of the dramatic campaigns to recover it that followed the loss of the Varian eagles.

2) The Varian Disaster of 9 A.D. was one of the worst defeats that the Roman army suffered in the Imperial period. Three eagles and three legions were lost, XVII Classica, XVIII Libyaca, and XIX Paterna. Their eagles were eventually recovered after campaigns undertaken primarily for that purpose, but these legions were never reformed. The three legions seem to have been attacked on the march and then overrun by the main body of German Cherusci before they could concentrate. The bulk of the legions fought to the last man, and the few who tried to surrender were sacrificed in the German manner.

Despite the magnitude of the disaster, there was a significant number of survivors from each of the legions. Holding garrisons had been left at the legion bases, Nijmegen, Xanten, and Cologne. Logistic supply points had been established along the legions' marching route and were, however lightly, garrisoned. And there were survivors who fought their way back through the tribesmen and reported what had happened. It may well be that 10-20% of the legionaries assembled back on the Rhine, albeit momentarily demoralized. These legions, however, were not reconstituted, and their numbers were never again reused.

3) In 61 A.D., the Boudiccan uprising broke out in Britain. IX Hispana sent a vexillation of some 2000 men plus cavalry, nearly half of its available manpower, south to the scene. The eagle did not accompany the vexillation. The Roman force was overwhelmed, and only the legate and a few scattered horsemen escaped from the battlefield. IX Hispana was reinforced and continued with its mission of pacifying Britain for another 60 years.

4) In 62 A.D., Lucius Caesennius Paetus was given command of IV Scythica and XII Fulminata plus auxiliaries, and ordered to reconquer Armenia from the Parthians. At Rhandeia, his force was smashed. Historical sources, which normally minimize Roman casualties, report that IV Scythica and XII Fulminata lost more than half of their legionaries and were forced to retreat from the province. The eagles, however, do not seem to have been lost. The legions were reinforced and served on in the provinces of Syria and Palestine.

5) XII Fulminata was rebuilt but does not seem to have recovered from its Rhandeian experience. A Jewish uprising blazed out in 66 A.D. and XII Fulminata was sent from Rafniyeh in Syria to Palestine to deal with it. In the first year of the war, led or misled by Cestius Gallus, it was ambushed in retreat from Jerusalem in the Beth Horon pass. The legion abandoned its artillery, its baggage train and, worst of all, lost its eagle, although it would appear only temporarily so. XII Fulminata stole away in the night sacrificing one full cohort as a rear guard. Subduing the Jewish uprising went on without XII Fulminata, and the Vespasian expedition to Italy left the legion behind. XII Fulminata was "exiled" to Cappadocia to watch over the newly organized XVI Flavia and continued its existence to the end of the Empire.

6) When Vespasian reached Rome in 69 A.D. to assume the purple, one of his first acts was to reorganize the army on the Rhine frontier. All of the seven Rhine legions had sworn allegiance to Vitellius. Three of them, V Alaudae, XXI Rapax and XXII Primigenia, plus I Italica from Lyon and vexillations from the other Rhine and British legions, had fought against the Vespasianic forces at Bedriacum II. They had suffered heavy casualties in the two battles and, at the end, the four full legions were forced to surrender. During that time, supporters of Vespasian had instigated an uprising in Gaul and Germany to distract the Vitellian forces. The rebel army, led by Civilis, annihilated one legion, XV Primigenia, and the headquarters personnel of V Alaudae at Xanten on the Rhine. The three remaining Rhine legions, I

Germanica, IV Macedonica and XVI Gallica committed the ultimate sin of swearing allegiance to Civilis and his New Gallic Empire. In the campaign that followed, these three legions surrendered to Cerialis, Vespasian's general, without a major battle.

The Vespasianic solution shows a mixture of realism and revenge. Four legions were officially disbanded: XV Primigenia from Xanten (which had been destroyed by Civilis), XVI Gallica from Neuss, I Germanica from Bonn and IV Macedonica from Mainz, the three that had forsworn their loyalty. The legions that had fought against the Vespasianic forces at Bedriacum II received back their eagles, were reinforced, and relocated elsewhere in Vespasianic service.

Two new legions were formed using the numbers carried by the disbanded legions: IV Flavia Felix, and XVI Flavia Firma. It would seem that, if Vespasian had wanted the memory of the disloyal legions erased, he would have chosen different numbers for his newly created units. There was already another IV legion, IV Scythica, in service, so symmetry is not the entire answer. It is probable that the survivors of the old IV Macedonica were not executed or discharged but were incorporated into the new IV Flavia. Raising an additional 5,000 new volunteers in the aftermath of what was considered to be a civil war would not have been easy. Trained legionaries were a military asset of great value. Their loyalty to Vitellius could be redirected by new officers. IV Flavia was posted to Kistanje, Dalmatia, a quiet backwater suitable for recruiting and training. XVI Flavia was raised in the East and went to Kelkit, Cappadocia where it would never be a threat to internal order.

VII Galbiana, formed by Galba in Spain in 68 A.D., had fought against the Vitellian forces and had been defeated. It was taken into the new army by Vespasian. It was re-named VII Gemina at this time, normally a sign that it had absorbed a large number of legionaries from another unit, in this case perhaps I Germanica and XVI Gallica which had sworn loyalty to Cerialis without a fight and had been disbanded. VII Gemina was sent back to Spain, also well away from Italy and the throne. XV Primigenia, which had been annihilated by the army of Civilis, was not reconstituted although its eagle was soon recovered.

While Vespasian appeared on the surface to have taken retribution on that part of the army that had stood against him, in reality few of the surviving Vitellian legionaries seem to have missed a payday. Their officers, the centurionate, would have received no mercy.

7) The disappearance of V Alaudae has been a matter of some controversy among historians. The Dacians raided across the Danube into Moesia in 85 A.D., and succeeded in killing the Roman governor who was trying to organize the defense of the province. A year later, a counteroffensive was launched against the Dacians, led by the praetorian praefect, Cornelius Fuscus. The expedition of 86 A.D. into Dacia turned into a total defeat. Fuscus was killed, a legion reportedly destroyed, and an eagle captured. Domitian sent reinforcements to Moesia including IV Flavia, and Tettius Julianus defeated the Dacians at Tapae in 88 A.D. The historical dispute is whether V Alaudae was destroyed in 86 A.D. or later in 92 A.D. in a campaign against the Jazyges.

The Moesian garrison in 85 A.D. had consisted of four legions. The transfer of IV Flavia in 86 A.D. would have brought the number to an unusual five had V Alaudae still been in existence. Domitian then divided Moesia into Upper and Lower provinces. V Alaudae would have made the third legion in the Lower province. Moreover, at the end of the 1st Dacian War in 102 A.D., Trajan's diplomacy recovered the eagle of V Alaudae from the Dacians. The Dacians must therefore have destroyed V Alaudae and this could only have occurred in 85/86 A.D. Consequently, it would appear that it was V Alaudae that was destroyed with Cornelius Fuscus.

8) The end of XXI Rapax is a riddle within a mystery. XXI Rapax was transferred from Mainz, Germany to Ptuj, Pannonia following its participation in the Saturninus revolt of 89 A.D. and its subsequent defeat by loyal legions at Besançon. It remained at Ptuj until it disappeared. Conventional wisdom has it that it was the legion destroyed by the Jazyges in 92 A.D.

Two pieces of archeological data seem to call this theory into question. Following its disappearance, XXI Rapax was replaced in Ptuj by XIV Gemina from Mainz in Germany, its companion mutineer from the Saturninus affair. XIV Gemina was replaced in Mainz by XXII Primigenia from Xanten. Tiles have been found at Xanten made by XXII Primigenia which were fabricated after 96 A.D., the date of Domitian's assassination, when XXII Primigenia dropped the 'Domitiana' from its name. Therefore, XXII Primigenia did not move to Mainz before that date. Mainz was garrisoned by the Roman army continuously from 16 B.C. until at least 355 A.D. It is extremely unlikely that Mainz would have been left empty, as it would have been had XIV Gemina left for Pannonia in 92 A.D., and XXII Primigenia had only arrived after 96 A.D. Consequently, XIV Gemina must have remained at Mainz until at least 96 A.D., and XXI Rapax' disappearance be dated after that date.

A second fragment of history is a memorial inscription to a certain Numisius Sabinus who is stated to have been a tribune in XXI Rapax and later curator of the Via Traiana construct-ed in 109 A.D. After this, he became legate of I Italica and II Traiana in Moesia. It is extremely unlikely that Sabinus could have been a tribune in 92 A.D. or before with XXI Rapax and 20 years or more later legate of I Italica. This would say that XXI Rapax existed for a number of years after 92 A.D. and was not annihilated then.

An argument can also be made that the granting of the number of XXX Ulpia to the legion formed by Trajan in 99 A.D. can only be interpreted to mean that it was the thirtieth legion in the Roman army. This would mean that either V Alaudae or XXI Rapax was still in existence at the beginning of the 1st Dacian War. There is general agreement that V Alaudae was the first of the two legions to disappear. Therefore, XXI Rapax must have survived until the 1st Dacian War.

That being the case, what happened to XXI Rapax? This legion had blundered and been reorganized twice in 20 years, once after it had sworn allegiance to Vitellius, and again after supporting Saturninus. Its transfer to Ptuj was in the nature of an exile, not to serve a vital need.

One clue may be found in analyzing the movements of other legions. VI Victrix was stationed at Neuss in Germany from the Vespasianic relocations until the end of the 1st Century A.D. VI Victrix served in the 1st Dacian War from 101-102 A.D., and returned to Germany before the 2nd Dacian War of 104-106 A.D. Upon its return, it was stationed in Xanten replacing XXII Primigenia, and not at its original base in Neuss. Neuss was never reopened. Logic would have it that XXI Rapax was disbanded or destroyed in the 1st Dacian War in 101-102 A.D. and that, at that time, XIV Gemina moved to replace it at Ptuj. XXII Primigenia then moved from Xanten to Mainz to replace XIV Gemina. VI Victrix, perhaps having suffered heavy casualties in the 1st Dacian War, replaced XXII Primigenia at Xanten, a base which was less sensitive at that time than Mainz, but this could have only have taken place after 102 A.D. when the 1st Dacian War was over. If XXI Rapax disappeared only in 102 A.D., then all of these legionary movements would fit a reasonable pattern. I Adiutrix received its "Pia Fidelis" in 102 A.D. implying that it had shown its loyalty to the emperor above and beyond the call of duty. I Adiutrix was then based at Szony rather close to Ptuj.

On two inscriptions at Vindonissa, Switzerland, a former base of XXI Rapax, the name of the legion was erased in "damnatio memoriae" indicating that it had disgraced itself. Trajan formed a new legion, II Traiana, at about this date which maintained the number of legions in the army and may have been intended as a replacement for XXI Rapax. The number XXI was retired forever.

9) One of the mysteries that has fascinated British historians is the disappearance of IX Hispana about 122 A.D. It had been based at York, Britain. In 122 A.D., VI Victrix was transferred from Xanten, Germany to York. IX Hispana is recorded as having transited Nijmegen, Holland, a base which had been closed since 101 A.D. There is no firm information as to its whereabouts at any base thereafter. Theories that it might have survived to be destroyed in Judaea in 132 A.D., or in Armenia in 161 A.D. seem to be the wildest speculation. There are no bases where IX Hispana could have been stationed for the next 20 or 40 years without leaving some trace. Two inscriptions, however, give cause for confusion. (a) L. Aemilius Carus, a former tribune of IX Hispana, was praetorian governor of Arabia in 143 A.D. and suffect consul in 144 A.D. (b) L. Novius Crispinus, a former tribune of IX Hispana, was praetorian governor of Numidia in 147 A.D. and suffect consul in 150 A.D. While it is not impossible that 25 years should have passed from the time these former tribunes were appointed to be governors, it is at least unusual.

Roman legions did not rotate from duty station to duty station. There would have been no precedent and no reason for transferring VI Victrix from Xanten to York, and replacing it at Xanten with XXX Ulpia from Pannonia, unless IX Hispana was unable to carry out its function in Britain. XXX Ulpia was replaced in Pannonia by II Adiutrix from Dacia. It would be equally incomprehensible to transfer a legion from northern Britain to the East where it would be wholly without training to carry out its mission, when a legion in Dacia, 2 months' march closer to the Eastern provinces, was available to be transferred there.

Tiles have been found at Nijmegen with the mark of IX Hispana. This would indicate that there was still a unit officially bearing that title at the time the troops moved to Holland. It is therefore most unlikely that the legion was annihilated in Britain or that it was disbanded there. An indication that IX Hispana was disbanded at Nijmegen is the posting of the auxiliary units that had been attached to it in Britain. It was customary at this time that auxiliaries were permanently assigned to a particular legion. Where the legion went, went also its support units. In the case of IX Hispana, the auxiliaries that had served with it at York were also transferred with the legion to Nijmegen. Some years later, these same auxiliaries were back in Britain. If IX Hispana had continued to exist, it would have had to acquire a new constellation of auxiliaries. This would have been a further departure from the Empire-wide system of army organization.

The most probable answer is that IX Hispana had suffered serious losses in battle with British tribesmen and, additionally, had disgraced itself beyond the point where it could be reconstituted. We hear of a revolt of the Brigantes at about this time and a self-proclaimed Roman victory in 119 A.D. York is not far from Brigantian territory. On the other hand, Hadrian's Wall, begun about 121 A.D. faces north toward the Caledonians and not south toward the bulk of the Brigantes. There is no trace of Hadrian's Wall being even partially constructed by legionaries from IX Hispana so the legion must have been rendered useless before 121. It is more probably that IX Hispana failed in front of the Caledonians. That the legion was considered not to be worth rebuilding indicates that something worse than battle losses had occurred. Its surviving legionaries would have been transferred to other legions, probably on the Rhine frontier, with the advice to forget where they had come from. The eagle of the IX was retired and no new IX legion was ever formed.

10) Toward the end of his reign, the emperor Hadrian attempted to Hellenize the eastern provinces with the idea that this would reduce the constant friction between the various cultures to be found there. The Jews in Palestine revolted under Bar Kochba in 132 A.D. against the Hadrianic edicts. An additional legion, XXII Deiotariana, was called in from Alexandria to assist in crushing the uprising. This legion disappeared from the list of active legions during the Bar Kochba War. As the Jews were fighting a guerilla war, it is difficult to see how a full legion could be destroyed or even defeated. Talmudic sources, however, refer to the destruction of a legion, and it can only be XXII Deiotariana which they mean.

XXII Deiotariana had been stationed in Alexandria for more than 150 years, and may have been unfit for open field operations. The theory that the legion was overwhelmed in Alexandrian riots while its sister legion II Traiana survived does not seem to hold water. In any event, XXII Deiotariana must have disgraced itself to the point where it could not be reformed.

Because Roman authors are so reticent about their defeats, it requires a lot of detective work as well as a modicum of fantasy to come to logical answers as to why a certain legion was disbanded. It appears that the temporary loss of an eagle was not the sole criterion to be used for the decision. Equally, the number of casualties was not controlling. A relevant factor to be considered is the number of years - three to five - that were deemed necessary to bring a new legion from a collection of soldiers to a unit fit to carry out its missions. If the number of qualified centurions - excluding those who had failed in their recent duty - fell below a certain level, then a legion was beyond repair, and it would have been better to start with a new unit as and when sufficient manpower resources were available. At the same time, if the core of the legion remained, and its morale was not wholly destroyed, the ranks could be refilled and the legion would be fit for service long before a newly formed legion could be ready. The basis for a decision to rebuild or to disband a legion was the practical consideration of whether a skeleton still existed which could be fleshed out with transfers and new recruits. This skeleton would have been an effective centuriate, without which no legion could function. It was not the prestige factor of the loss of the eagle.

Selected Bibliography

Alföldy, G., Die Truppenverteilung der Donau Legionen am Ende des I. Jahrhunderts, (Acta. Arch. Hung. ll, 1959)

Biernacke-Lubanska, M., The Roman and early Byzantine Fortifications of Lower Moesia and Northern Thrace (Warsaw 1982)

Birley, E. B., The Fate of the Ninth Legion in Soldier and Civilian in Roman Yorkshire, pp. 71-80 (Leicester 1971)

Le Bohec, Y., L'Armée romaine sous le Haut-Empire (Paris 1989)

Le Bohec, Y., Les legions de Rome sous le Haut-Empire, Proceedings of a conference held at Lyon 1998 (Lyon 2000)

Bowersock, G.W., Roman Arabia (Cambridge 1983)

Breeze, D. & Dobson, B., Roman Officers and Frontiers (Stuttgart 1993)

Brewer, R.J. (ed.), Roman Fortresses and their Legions (London 2000)

Campbell, J.B., The Emperor and the Roman Army 31BC - AD235 (Oxford 1984)

Cataniciu, I.B., Evolution of the System of Defence Works in Roman Dacia, British Archaeological Reports, International Series 116 (Oxford 1981), pp. 1-115

Dabrowa, E., Legio X Fretensis, Historia 66 (Stuttgart 1993)

Dabrowa, E., The Commanders of the Syrian Legions in the Roman Army in the East (Ann Arbor 1996)

Domazewski, A., Die Rangordnung des römischen Heeres (rev. B. Dobson) (Cologne 1967)

Ferrill, A., The Fall of the Roman Empire (London 1986)

Filow, B., Die Legionen der Provinz Moesia von Augustus bis zu Diocletian (Leipzig 1906)

Forni, G., Il reclutamento delle Legioni da Augusto a Diocletiano (Milan 1963)

Freeman, P., The Annexation of Arabia and the Imperial Grand Strategy, The Roman Army in the East, Journal of Roman Archeology Supplement 18, (Ann Arbor 1996), pp. 91ff.

French, D., Legio III Gallica, The Roman and Byzantine Army in the East, pp. 29-46 (Krakow 1994)

Goquey, R. and Reddé, M., Le Camp légionaire de Mirebeau, Roemisch-Germanischen Zentralmuseum Monograph, Vol. 36 (Mainz 1995)

Grant, M., The Army of the Caesars (London 1974)

Hoffman, D., Das spätrömische Bewegungsheer und die Notitia Dignitatum (Duesseldorf 1969)

Holder, P.A., The Roman Army in Britain (New York 1982)

Isaac, B., Legio II Traiana in Judaea, Zeitschrift fuer Papyrologie und Epigraphik 33, (Bonn 1979), pp. 149/156

Isaac, B., The Limits of Empire (Oxford 1992)

Josephus, Flavius, The Jewish War (Philadelphia 1848)

Keay, S., Roman Spain (London 1988)

Kennedy, D.L., The Garrisoning of Mesopotamia in the Late Antonine and Early Severan Period, Antichthon 21, pp. 57-66 (1987)

Kennedy, D.L. & Riley, D., Rome's Desert Frontier from the Air (London 1990)

Keppie, L.J.F., The Making of the Roman Army (London 1984)

Keppie, L.J.F., Legions in the East from Augustus to Trajan; Freeman, P. and Kennedy D.L. (eds) The Defence of the Roman and Byzantine East, British Archeological Reports, International Series 297, (Oxford 1986), pp. 411-429

Keppie, L.J.F., The Fate of the Ninth Legion; A Problem for the Eastern Provinces, British Archeological Reports, International Series 553 (Oxford 1989), pp. 247-255

Keppie, L.J.F., The History and Disappearance of the Legion XXII Deiotariana, Greece and Rome in Eretz Israel, eds. A. Kasher and G. Fuks, (Tel Aviv 1990), pp. 54-61

Keppie, L.J.F., Legiones XVII, XVIII, XIX – Exercitus Omnium Fortissimus, Roman Frontier Studies 1995, pp. 393-397

Lepper, F.A., Trajan's Dacian War (Oxford 1948)

Lesquier, L'armée romaine d'Egypte d'Auguste à Diocletain (Cairo 1918)

Luttwak, E., The Grand Strategy of the Roman Empire (Baltimore 1976)

Marcos, V.G. & Hernandez, F.M., A New View on the Military Occupation in the Northwest of Spain during the First Century: The Case of Leon, Roman Frontier Studies 1995, pp. 355-359

Mattern, S.P., Rome and the Enemy (Berkeley 1999)

Millar, F., The Roman Near East 31 B.C. - A.D. 337 (Cambridge 1993)

Mitchell, S., Armies and Frontiers in Roman and Byzantine Anatolia (British Archeological Reports, International Series (Oxford 1983)

Mócsy, A., Pannonia and Upper Moesia (London 1974)

Mor, M., The Roman Army in Eretz-Israel in the Years 70-132 A.D.; Freeman, P. and Kennedy, D.L. (eds) The Defence of the Roman and Byzantine East, British Archeological Reports, International Series 297, pp. 575-602 (Oxford 1986)

Oldenstein-Pferdehirt, B. Die Geschichte der Legio VIII Augusta, Jahrbuch des Römisch-Germanischen Zentralmuseums (1984)

Parker, H.M.D., The Roman Legions (rev. Watson, Cambridge 1971)

Ritterling, E. & Kubitschek, W., Legio, Pauly-Wissowa, Realencyclopaedie der Klassischen Altertumswissenschaft (Stuttgart 1924), Legio, XII, 2

Le Roux, P., L'Armée romaine et l'organisation des Provences ibériques d'Auguste à l'invasion de 409 (Paris 1982)

Schönberger, H., Die römischen Truppenlager der frühen und mittleren Kaiserzeit zwischen Nordsee und Inn, Bericht der Römisch-Germanischen Kommission 66, pp. 322-496 (1985)

Sayer, R., Untersuchungen zu den Vexillationen der roemishen Kaiserheeres von Augustus Bis Diocletian; Epigraphische Studien 1 (Koln-Graz 1967)

Soproni, S., Die Letzten Jahrzehnten des Pannonischen Limes (Munich 1985)

Speidel, M.P., Augustus' Deployment of the Legions in Egypt, Chronique d'Egypte, LVIII (1982) pp. 120-124

Strobel, K. Die Donaukrieg Domitians (Bonn 1989)

Syme, R., The First Garrison of Trajan's Dacia; Laureae Aquincenses (1938)

Syme, R., The Conquest of North West Spain; Legio VII Gemina, pp. 83-107 (Leon 1970)

van Berchem, D., L'Armée de Diocletien et la réform constantinienne (Paris 1952)

Wagner, J., Legio IIII Scythica im Zeugma am Euphrat, Studien zu der Militärgrenze Roms, (1977) pp. 517-539

Wagner, J., Die Römer an Euphrat und Tigris, Antike Welt 16 (1985), pp. 3-72

Webster, G., The Roman Imperial Army (London 1985)

Webster, G., Fortress into City (London 1988)

Wellesley, K., The Long Year A.D. 69 (London 1975)

Welsby, D.A., The Roman Military Defence of the British Province in its Later Phases, British Archeological Reports, International Series 101 (Oxford 1982)

Williams, D., The Reach of Rome (London 1996)

www.ingramcontent.com/pod-product-compliance
Lightning Source LLC
Chambersburg PA
CBHW041705290426
44108CB00027B/2866